DEEP SKIN

DEEP SKIN

Elizabeth Bishop and Visual Art

PEGGY SAMUELS

CORNELL UNIVERSITY PRESS

Ithaca & London

First published 2010 by Cornell University Press

Printed in the United States of America

Library of Congress Cataloging-in-Publication Data

Samuels, Peggy.
    Deep skin : Elizabeth Bishop and visual art / Peggy Samuels.
        p. cm.
    Includes bibliographical references and index.
    ISBN 978-0-8014-4826-3 (cloth : alk. paper)
    1. Bishop, Elizabeth, 1911–1979—Criticism and interpretation.   2. Art
in literature.   3. Visual perception in literature.   4. Aesthetics in
literature.   I. Title.
    PS3503.I785Z856 2010
    811'.54—dc22   2009036862

Cornell University Press strives to use environmentally responsible suppliers and materials to the fullest extent possible in the publishing of its books. Such materials include vegetable-based, low-VOC inks and acid-free papers that are recycled, totally chlorine-free, or partly composed of nonwood fibers. For further information, visit our website at www.cornellpress.cornell.edu.

Cloth printing   10 9 8 7 6 5 4 3 2 1

To the irrepressible, Rabelaisian, and deeply loved Lester Schwalb

CONTENTS

ILLUSTRATIONS

ACKNOWLEDGMENTS

In undertaking the pleasant reverie of calling up the people who have contributed to the making of this book, I begin with Peter Sacks, who introduced me to Elizabeth Bishop and whose descriptions of poems have stayed with me for many years. It is with affection and gratitude that I recall the patience, intellectual rigor, and inspiration so freely granted to me by my teachers, the late Martin Stevens, Joseph Wittreich, Angus Fletcher, and especially Rich McCoy, whose generosity, acuity, and sheer human decency have been a model to me as I continue to develop as a teacher and a scholar. I thank Rosemary Mahoney and David Kohn, who told me to write a book and whose own writing combines instruction with delight. This project would not have come to fruition without Cassandra Laity, who took me into the fold of modernist scholars, shared with me her insights about the period, and took the time to read parts of the manuscript and gave me invaluable editorial suggestions. Among those modernists, I am grateful to Brett Millier, who graciously answered my earliest queries, and to Bonnie Costello and Charles Altieri, readers for Cornell University Press, whose suggestions helped me to improve the book and whose encouragement meant everything to me.

Throughout the project, I have also felt keenly the goodwill and encouragement of my colleagues in the Drew English Department: Frank Occhiogrosso; Gerry Smith-Wright; Bob Ready; Charli Valdez; Patrick Phillips; Tiphanie Yanique; Neil Levi, who gave me crucial reading suggestions and lent a willing ear; Nicky Ollman, whose optimism and encouragement have been pleasantly contagious and truly sustaining; Sandra Jamieson, who in the midst of hundreds of projects always had time to offer practical, seemingly prescient, advice and support; Wendy Kolmar, whose concern, interest, conversation, and advice kept me afloat over the long years of my engagement with this project; and Jim Hala, whose unflagging, genial, and heartfelt encouragement I found restorative in the deepest sense of the term. I am grateful also to Walter Jacobsohn, whose sensitive response to a piece of the manuscript buoyed my spirits and gave me the confidence to proceed. As I found myself wandering into other disciplines, I have benefited from conversations with Jeff Halpern and Sharone Ornstein; Mona Hadler; and Sarah-Henry Corrington, who shared with me her knowledge of Paul Klee. I am indebted to Deborah Jerome, who wielded her expert editorial help as I was struggling with an early version of chapter 1. Gamin Bartle, Krista White, Sarah Ashley, and John Saul, staff members in technology services at Drew University, excelled not only in technical expertise and instruction but also in patience and good humor in the face of more interruptions than one faculty member reasonably should be allotted. Jody Caldwell and Bruce Lancaster—Drew University librarians—have also contributed to this book, and I thank them for not only their expertise but also their willingness to share it with me, often when I accosted them in the midst of other endeavors.

Michelle Harvey, associate archivist at the New York Museum of Modern Art, graciously helped me to navigate the wealth of material in the archives. I am especially grateful to Adrian Sudhalter, who so generously shared with me materials that she had uncovered at the Museum of Modern Art and who tactfully saved me from errors. Dean Rogers at Vassar Library Special Collections made me feel welcome as a reader, efficiently and graciously gave me access to materials, and never seemed to tire of my requests. I am grateful to Joanne McCann, who helped me with her organizational and problem-solving skills, willingness to roll up her sleeves, and upbeat spirit. I also thank Drew University for allowing me to benefit from a research leave and two research grants, giving me the time and money necessary to complete the project. I am indebted to Karen Laun and John Ackerman at Cornell University Press and to copyeditor Julie Nemer, who gave me sound advice, saved me from errors and strengthened my work.

I thank Esther, David, Mimi, and Jake for their love and support and for providing many fun interludes. I am grateful to my brothers

Rick and John Samuels, whose concern grounds all my endeavors, and to my mother Marlene Silverman Samuels and my late father Richard Samuels, both of whose own intelligence, honesty, and genuineness provided me with the human qualities necessary for this scholarly project. Finally, and most important, I thank Lester Schwalb, whose tolerance for obsession and distraction and whose humor, respect, and love made all this work possible to perform, and Nate and Ella Schwalb, young writers who have inspired me to keep revising and whose self-reliance and easy-going loving natures gave me the liberty to pursue my path.

Chapter 1 was first published as "Verse as Deep Surface: Elizabeth Bishop's New Poetics, 1938–39," *Twentieth-Century Literature* 52, 3 (Sept. 2006): 306–29 and is reprinted by permission. Chapter 2 was first published as "Elizabeth Bishop and Paul Klee: Selected Notebook Drafts and A Cold Spring," *Modernism/Modernity* 14, 3 (Sept. 2007): 543–68, © The Johns Hopkins University Press. Excerpts from Elizabeth Bishop, *The Complete Poems 1927–1979* (copyright © 1979, 1983 by Alice Helen Methfessel), are reprinted by permission of Farrar, Straus and Giroux, LLC. Excerpts from Elizabeth Bishop, *Edgar Allen Poe & the Juke-Box: Uncollected Poems, Drafts, and Fragments,* edited and annotated by Alice Quinn (copyright © 2006 by Alice Helen Methfessel, introduction copyright © 2006 by Alice Quinn) are reprinted by permission of Farrar, Straus and Giroux, LLC and Carcanet Press Limited. Excerpts from unpublished letters to Loren MacIver and Margaret Miller, notebooks, drafts of poems, fragments from unpublished poems or prose, and notes on essays by Elizabeth Bishop (copyright © 2009 Elizabeth Bishop Estate) are printed by permission of Farrar, Straus and Giroux, LLC on behalf of the Elizabeth Bishop Estate.

DEEP SKIN

INTRODUCTION

Elizabeth Bishop responded to Randall Jarrell's praise of her second book by simultaneously confiding and disowning a secret desire:

> [Your review] made me so happy that I really can't put off writing a note about it any longer. . . . I still from the bottom of my heart, honestly think I do NOT deserve it—but it has been one of my dreams that someday someone would think of Vermeer, without my saying it first, so now I think I can die in a fairly peaceful frame of mind, any old time, having struck the best critic of poetry going that way. (Bishop 1994, 311–12)

Such a profound and long-standing desire to be understood as the written equivalent of Vermeer accords with Bishop's other offhand remarks through the years that she would rather have been a painter (Brown 24; Johnson 100).[1] Bishop's attraction to the visual arts has long been noted; but, because of the diversity of her interests, from Johannes Vermeer to John Constable to Paul Klee and beyond, the traces of her encounters with paintings and painters in her correspondence, notebooks, and poems seem to scatter, without any means of cohering. Given this difficulty, Bonnie Costello chose to focus on the poems themselves, and in one careful reading after another, she shows the extent to which Bishop's poems use visual perception—"experiments with odd and multiple perspectives, with radical shifts of frame and scale, with temporal conditions of observations"—to

I

represent "a fluent, temporal subjectivity" (Costello 1991, 45).[2] The richness of Costello's study makes apparent the likelihood that Bishop sought modes of conceptualizing subjectivity by turning to experiments in the visual arts. Yet, although Richard Mullen and Lorrie Goldensohn established that Bishop was moved by and subsequently distinguished herself from surrealism, no scholar has yet undertaken a sustained study of Bishop's relationship to the visual arts and to those painters whom she identifies as primary to her work: Paul Klee and Kurt Schwitters (Mullen; Goldensohn 1992, 121–30).[3]

Such an undertaking is possible only by taking into account the contemporary discourse about visual art, which provides a mediating context for Bishop's understanding of painters. The closest intellectual context for Bishop was supplied by her friendship with Margaret Miller, her former college roommate, who worked as a research associate and, later, as an associate curator at the New York Museum of Modern Art (MoMA). Bishop's sustained interest in both Klee and Schwitters probably derives from Miller's own passionate interest in those two artists. In addition, Miller's and Lota de Macedo Soares's roles in the early reception of Alexander Calder impacted Bishop's conception of possible structures for verse. From the late-1930s through the mid-1950s, Bishop drew on visual art intently to work out her own aesthetic. In this book, I focus on the work of that period, although I extend the discussion to a few later poems that crystallize some of the earlier aesthetic developments. I draw on Bishop's correspondence, notebooks, unpublished drafts, published poems, and amateur artworks, as well as on MoMA exhibition and correspondence files and mid-century art criticism to tell the story of Bishop's use of visual art to fashion her own poetics. By placing Bishop's concerns in conversation with the visual arts, we see painters' experiments and the discourse about those experiments pulled through the reacting sensibility of a poet working on her own affective and aesthetic concerns. Bishop used the visual arts to distinguish her own poetics from the compositional methods of her modernist predecessors, particularly the work of Marianne Moore. In regards to broader trajectories in literary history, these interart relations unveil a particularly illuminating strand in the multiple transitions between modernism and postmodernism.

The Surface of Painting, the Surface of Verse

In this book, I argue that the surface of a painting, understood as a kind of boundary, became one of the most important sites for Bishop's inventiveness. I explore Bishop's complex conception of the surface of the page of poetry as akin to the surface of a painting and of both as the boundary at which interior and exterior encounter one another. The surface of verse, like a semipermeable skin, becomes a corollary for the mobile membrane that allows materials from the world to cross into the self. This book therefore traces a complex and rich four-way metaphor: surface of verse, surface of painting, skin, and interface between mind and world. These associations allowed Bishop to reconceive the nature of lyric as a material where the pliable lattice of the poem's lines becomes a site for the embodied mind to open toward, receive, and tactilely interact with the world's disparate materials. Lyric becomes a membrane that allows layers of human experience—physical sensation, visual image, memory, word, emotion, thought—to meet, cross, absorb, and alter. By the late 1930s, Bishop was using the art historical discourse about Impressionism's conception of the surface of the painting as the record of the encounter between the interior of the artist and nature to think about the surface of verse. Experiments in the visual arts with the surface of painting became productive for her invention of a poetry that could produce complex relations between interior and exterior and could reposition the lyric speaker. Often Bishop's poems start farther back than the "I," in a position of openness to the world, and then, as the poem collects sights and sounds, eventually they reach a more condensed "I." Mid-century visual artists who released the figure from the bound line and invented new modes of orienting the subject in three-dimensional space provided Bishop with methods of experimentation in lyric.

By using the term *deep skin*, I mean to draw attention to Bishop's widening of the arena for positioning the lyric subject in the materials of verse and world. The "skin" of page or canvas becomes activated and mobile as the boundary between interior and exterior; it is also a boundary that opens toward different kinds of depth. Bishop invented a poetics that used the "skin" of verse to replace the skin of the body that would hold disparate interior materials in an illusory separation from the disparate and mobile materials of the environment. Imagining verse as an immersible net and as a fabric, Bishop began to experiment with the thickening, dispersion, turning, and tilting of verse that could "touch" or incorporate the realms of real nature and interior ideas and feeling. On the cusp between a modernist fascination with depth and a postmodernist turn toward surface, Bishop creates an alternative that allows for the temporary and fluid production and disappearance of depth and revolutionizes our understanding of the variety of kinds of depth in human life.

One material became crucial for Bishop's imagining the "skin" of verse and provided immense flexibility for her positioning of the lyric subject. In a striking metaphor, fleetingly mentioned but sustained over a number of years in notebook drafts, prose, and poetry, Bishop likened the surface of verse to the surface of water. Water has a special kind of surface because it necessarily holds a mobile volume "behind" it and the surface or skin that contains that volume fluidly bounds. It constantly hints at the plane as an illusorily stable boundary between inner and outer.[4] Imagining the surface of verse as "glassy water" and water as a kind of skin that has a volume "behind" it, Bishop develops a productive metaphor in which the materiality of the verse becomes a kind of second skin. The surface of verse loosely bounds subjectivity and yet also opens to both the interior depth of the subject and to an exterior depth, to the extension of outer landscape. In choosing to imagine the surface of verse as like the surface of water, Bishop could take advantage of the activity that "opens" or "turns" a surface upward or downward into depth, induces reflection or absorption, turns light or heavy, or creates a multitude of other effects that could reproduce the variable reciprocity of the oddly angled encounters between the interior of the subject and the exterior world, using verse as the mobile threshold between them. She creates a deep skin that opens inward and outward through the materiality of verse.

Part of the impetus for metaphorically linking the surface of water, the surface of verse, and the surface of painting probably derived from Paul Claudel's writing on Vermeer. Claudel's short essay on Dutch painters (1935) was widely read in Paris in the years that Bishop was there.[5] In distinguishing Vermeer from the other Dutch painters ("more perfect, more rare, more exquisite," [Claudel 20–21]), Claudel remarks particularly on one quality, switching from French to English to capture precisely his sensation: "if other adjectives were necessary, it would be those offered to us only in the English language: eery, uncanny" (Claudel 21).[6] For Claudel, the Dutch landscape itself, with its many bodies of water and its clarity and stillness, lent itself to an unusual and eerie thinness of boundary between reality and the reality reflected in mirrored, silvery surfaces. Holland, with its "sheet of water [that] extends everywhere" is "where reality and reflexion interpenetrate and communicate by the most delicate and subtle veins" (Claudel 31). Claudel declares, "Dutch art has its beginning in water, and, to state it more exactly, in that water which, when purified, hardened, and well-defined, becomes a mirror or a glass over silver" (Claudel 37–38). According to Claudel, in Vermeer's painting the eeriness or mysteriousness comes from the way that the watery, reflective environment, when precisely and realistically rendered, becomes the wavery, unstable, silvery, nacreous, and therefore mysterious or "supernatural" surface in Vermeer's painting. It is the place where solidity and uncertainty, reality and reflection, interpenetrate. Claudel himself makes the analogy between the surface of painting and the surface of the page:

> It would not be correct to say the painter (I speak of the painter in general) has the pretension of raising the curtain between the exterior world and ourselves. It would be better to say that he has tightened it at the four corners. It has stopped fluttering; the vague field of vision has become a page, a limited and well-defined screen upon which the artist projects his interior vision of an intelligible whole, a composition with a view to the effect, something that, by the relationship of its various elements, constitutes a meaning, a spectacle, something that is well worth the trouble of the time one passes in looking at it. (Claudel 35)

In these remarks, and in that comparison of canvas with page, Claudel lays out some of the major lines of analogy that will become crucial for Bishop's relationship with the visual arts. In poems that combine precise and realistic renderings with the wavery and unstable, Bishop works with the tautness of a surface that can also flutter, reflecting and serving as plane of encounter between landscape and self, natural and supernatural, the real and art.

From the beginning moments of the reception of Bishop's work, critics have noted the strange quality of the surface of her verse. At first, reviewers decried her poetry as "all surface" and "mere surface." Later, critics defended her by unveiling the depth of emotion that lay under that surface (Storace; McCabe). Alan Williamson, writing about the poems in *A Cold Spring*, even while praising Bishop, locates emotion under the surface ("the just balance between surface archness and detachment and subliminal emotional intensity is finally struck"; Williamson 103). Even more recent critics, such as Jeredith Merrin and Camille Roman, who have illuminated the dynamics of gender and politics in Bishop's poetry, have tended to conceptualize the poems as having a "deeper" and "hidden" or "repressed" content (Merrin 1993, 159; Roman 15). Yet this description of the relation between surface and depth in her poetry corresponds much more closely to the late-1950s style of her close friend and contemporary Robert Lowell than to her own work. Early criticism of Lowell claimed that the "visual element is supreme" in the first section of *Life Studies* in which the poems

> attempt to imitate in verbal form the visual effect of a photograph. They therefore seem to lack depth. We learn from them what Lowell's eye has seen but we do not learn directly what his heart has felt. Unlike *Lord Weary's Castle*, where the outer world was at times blocked from view by the presence of the poet's own gesticulating consciousness, *Life Studies* gives us a world of characters in full view, with the consciousness of the poet reduced to the thickness of a camera lens. Yet this effect of two-dimensionality is somewhat misleading. The surfaces of the poems may seem flat, but just below the surface one senses the poet's immense emotional pressure, which once or twice forces through in the form of tears and anguished exclamations. (Axelrod 119)

These poems were "photographs of experience" that periodically— but only occasionally—revealed the emotional depth that lay under the surface. In contrast, Bishop's self-education in the visual arts gave her a rich set of concepts and vocabulary to reimagine and reinvent a mobile and dynamic interaction between two and three dimensions. In describing Bishop's poetics, Costello writes that "the self is projected into the world and, conversely, the mutable world enters the domain of the self. *Bishop sees at the threshold, along the pane of glass*" (Costello 1991, 60). Lorrie Goldensohn writes of her sense that "consciousness playing in [Bishop's] work feels like a sympathy without skin extending deeply and unnervingly everywhere" (1992, 56).[7] Both scholars are describing the strangeness of a mind that somehow lacks the usual membrane between itself and the surrounding world or, put another way, a membrane that has become so porous, transparent, and extensive that it no longer bounds in the usual way. Particularly in the poems of *A Cold Spring* from Bishop's middle period, the lyric speaker's partial effacement allows the camera lens to extend outward and thicken, extending subjectivity into the intricate density of materials arrayed across multiple interior and exterior boundaries.

Bishop, of course, found her way to her own poetics by making discoveries and choices about her literary predecessors and contemporaries. Although this book necessarily excludes an extensive discussion of Bishop's literary relations, I do show that her encounters with the visual arts opened new means of navigating those relations and, especially, gave her a means of differentiating her own aesthetic from the work of her closest influence and mentor, Marianne Moore. Bishop's invention of a poetics distinctively her own involved three closely interconnected discoveries: a new mode of conceptualizing surface-depth relations, a new way of holding the lyric speaker, and a new means of conceptualizing the relationship of verse materials and materials of nature and mind.

For Marianne Moore, attentiveness to surfaces involved an ethics of respect for the natural world, a correlative human response to that world's ability to instruct. Almost in the way that seventeenth-century Protestant poets discovered a legitimacy for their own "curled" aesthetics by finding evidence of that "curling" in God's Word and world, Moore legitimated her poems' detailed surfaces by finding similar surfaces in nature. As Costello notes in discussing "The Jerboa," Moore's "eye clings to the desert rat's surfaces, finding in them ideals of economy and modesty that become aesthetic standards" (1984, 142). Surface of verse for Moore had much to do with her concept of "neatness of finish" of an aesthetic object and its relation to hard labor, discipline, asceticism, and "relentless accuracy" (Molesworth 185). Ultimately, she observed surfaces—surfaces of the world and surfaces of art objects—in painstaking detail, displaying them for her reader because they glimmered with a moral significance. This fine attunement to surfaces displayed the moral stance of a mind that had the humility to take exquisite care in recording and reflecting on fine distinctions.[8]

The attentiveness to and valuation of the surfaces of the world effectively enabled Moore to construct not only a particular style for the surface of verse but also a particular kind of lyric speaker. Her lyric speaker had a "cerebral, civilized manner on the page" (Costello 1984, 138). Although, as Cristanne Miller argues, Moore did not go so far as to construct a lyric of "impersonality"; nevertheless, as Miller herself shows, Moore emphasizes "the constructed quality of her verse" with her use of rhyme, quotation, allusion, and "density of interwoven voices" (Miller 1995, 77).[9] The difficulty of the surface of Moore's verse, its glistening, "polished," hard-edged sharpness drawing attention to its own constructedness, was designed to mark the lyric speaker's "inquisitive intensity" and demand a responding inquisitive intensity of the reader (Miller 1995, 38). The technique resulted in a particular characterization of the lyric speaker; Miller uses the term *unembodied* to describe Moore's lyric persona (Miller 1995, 38). The "individuality" that Moore creates, according to Miller, is of an "aesthetic, philosophical, political position rather than of a personality of 'I'—even though that 'position' has marked attributes of idiosyncrasy and charm" (Miller 1995, 33). Miller argues, "Moore's distance from any ordinary or unexamined sense of poetic voice, as well as from a characterized speaker that centers an ongoing, dramatic relationship between reader and poet" does not present a continuous "sense of 'voice' or form as an extension of the physical body" (1995, 74).

Experiments in the visual arts helped Moore to conceptualize and legitimize these relations of mind to poetic materials, both materials of the world and linguistic materials. Deploying a linguistic equivalent of the cubists' superimposition of multiple perspectives, in "Peter," for example, she arranged jarring multiple interrogatory and descriptive angles of observation while providing the naturalistic image of "cat" to contain the dispersal (Costello 1981, 206). As Costello has shown, Moore also used the aesthetics of collage, understood as an "explosive bond created on the canvas by multiple incongruous representations and materials" (1981, 212). According to Costello, "Collage gives [Moore] an opportunity to affect distance from the claims of the poem (she has only 'found' the words of others" (1981, 212).[10] By juxtaposing perspectives and perceptions, Moore could sharpen contrasts and ironize the positions and attitudes of others whom she wished to interrogate or critique.

Bishop's other significant modernist precursor, Wallace Stevens, also looked to visual art to imagine, validate, and represent the compositional powers of the mind and the mind's freedom (Altieri 1989, 25). Glen MacLeod has shown how closely and extensively the development of Stevens's solutions to aesthetic problems derived from his changing engagement with controversies and experiments in the arena of visual art. Stevens used the ready-made to help him to conceive of art as "the act of the mind" (MacLeod 21), defined his own aesthetic in relation to surrealism in "The Man with the Blue Guitar" (MacLeod 66), and used Mondrian's geometric abstractions to "come to terms with the highly intellectual quality of his own poetry" (MacLeod 122).[11] MacLeod also tracks the trajectory of some of Stevens's aesthetic projects in relation to the shift in the aesthetics of the abstract expressionists from the mid- to late 1940s; like the abstract expressionists, Stevens moved from wanting to develop a "new myth" and work with tragic and timeless subject matter (MacLeod 152, 155) to "a purely abstract substitute for myth" and an interest in "kinetic abstraction" (185, 187).

Partly by drawing on models available in visual art, then, both Stevens and Moore invented a poetics that could accommodate perceptual, sensory attentiveness to the surface of the world and the discursive energies of the mind. Yet, in these modernists' poems, the lyric speaker's discursiveness bristled with a kind of defensiveness and willfulness that continually reasserted its own right to exist. Moore's lifting of the status of surfaces involved a defensiveness against the part of Christian tradition that relegated appearances and objects to the dust (Molesworth 193). Her "use of sharp rather than vaporous detail, the emphasis on aesthetic distance as opposed to sentiment or even presumed empathy, and the notion of juxtaposed details and perspectives" derived from her need to distance herself from the sentimentality associated with the female poetess (Molesworth 81). In Stevens's poetry, for all the joyous embrace of sensuous particulars, the mind throws its energies, conceptions, and desires at the world in a declaration of the legitimacy of its own freedoms and pleasures. In Moore, the discursive, interrogating mind arranges the fragments of the world, ironizing by juxtaposition, to counter less acceptable modes of life and thought. Looking to visual art to liberate and legitimate the full play and range of the powers of the mind, both of the modernists closest to Bishop, therefore, enforced the divide between mind and world in a highly discursive and rhetorical mode of the ultimately disembodied voice.[12]

In contrast, beginning in the late 1930s, Elizabeth Bishop founded her poetics on an embodied lyric speaker, a mind held by materials of verse that intricately and deeply interacted with materials in nature and so exponentially expanded the interactions between surface and depth. Although Stevens's *Harmonium* held a particularly significant place in her development, Bishop also expressed dissatisfaction with Stevens's discursiveness, writing in one of her Key West notebooks, "What I tire of quickly in Wallace Stevens is the self-consciousness—poetry so aware lacks depth"(VSC 75.3A, 89).[13] The significance of tactility in avoiding that self-consciousness is revealed in one of the Key West notebooks, where, in the midst of thinking about visual art, she confesses, then mostly crosses out, her dissatisfaction with one of the great practitioners of her own linguistic medium: "Yeats'[s] poetry leaves me cold. . . . It all seems 'made-up.' . . . he seems too busy being a poet to . . . really get in touch with anything" (VSC 75.4B, 141). In the last phrase, she makes clear that she will be satisfied only with a poetry that has the warmth of coming into touch with reality. Poetry that "lacks depth" and feels "made-up" must be replaced by a poetry that feels more real, can touch, can become less cold. For Stevens, Mondrian provided a means to legitimate his move into a colder, more intellectualized, abstract discursiveness; Bishop, to escape this discursiveness, instead looked to those visual artists whom critics considered the alternatives to Mondrian's coldness and his unreality.[14] She did not turn toward surrealism, which critics characterized—because of its biomorphic shapes and representation of the real—as one kind of alternative to geometric abstraction. Instead, she looked toward Paul Klee's experiments, so influential for a new generation of American artists. Mid-century critics of Klee's work emphasized that the viewer of a Klee painting became immersed in a deep space, having to find his way with all his senses, including hearing and touch. Critics drew attention to the feeling of the undefined, miniscule subject wandering, tactilely, among floating motifs in a field that had no defined frame. Bishop also turned to the aesthetics of Kurt Schwitters, whose collages in the early 1920s, in contrast to other dadaist or cubist collage, did not concern itself predominantly with jarring juxtapositions.[15] Instead, Schwitters arranged materials to interpermeate or modulate into one another. Bishop translated Schwitters's concept of interpermeating materials using the materiality of verse to hold the world's surfaces, its materials in a softer, deeper, more tactile, and more mobile encounter with the materials of the lyric speaker's mind.

These visual artists became crucial figures for Bishop because they not only widened the arena for tactility in the visual arts but also experimented with new experiences of depth and new ways to position a wandering and tentative subject. For Bishop, particular categories became crucial constituents of experience: absorption, weight, density, diffusion, condensation, saturation, fragility, solidity, and lightness—all the ways that one material brushes past, hovers over, or sinks into another. These qualities became the crucial mode of the materiality of verse, serving as the site of the encounter between the materials of mind and the materials of world. Conceptualizing verse's relations of surface and depth in this way allowed Bishop to invent a means of limiting the lyric speaker's move into the discursiveness of metaphor and meaning: the idea can emerge quietly from and sink back into the material of the sensory world. Unlike her predecessors, Bishop was much more likely to allow verse to carry a line of thought or emotion that then gently dropped back into sensory feeling. Increasingly in her middle period, Bishop's verse tends to turn or rise, brush past, or sink from one register of human experience to another. Whereas Moore continually inflected her attentiveness to surface in a thematics of simplicity and humility versus the overly ornate, prideful, and superfluous, Bishop let go of those thematics and engaged more thoroughly in the intricate interplay of infinitely variant materials and densities as they touched one another. Her poetics is very much about the touch of the materials of the mind and world inside the materiality of verse.

Orientation

A late poem draft, from Bishop's experience on the Amazon, registers the tactile perception of the environment as it is experienced by a lyric speaker who never emerges into "I":

It [the river] moves, it moves, it lives
it is easy in its bed, it sleeps and wakes
        the bronze and red bird flying low along the bank
. . . .
Round paddles. The paddler cross legged in the bow
and the canoe rising like a leaf behind him, out of the water
. . . .
Look! A tree of birds. A candelabra
of birds risen out of the water
all white, sleeping, vigil lights
then another, and another—all along the bank now—
they don't move.
a few lights, candles or small lamps
coming and going as the trees move in front of them—
the ships lights show mud mud and trees
one sweeps along the deck

The tiny plank goes out—out—like a finger
a flashlight on the bank, no one speaks—
a rope is thrown and falls like lead
—the wand-like plank has hit on something—mud—
the whisker the wand—we have found land touch something
or almost land—
. . . .
land-for-a-while—until it drifts to move on, too— (VSC 68.1)

The draft of the poem's tactile empathy illustrates beautifully Lorrie
Goldensohn's description of Bishop's "sympathy without skin extending deeply and unnervingly everywhere" and Bishop's method: "in
poem and picture, the depths and interrelations of space are characteristically resolved upon by groping from point to point *in situ*, and are
fastened and probed, by contiguity, not by imperial overview" (Goldensohn 2001, 105).[16]

The traditional means of gaining an "imperial overview" in Western art has been through perspective, which organizes and hierar-
chizes attention by foregrounds, backgrounds, and focal points.
Bishop's remark to Ashley Brown explicitly translates categories of
perspective from the visual arts into the practice of poetry: "switching
tenses always gives effects of depth, space, foreground, background

and so on" (quoted in Brown 26). The remark shows that Bishop did consider the organizing devices of the visual arts when creating structures for poems and reveals that she considered poetry as an arena not just for "groping *in situ*" but for orientation.

Given that Bishop reportedly carried a compass with her everywhere and slept with her head pointed to the north, we can assume that she found orientation in three-dimensional space to be crucial (Goldensohn 1999, 167–68). Critics have linked these habits metaphorically to Bishop's sense of homelessness, and I take seriously, and somewhat more literally than other scholars, that for Bishop orientation meant making a home by positioning the subject in a real space wider than a room or a house. In this respect, I draw on the work of David Summers in *Real Spaces: World Art History and the Rise of Western Modernism*. Summers explains that orientation is fundamentally related to our own cardinality—"uprightness, symmetry (including the asymmetry of handedness) and facing")—and that art provides conditions for the cardinality of the human body, its need to face something and to align itself (Summer 37). Summers extensively documents the premodern sense of space, in which cardinality is aligned to the larger order of the world through centers, boundaries, paths, and precincts. He documents the way that premodern spatial art uses alignment and pilgrimage, a facing toward an object with presence or power that then orients attention, movement, and activities. In modernity, with, as Costello remarks, its "many anxieties of location . . . among them the collapse of distance, the violation and evacuation of the personal, the inhuman scale and power of the public realm" (2008, 18), the need to find a means of orientation becomes a crucial personal and artistic project.

Bishop's passion for visual artists focused on painters who invented solutions for reorganizing the orientation of the viewer beyond the means of traditional Western painting with its foregrounds and backgrounds and frontal, virtual perspective. Klee, Schwitters, and Calder conducted visual experiments that involved reorienting the subject in three-dimensional space. And Bishop used these artists' work, as well as their writing, to reimagine the structures that could be made inside of the "intricacy of density" and flux (VSC 75.2). Through her engagement with visual art, the conceptual vocabulary about orientation from the discourse of visual artists and critics became available to Bishop for imagining her own work. Her published and unpublished poems reveal that Bishop drew on and inventively redeployed concepts coined by Klee: his "taking a walk with a line," "eye in a landscape" "complex of movements," and "spatial organization through three dimensional energies (fish swimming in all directions)."[17] Likewise, Bishop drew on Kurt Schwitters's "interpermeating surfaces," and "lines that thicken into surfaces," and Alexander Calder's "shifting relations" among disparate bodies and his "composing motions." This terminology has not entered literary criticism, but the concepts and experiments in visual art became crucial tools in Bishop's invention of responses to the questions of disorientation in modernity.

Some of the problems of orientation have been previously laid out in the work of Thomas Travisano. His *Mid-Century Quartet* shows that Bishop, along with Robert Lowell, Randall Jarrell, and John Berryman, invented a postmodern aesthetics that attempted to create an "uncertain refuge in a dangerously decentered world—a refuge that was itself unsettling, permeable, and fragmentary" (Travisano 1999, 13). Tracing Bishop's poetic interactions with the visual arts offers new models for conceptualizing the postmodern attention to "flux," "mobile flexible exploratory aesthetic," "stripping away of authorial priviledge," "perceptual mobility," and "multiplanar" delineated by Travisano (Travisano 1999, 114, 189, 190, 191). Her poetry adheres to Richard Sheppard's claim that the "essential feature of postmodernism is its acceptance of modernity with its decentered plurality, ephemerality, fragmentation, discontinuities [and] indeterminacy."[18] She accepts knowingly, with a combination of resignation, humility, and humor, the features of the universe that the modernists often responded to in a mode of crisis, with a theatricality sometimes veering into the apocalyptic. But she forged that acceptance partly by the use she made of the experiments in the visual arts, particularly of Paul Klee, Kurt Schwitters, and Alexander Calder. She allowed for but contained fragmentation by orchestrating modulation across different registers of experience. She expressed—but also created alternatives for—isolation and dispersal by using interpermeating materials and surfaces that open and close. Instead of a chaotic flux, she oriented the embodied subject by suspending it in a complex of motions, inside shifting relations among disparate objects with varying speeds, scales, and trajectories. Instead of retreating to mere surface bereft of depth or becoming enamored only of mythic and tragic depths, she tracked the momentary production and disappearance of depth. By attending to the scale and duration of phenomena, by weighing different registers of experience against one another (the sensory and the discursive, the scale of the deep cultural past against a particular present, the many degrees on a continuum between willed and unwilled movement), Bishop distinguishes her aesthetic from the postmodernism that commentators have described as a "flux [that] precludes either cathexis or historicity," in which materials circulate in a homogenized, unprioritized, unweighted, "perpetual present, where retro-styles and images proliferate as surrogates of the temporal" (Anderson 56). Bishop translated the mid-twentieth-century explosion of visual artists' experiments with tactility, materiality of surface, suspension among floating motifs and orbits, surfaces opening into depths, deep space, modulation from two to three dimensions, mobility of figure to ground, lines loosely bounding forms, and layering to reconceptualize the relation of surface to depth in her poetics and to resituate the place of the lyric speaker in the materials of verse and environment. In doing so, she provided a solution to the question of depth that contrasts sharply with the later visual artists such as Jasper Johns and Andy Warhol, who became obsessed with the status of depth but pronounced depth to be only an illusory category. For example, Jasper Johns's "Drawer" (1957) tempted the viewer to open the two knobs of a drawer and see what was "behind" the picture plane, where of course there could only be the wall on which the painting had been hung. In contrast, Bishop invents new means of conceptualizing depth and considers variant kinds of depth to be crucial for human experience.

Access to Bishop's Knowledge of Art

In the course of her life, Bishop experienced intense and disparate enthusiasms for a divergent list of artists, belonging to no one school: Rembrandt, Pierre Bonnard, Loren MacIver, Ben Shahn, Vincent Van Gogh, Max Ernst (for his photomontages), Honoré Daumier, Joseph Cornell, Vermeer, Edouard Vuillard, Klee, Schwitters, Constable, Jackson Pollock, Willem de Kooning, Francis Bacon, Calder, Georges Seurat, Giorgio de Chirico, Oskar Kokoschka, Hyman Bloom, and John Marin. And she expresses considerable enthusiasm about her reading of art historians Reginald H. Wilenski, Erwin Panofsky,

Meyer Schapiro, Daniel-Henry Kahnweiler, Ernst Gombrich, and Arnold Hauser. This wide range of experiences with the visual arts, combined with Bishop's reluctance to describe in detail her responses to specific art works, has prevented critics from fully analyzing her relationship to the visual arts.[19] Nevertheless, there are several avenues of investigation that yield plenty of information. It is necessary to acknowledge at once Bishop's distaste for poems that are based on particular paintings. In a letter to May Swenson, Bishop warns the younger poet against relying on paintings as subject matter, making clear that she considers it to be an evasion or short cut of the real work of writing. The technique, she suggests, will result in poems suffused with allusions, poems that are full of "culture" and "too 'literary'" (letters to May Swenson, February 18, 1956, and December 26, 1960, WUL). With the exception of four poems in her oeuvre, the use that Bishop made of visual art lies elsewhere, not in ecphrastic poetry that describes or takes off from a particular painting.[20]

Moving away from the exploration of the ecphrastic, we can turn to other means of tracing Bishop's reflections on painting. First, Bishop's letters do occasionally mention particular paintings and sometimes include enough descriptive phrasing to provide insight into her reflections on specific paintings or artists and her preferences for particular artists. Occasionally, a letter allows us to see Bishop's comments on interart relations.

Second, contemporary conversations about the visual arts, circulating among art historians and reviewers, provide discourses that shaped her experience of visual art and informed her poetics. The categories used in talking about visual art have relevance for aesthetic problems for which Bishop needed to find solutions. Occasionally, we can see these categories appear in Bishop's notebooks, drafts, and even published poems. Her notebooks contain comments on tactility, on "wholes," on surfaces, and on representation. She sometimes draws on the exact word choice of art historians. For example, Alfred H. Barr, in a standard critical work of the mid-1930s, *Cubism and Abstract Art*, articulated the dichotomy between the geometric and the biomorphic with the phrase "the shape of the square confronts the silhouette of the amoeba" (Barr 1935, 19). Bishop uses the word *amoeba* in "Pleasure Seas" when she explores the dichotomy between the rectangle of the pool and the more fluid shapes of the movement of clouds, tides, and sea. In this case, her own reflections on the way that verse lines and form can contain experience clearly engages with a similar conversation that was taking place about the visual arts. Although Bishop's written commentary on art criticism is not extensive, her notebooks do contain brief and ultimately illuminating remarks about the development of her own aesthetics in response to painters' experiments. In addition to providing a view of Bishop's use of categories from the visual arts, the unpublished material allows access to Bishop's habitual mode of composition, which often begins with an almost passive registering of the environment, a kind of tactile perception that records the relations among the weights, textures, drift, and stability of elements of the environment. These unpublished poems, along with prose notebook entries, can help us characterize Bishop's habitual modes of perception. Unpublished drafts also reveal Bishop's trying out compositional methods in response to visual artists' own writing about art.

Third, beyond the general conversation about the visual arts available to Bishop in art books, journals to which she subscribed, newspaper reviews, and catalogues of exhibitions that she attended, Margaret Miller provides the closest intellectual context for Bishop's understanding of art.[21] The intimacy of Bishop's relationship with Miller is recorded both by Frank Bidart, who comments on Bishop's obsession with Miller, and by Bishop's letter to Lowell, explaining that through the 1940s, Bishop sent every one of her poems to Miller (Fountain and Brazeau 70; Bishop 2008, 73). Miller began to publish on the visual arts as early as 1934, her senior year at Vassar, went on to earn a masters in art history at New York University, and eventually worked at the MoMA, becoming a deeply knowledgeable, strongly opinionated, and articulate professional. In the many years of correspondence, Miller shares news of her work, reports to Bishop on gifts or purchases of art books, lends some of these art books to Bishop, and shares reflections on reading.[22] Miller's correspondence with Bishop also shows that the two friends engaged in comparisons across the two media of painting and poetry.

Bishop's enthusiasm for Paul Klee was certainly influenced, if not led, by Miller's enthusiasm. Miller worked on the 1945 MoMA publication about Klee, which reproduced some of his writings and made them widely available to an English-speaking American audience. Miller's excitement about the special issue on Klee of the major European art journal *Cahiers d'Art* provides a crucial source for Bishop's own early understanding of Klee, especially important because the sheer number of Klee's paintings and their immense variety constitute an obstacle to understanding Bishop's specific interest in his work. It seems likely, as well, that Bishop's enthusiasm for Kurt Schwitters had its roots in Miller's role as an early and ardent supporter of Schwitters in the United States well before the 1950s, when he became widely acknowledged by the art community (Orchard 284). Correspondence between Miller and Schwitters, as well as between Miller and the MoMA staff, reveals that Miller had an especially empathic connection to Schwitters at a time when his desperate circumstances were not fully understood or addressed by the museum administration.[23] Miller advocated on behalf of Schwitters for a fellowship to complete and restore his major artistic project, the Merzbau, that the Nazis had destroyed, and she also sent food parcels to Schwitters, suspecting that he was too scrupulous to spend the fellowship money on food rather than art materials (Orchard 281).[24] Schwitters sent Miller thirty-nine collages for an exhibit that Miller was curating for MoMA, originally planned for 1947. Because of delays in the mounting of the exhibition, for two years Miller was in possession of collages that very few other Americans had seen. It is possible that Miller and Bishop felt that Schwitters was, in some sense, their shared secret, given that so few people knew his work. Some of Miller's own work on collage theory, although never published in a catalogue, can be gleaned from correspondence with artists and dealers. Miller was also responsible for sending Bishop a book on Oceanic art in 1946, during the period that Bishop began to compile the notes that built the foundation not only for some of the poems of *A Cold Spring* but also for the autobiographical prose that led into *Geography III*. Finally, although Bishop's enthusiasm for Alexander Calder may have arisen independently of Miller,[25] Miller worked as research associate on the 1943 catalogue for the MoMA exhibit on Calder organized by James Johnson Sweeney, who was the most important and earliest American curator to develop an enthusiasm for Calder and who popularized the terms for conceptualizing his work.

Fourth, in addition to looking at the intellectual context for Bishop's understanding of visual art, periodically I attend to Bishop's own amateur paintings when some of the details of the paintings illuminate features in the poetry. While scholars have consistently invoked the term *primitive* to classify Bishop's art work, we would do well to remember that art critical discourse may have played a large role in her paintings. Lorrie Goldensohn, who first explored the interconnection between the two bodies of Bishop's work—painting and poetry—captures in her own magnificent prose the odd angles at which some of the paintings are pitched and the way that Bishop handles her "black, calligraphic line" so that it "hesitates expressively between serving as writing or as representation" (Goldensohn 1999, 171). In many ways, this project builds on qualities that Goldensohn described as features of Bishop's painting where "space becomes either exhilarating or terrifying in its elasticity," where "interiors . . . have flat, tippy surfaces, with shallow and irregular depth" (Goldensohn 1999, 168, 171). The mid-century discourse about the visual arts widens the field of significance for Bishop's seemingly quirky pictorial strategies and offers further insight into the relationship of those strategies to her poetics. For example, the choice of perspective corresponds quite closely to the description of Henri Matisse in an early and widely read essay by Meyer Schapiro, the art historian under whom Miller began her masters thesis: "Within more intimate subjects—interiors and still-life—the spatial framework was complicated by an accidental viewpoint, the whole being seen at a sharp angle, or from above (whereby the horizontal surfaces are perpendicular rather than parallel to the glance) and the main, as well as peripheral objects, being cut by the frame" (Schapiro 1932, 26).[26] Schapiro has much to say about the inventiveness of visual artists once they had left behind them the "definiteness in the relations between the objects and . . . the very space in which they are set," and his commentary on perspective and other matters provides a context not only for Bishop's choices in her paintings but also in her poetics (Schapiro 1932, 33). Likewise, the mid-century art historical discourse about the "wandering line" versus the straight-edged line, the discussion of the means by which a line tightly bounds a form, holds loosely, or disintegrates can help us not only to understand the variety of "lines" (electrical wires, kite strings, flag pole wires, etc.) that Goldensohn first noticed reappear in Bishop's paintings but also to better understand one way that Bishop conceived of the verse line.

There are certainly limits to our ability to access Bishop's response to the visual arts. Much of her engagement with visual art simply remains within a private realm that is forever closed to scholars. Even in cases in which her correspondence contains a record of a strong reaction—for example, in her declaration that two Daumiers made her feel that her whole life had been wasted—the content of the experience can only become guesswork.[27] Although it is sometimes possible to pinpoint the moment when her opinion of an artist altered (e.g., with Mondrian and Henry Moore), the fluctuations in her interests and tastes sometimes remain inaccessible, as do the full range of her interests in an artist. Surely, her engagement with Klee, especially, must have altered through the course of her life, given that she began to be interested in his work in 1937 and continued that interest through at least the mid-1960s, if not longer (Millier 219), yet it is impossible to track the nuances of these shifts. Furthermore, some aspects of Bishop's attraction to an artist, although profound, provide little basis for scholarly commentary. For example, Bishop's affinity for Klee surely had to do with his humor and with the sheer freshness and inexhaustibility of his inventiveness, yet it does not get us very far to note that Bishop used Klee as a model for her own freshness of invention. In some cases, the use of particular proper names, diction, images, or specific references in letters allows for certainty in describing Bishop's translation of elements of the visual arts into her own linguistic medium, whereas in other cases, perception of the affinity between works of visual art and Bishop's poems must also be used. In those cases for which my argument relies on claims about affinities, I have grounded my assertions in knowledge about Bishop's attendance at particular exhibitions and worked as closely as possible with the mediation supplied by her closest intellectual contexts. The language of criticism, both written and—far more elusive—the oral commentary of the highly articulate Margaret Miller, brought the visual arts closer to Bishop's own linguistic medium. It is in the poems themselves that we can watch how Bishop further translated those linguistic statements into methods of composition so that visual art could play a significant role in the complex process of composition that has so many points of origin and influence.

Objects and Materials

This book focuses on aesthetics and has very little to do with Bishop's biography. Yet there are recurrent interests in Bishop scholarship about the poet's early memories that I will recall and adjust as a way to think about relations between surface and depth. There is no question that Bishop's primary experience of depth was one of fear, associated with her mother's disappearance. As Alice Quinn has noted, Bishop repeatedly imagined a scenario of falling into loneliness (Quinn 287). And the usual scholarly rehearsal of primal psychological moments from Bishop's early childhood leans heavily on such moments—the floating on the swan boat, from which the swan emerges to bite the mother's hand, has that sense of a dangerous depth into which the child could drop, as does the frequently cited unpublished draft of Bishop as a young child standing precariously on the "crust" of snow, as her mother "fell through it" and disappeared back into the house to retrieve the snowshoes (Bishop 2006, 155–57). These moments' resonance with "the sensation of falling off / the round, turning world / into cold, blue-black space" that appears many years later in "In the Waiting Room," indicates that depth was associated with a fall into the immensity of loss and disconnection (*CP*[28] 160).

David Kalstone first suggested the means by which writing could serve to prevent such a fall. Focusing on the prose memoir "In the Village," Kalstone worked out a compelling explanation for the relationship between the radiant surface of objects in Bishop's work and the psychological depth of her early loss of connection to her mother, explaining that the objects become "radiant" because they serve as distractions, holding off the child's grief (Kalstone 220; Keller 1987, 117–18). Suspended and arrayed around the child, the objects tentatively and precariously hold the child from collapsing into herself, into knowledge of sorrow and into a state of being overwhelmed by sorrow. The child, with the intensity of her attentiveness, holds on to the objects like life rafts; and, for Kalstone, the speaker of the poetry likewise arrays the objects in balanced arrangements around herself. Victoria Harrison, revising and extending the work of David Kalstone, argues that Bishop's attentiveness to objects derives from their function not only as distractions from grief and carriers of grief but as substitute objects that can carry the "connectiveness" missing because of the mother's absence. According to Harrison, Bishop "sought in her published writing to decenter the mother-child dyad and discover among her familiar objects and family members a continuity that would make a place for the mother's disconnection" (Harrison 110). In Harrison's view, a poem's or story's details all "together enable the child to bear the family emotions" (120). Harrison adds to Kalstone's insight the important category of emotional *connection*. The radiant objects in the literary texts are not merely arrayed around the speaker, distracting her from the danger of overwhelming grief but, rather, the objects' tensile relationships with one another create the connectiveness missing in Bishop's relationship with her mother.

Other memoir fragments can alter our sense of that relationship between aesthetic experience and a fall into deep sorrow or loneliness. Two early memories of Bishop's maternal grandparents' house at night, one published recently by Jonathan Ellis and the other published by Alice Quinn, establish Bishop's reconstruction of an early memory in which the child is sealed between layers of unlike materials that shift where their edges are located in relation to one another:

> The starlight [viewed through a skylight] made the silence of the house separated [sic], there was silence, itself, and then sleep, as illustrated by an occasional snore from my grandfather—or the other noises I was waiting for. But on dark nights the sky and the silence and the house full of sleep merged all together. (quoted in Ellis 37)

> [In the parlor, with grandparents] I sat silent and made the wallpaper come off the wall. Small bouquets of red-gray roses, thin trellaces [*sic*] of golden wires, swayed, retreated and advanced, in space out from their background of wide white and faint silver stripes—up&down—Where a lot of wallpaper showed . . . the gilt and rose skimpy summer house advanced as far as the lamplit blur of Gammie's white hair. . . . [and upstairs in bed] That arbor, bower—summer house—I had not words for it—I didn't know where I'd go—where I'd be—anything—sealed between downstairs and upstairs dark, warm, smelling a little of dog, kerosene, geranium blooms. . . . (Bishop 2006, 213–14)

These passages situate the self in relation to both intimate and vast spaces, not by grounding the self but by suspending it in layers of materials composed of varying kinds of substances—sleep, silence, and the night sky; lamplight and wallpaper, the unfolding odor of geraniums held against an enveloping extensive darkness.[29] To grasp the primary feeling of subjectivity here, we must note that the "I" hangs suspended, enveloped, and almost tilting as different kinds of materials and shapes appear to sway forward, emerge into distinctness and subside, touch one another along long and shifting edges while the consciousness of the speaker also sways out and subsides in acts of multisensory perception. The mind "hides," closed in on itself within its own sense of circumference, and sways out to see feelingly, in an act of tactile empathy, other materials in the periphery that become other "skins," other circumferences.

In extending Kalstone's and Harrison's formulations and proposing different memoir fragments as foundational, I seek not to undo their accounts but to redirect the focus of our attention from objects to materials. It is by focusing on the array of different kinds of materials in the environment that we can then look not only at radiant objects in the literary texts but at the materiality of the verse that itself functions as one of the infinitely flexible substances forming a layered connectiveness in which the speaker is suspended. In the memoir fragments, the array of materials, some of which have considerable depth themselves and which reach across or are layered over one another, enwrapping the child's body, then becomes an alternative experience of depth, less dangerous and more containing.[30] For Bishop, the depth created by folding material against and into other materials replaces and guards against the more frightening depth of loss. Bishop's intensity of feeling for intermingling, layering, and interpenetrating materials produces her special feeling for the materiality of verse. And it is her passionate handling of the materiality of verse that provides the matrix for her contact with the visual arts. To understand Bishop's use of visual art, it is crucial to see that Bishop used not only objects but the "skin" of materials of different textures and densities to arrange against or provide a counterweight for the danger of disconnection.

Her aesthetic solution arose from a discovery that she could focus on the infinitely variable interfaces between materials. In the midst of working on her essay about Marianne Moore, "Efforts of Affection" (begun sometime in 1946), Bishop writes, "Miss M's method applied to interstitial situations" (VSC 73.3b, 189). The beauty of this subject was its magnitude and flexibility because interstices multiply to include the encounter between as many materials as the world holds.[31] Once *materials* comes to mean words, feelings, ideas, visual images, reminiscences, people, animals, objects, and nature, the range of untold encounters becomes infinitely expandable. Bishop concentrates on the way that these materials can interpermeate, resist, subside, tilt into or against one another, shift toward or away, condense, disperse, diffuse, reflect, modulate, absorb, and diverge.

This book emphasizes the way that Bishop created her own post-modernist poetics partly by deploying, in her own medium, the experiments of visual artists with absorption, incorporation, or suspension in a mobile space that holds, diffuses, condenses, balances, counter-weighs, moves, and orchestrates differences in scale, directionality, and speed. In exploring this terrain, it is possible to uncover not only another case study in what Charles Altieri has called the modernist "dialectic between painterly achievements, writerly appropriations, and painterly responses" (1989, 178) but also a novel and illuminating channel in the multiple currents of transition between modernism and postmodernism. In the modernist shift away from the orienting function of an upright figure, bound in space, and facing a frontal screen or virtual space organized around a single perspective point, Klee, Schwitters, and Calder created innovative ways to reorient the subject in a three-dimensional space not organized by the virtual. These artists emphasized the way that orientation in space impacts and organizes the sense of self and experimented with tactile empathy and with atmospheres of lucidity and clarity that darken and deepen. Klee and Calder both worked with a mobile field from which an event emerges and that frames us. In Klee, the release of the line from bounding the figure is closely related to the subject's sense that the surface of the body is incompletely and incoherently sensed from inside, cannot properly bound the ego, and is open to and entangled in the environment. Ultimately, Bishop's sense of an "I" comes closest to the mobility of visual art's staging of an event in which an object appears in a field that did not contain it before but that immediately rearranges itself, opening, to hold it. The self is not the center of that occurrence. The "I" is itself a kind of field, the borders of which are continuously altered by occurrences outside its bounds.

୬୧

This book begins by reopening the discussion of the aesthetic challenge that Marianne Moore thrust at Bishop in 1938, the challenge to work out a deeper, more profound poetics. Although Moore herself continuously took the rehabilitation of surface as one of her central subjects, she ultimately grounded her poetry in the depths of ethical inquiry and pronouncement. As others have noted, Bishop could not validate her own poetics by grounding it in Christian ethics and had to find another solution to Moore's challenge and a means of redressing her own dissatisfaction with a poetry that came dangerously close to the merely picturesque (Lucie-Smith 13; Ribeiro 15).[32] In chapter 1, I show that Bishop's poem "Pleasure Seas" (composed in 1938–1939) is an intellectualized early solution to the problem of depth. In "Pleasure Seas," Bishop uses the impressionist space of the sea surface—sea, sky, light, atmosphere—as the object against which the mind plays out its possible relations. John Dewey's *Art as Experience* and Meyer Schapiro's famous essay "Matisse and Impressionism" supply much of the thematics of Bishop's poem, and Bishop attends to the postimpressionist painter Seurat to move beyond impressionism and its attraction to surface. The poem reveals the reason that "glassy water" became so central to Bishop's poetry. Glassy water exhibited a "perspectival tension between two and three dimensions" that resembled the dynamics of verse.[33] In its sequence of glassy surfaces, "Pleasure Seas" launches a complex set of images that posits verse as a kind of deep threshold open in two directions: to nature and to the interior of the poet. The surface of verse, like the surface of water, becomes a threshold that registers but also intensifies, transforms, and refracts the variety of the mind's as well as nature's materials. It is a surface that faces both ways: toward an exterior nature, which it refracts and records, and toward an interior subjectivity, which it also refracts and records. In this way, Bishop found a means of working with the "depth of experience" that Moore had pronounced unavailable.

In chapter 2, I argue that Bishop used Klee's experiments with deep space to move beyond the intellectualized solution to the problem of depth that she had produced in "Pleasure Seas." By drawing on Klee's experiments, Bishop widened her sense of the surface of verse so that it became deeper and more coextensive with the interior of the lyric subject. She also positioned the lyric subject as suspended and moving among orbiting and unfolding motifs and atmospheres.

The reception of Klee's paintings in the late 1930s to mid-1940s stressed that the viewer must step through the surface of the painting and become identified with an eye in the painting so that the viewer's body became partially coextensive with a mobile landscape. Such an effacement of the skin of the viewer could become deadly. In two paintings that particularly intrigued Bishop, Klee expressed the extreme anxiety caused by the invasion of a force from outside that enters the self and severs its integrity. In these paintings, subjectivity became catastrophically open to the surround that violently encroached on and crossed the membrane of skin or consciousness. But Bishop also used Klee's experiments with deep space to protest that invasion and to redress it. Drawing on the aesthetics of Klee—as made available to an American audience through the 1945 MoMA publication edited by her friend, Margaret Miller—Bishop created poetic structures that allowed for the relation to external forces to be held at a distance, where differences in scale and speed do not threaten the self but are ranged around it in a variety of shapes or orbits. Contemporary criticism on Klee also described an alternative structure for engagement with forces outside the self, stressing the suspension of the subject in relation to floating motifs and the variety of colors and textures that cross into but do not threaten the self. In this mode, openness allows for a genial, capaciousness, gentle emotional warmth and response to the surprise of encountering motifs and textures that emerge in the environment. The critical discourse about Klee gave rise to compositional methods that Bishop continued to use in her drafts through the 1950s.

In chapter 3, I explore the compositional methods that Bishop derived from the work of Kurt Schwitters's collages. Schwitters arranged materials to modulate toward and away from one another by tiny resemblances and differences; and most visibly in "Cape Breton" and "At the Fishhouses," Bishop used his method to conceptualize poems as staging the interfaces among materials. In the Schwitters's collages, not only are the real objects of the culture brought inside the frame of art—a feature common to most twentieth-century collages—but also the materials of art are sequenced in tiny intervals of modulation toward the real. Schwitters arranged sequences from airiness to dense reality using transparent, semitransparent, and opaque papers. Transparent fragile materials gain color, density, and weight, and line modulates to surface and then to three-dimensional object, "crossing over" into the real by gaining density, weight, and saturation of color. In organizing modulations from art to life and across representational levels, Schwitters provided Bishop with a model for imagining the poem as a site of assemblage or collage, where the layers of human experience—visual image, personal reminiscence, a physical feeling, an emotion, an idea, a word—are brought together to interact as layers opening on to or into one another with varying weights, densities, and durations. Schwitters's ideas about lines that thickened into planes, fabrics that loosened into nets, and nets that disintegrated into lines or thickened into wires considerably altered Bishop's understanding of verse as a fabric that interfaced with other fabrics in the world and gave her one means of gently incorporating human ideas and metaphors into embodied experience. Linguistic metaphors become one kind of "deposit" that the human mind lays quietly or jarringly in different degrees of "touch" on the materials of landscape, animals, and the interior world.

In chapter 4, I argue that Bishop experimented with the verse line hovering over and sinking into landscape, incorporating objects, and holding subjectivity. I return to several Klee images that Bishop would have seen in 1948–1950, in which the artist uses a wandering, loosely drawn line that expressively rendered the human figure as open to and entangled in the environment or the human figure as partially hidden or embedded in the environment. Bishop's "View of the Capitol from the Library of Congress," "Insomnia," "The Prodigal," and "Argument" thematize lines and surfaces, hold the lyric speaker entangled in or hidden within an environment, and present the lyric speaker as falling into various kinds of extent. Bishop's poetic sequence "Four Poems" can be read as a radical experiment in imagining the lyric speaker held, entangled in, and opening toward lines and surfaces in the interior and exterior landscapes. The poem sequence constitutes the extreme version of Bishop's complex correlation of the surface of verse with skin and the membrane of the mind.

Bishop never again repeats the extreme style of "Four Poems," and in chapter 5, I show her use of Calder's aesthetic to ameliorate the anxiety associated with the dissolution of the surface of verse and extreme disintegration of the lyric speaker in "Four Poems." I trace the mid-century critical reception of Calder, known to Bishop because both Margaret Miller and Lota Macedo de Soares played important roles in that reception. Calder's aesthetic strategy of "composing motions," in which he orchestrated "contrasting movements and changing relations of form in space" became associated with buoyancy, humor, and pleasure, a counterweight to the despair and grief of the war (Sweeney 1943, 30). The system of the mobiles allowed one to feel the disparities between the elements so that the randomness and "accidents" felt peaceful, gentle, and orderly without becoming fixed or rigid. Through a catalogue description by Jean-Paul Sartre, the weightlessness, mobility, freshness, and surprise of the mobiles were characterized as a "private celebration" (quoted in Giménez and Rower 69) Sartre's comments associated the mobiles with the philosophical thematics of inclining from passive to active or a hesitation between being acted on and acting. In all these respects, Bishop's title poem, "A Cold Spring," situates itself in the realm of Calder's aesthetics. "Arrival at Santos" (originally part of the volume *A Cold Spring*), notebook passages from the 1950s, "Armadillo," the unpublished poems "Gypsophilia" and "St. Iphigenia, and "The Moose" all show Bishop's working inside Calder's aesthetic to organize the elements of her poems. In many of these poems, and especially in "North Haven," Bishop combines Schwitters's focus on materials of variant densities with her characteristic revision of Calder's hesitant inclining toward movement so that it is also an unfurling toward both emotional and spatial depths. In "North Haven," the dead body of Robert Lowell becomes the motionless counterweight to the drifting "constellation" of the moving world in all its freshness, lightness, gentle improvisation, and surprise. "North Haven" reads as a masterpiece that reprises, with consummate ease, Bishop's profound and long-standing engagement with the visual arts and the discourse about it at mid-century.

ONE

VERSE AS DEEP SURFACE

I don't think I ever said how interested I was to hear about the
glass painting—is it still going on? . . . It is a very—well—without
getting metaphysical all one can say is "interesting medium"
I suppose.

—Elizabeth Bishop to Kit Barker, January 26, 1956

In 1938, Marianne Moore set the problem of depth explicitly
for her young protégé in a letter that Brett Millier, Bishop's biographer,
considers "may have been the most important single piece of criticism
Elizabeth ever received" (Millier 137). Moore wrote:

You and Dr. Niebuhr are two abashing peaks in present experience for me. . . . Dr. Niebuhr says Christianity is too much on
the defensive, that it is more mysterious, more comprehensive,
more lastingly deep and dependable than unsuccessfully simpler
substitutes which objectors to it offer; and I feel that although
large-scale "substance" runs the risk of inconsequence through
aesthetic impotence, and am one of those who despise clamor
about substance—to whom treatment really *is* substance—I can't
help wishing you would sometime in some way risk some unpro-
tected profundity of experience; or since no one admits profundity of experience, some characteristic private defiance of the
significantly detestable. . . . I do feel that tentativeness and interiorizing are your danger as well as your strength. (1997, 390–91)

The letter marks a particularly sensitive moment in a sequence of inter-changes in the evolving dynamic between the two poets (Keller 1983, 418, 421). As Costello argues, "by confronting Bishop with aesthetic and moral principles [Moore] forced the young poet to consider her own artistic decisions on a larger scale" (1984, 137). The May 1, 1938, letter was received by Bishop during the period crucial for Bishop's transition to a poetics that moved beyond her early more introspective, fantastic poems (Kalstone 61–75; Travisano 1988, 19, 56; Page 1993, 200–206). In the 1930s climate of pressure to write a more politically engaged poetry, Moore urged Bishop to turn, as the older poet herself had, to the "deeper" moral and metaphysical Christian critique of cul-ture provided by Reinhold Niebuhr—hence the swerve in Moore's phrasing from a wide arena for poetic practice ("profundity of experi-ence") to the more constricted arena of morality ("private defiance of the significantly detestable"). Although Bishop admired Niebuhr and read some of his work, she could not rely on Christian metaphysics to provide a ground or create depth for her work.

Bishop felt the May 1, 1938, letter as an attack. In fact, Moore her-self used the term *attack* in a handwritten addendum at the bottom of the typed letter: "Don't interrupt yourself to answer this deference & attack" (Moore 1997, 391). In her reply, Bishop told Moore that she had "been having some meditations this morning" on the subject of the letter, where "meditations" clearly has a seventeenth-century Prot-estant aura of severe self-scrutiny (Bishop 1994, 73). The self-doubt that the letter engendered can be felt in the fact that Bishop's respond-ing letter asked Moore point blank whether it was worth her while to go on writing poems ("I wish sometimes you would tell me quite frankly if you think there is any use—any real use—in my continuing with them"; Bishop 1994, 73). She understood the remark as a call to write something more "important." In this, she heard Moore's advice correctly; as Charles Molesworth tells us, "for [Moore], 'depth of ut-terance' came more and more to mean a way of speaking with moral seriousness" (Molesworth 318).

There is some indication that Moore, herself, considered this letter and the terms of its critique to be crucial for her relationship to Bishop. Many years later, in the last paragraphs of her 1946 review of Bishop's first book, *North & South,* Moore returned to the terms of the critique laid out in the 1938 letter and systematically undid them. Reappearing only to be transfigured, the themes arrive: "interiorizing" and "tentativeness," lack of "depth," aesthetics divorced from morality, the reference to Niebhur, and the implied directive to pronounce moral dicta. These concluding paragraphs of the review also contain what appears to be a private request for forgiveness. Moore begins this section of the review by quoting from Bishop's poem, "The Imaginary Iceberg":

> Art which "cuts its facets from within" can mitigate suffering, can even be an instrument of happiness; as also forgiveness, symbolized in Miss Bishop's meditation of St. Peter by the cock, seems essential to happiness. Reinhold Niebhur recently drew attention in *The Nation* to the fact that the cure for international incompatibilities is not diplomacy but contrition. Nor is it permissible to select the wrongs for which to be contrite; *we are contrite; we won't be happy till we are sorry.* Miss Bishop's speculation, also, concerning faith—religious faith—is a carefully plumbed *depth* in this small-large book of beautifully formulated aesthetic-moral mathematics. The unbeliever is not ridiculed; but is not anything that is adamant, self-ironized?

> > . . . Up here
> > I tower through the sky
> > For the marble wings on my tower-top fly.

> With poetry as with homiletics, *tentativeness* can be more positive than positiveness; and in *North & South,* a much instructed persuasiveness is emphasized by uninsistence. At last we have a prize book that has no creditable mannerisms. At last we have someone who knows, who is not didactic. (Moore 1986, 408; emphasis added)

The densely packed passage withdraws all the terms of the critique in the May 1, 1938 letter, retrieving each term in order to turn it into praise. First, Moore commends rather than critiques an interiorizing poetry ("art that cuts its facets from within" can serve a significant, almost Christian, purpose, to "mitigate suffering"). Then, reinvoking "tentativeness" by name ("tentativeness can be more positive than positiveness"), she immediately redeems it, insisting that "uninsistence" is stronger and more persuasive than the didactic. The seemingly arbitrary movement to mentioning Niebuhr creates a structure that aligns the theologian's and Bishop's views, in contrast to the earlier letter that had used the theologian to "abash" the poet. In her newly invented term "aesthetic-moral mathematics," Moore withdraws her previous critique that Bishop's poetry failed to risk the move into morality. The seemingly arbitrary swerve into reflections on the theme of forgiveness leads up to a moment of contrition ("we are contrite; we won't be happy until we are sorry"), a statement that disguises personal apology as impersonal pronouncement.[1]

But, although in 1946, Moore herself could acknowledge, albeit in coded language, that Bishop had successfully met the challenge to create a poetry of sufficient depth, the road to that success had not been self-evident in 1938. At first, Bishop did attempt to follow Moore's suggestion to turn to Niebuhr. The correspondence with Moore shows that Bishop had purchased Niebuhr's *Beyond Tragedy,* was searching for it among recently unpacked boxes, and then had started to read it (letters from Bishop to Marianne Moore, May 1, 1938, VSC; January 14, 1939, in Bishop 1994, 78). Even if she never got past the first few pages of the book, she would have found Niebuhr to be articulating a philosophy of artistic creation diametrically opposed to the one that Bishop herself had developed in her early essays. In his description of an artist at work, Niebuhr assumes that the artist would have in mind a "meaning" that could prioritize all of experience, arranging and necessarily falsifying some things in order to portray a composite deeper meaning of experience (Niebuhr 6). In contrast, in her 1934 essay "Dimensions for a Novel," Bishop had argued passionately that continuous acts of retrospection reinterpreted experience, always reconfiguring a meaning that could not be fully known.[2] Bishop needed a theory that did not skip over the problem of tentativeness to reach depth or certainty of knowledge. She found aesthetic theories that were much more congenial and useful to her in the writings of John Dewey and the art historian Meyer Schapiro who had assisted Dewey in writing about visual art.

John Dewey and Meyer Schapiro

On February 13, 1939, a month after Bishop mentions reading Niebuhr's *Beyond Tragedy,* Bishop first met John Dewey, and on February 14, she tells Moore that she would like to read something by Dewey and asks Moore to suggest a book (Bishop 1994, 80). It is likely that whatever else Moore suggested (there is no record of her response to Bishop's query), Bishop would have read the work by Dewey that focused on her own interest, that is, on art; and Bishop's 1939 poem, "Pleasure Seas," provides evidence that she did so.[3] The poem also functions as a somewhat intellectualized, early theorization of Bishop's own developing poetics. Bishop's response to Moore's letter revealed that she was looking for a theory for writing poetry comparable to the one that she had experimented with in writing her short stories (Bishop 1994, 73). Although Bishop never formally recorded that theory in any prose treatise, the poem "Pleasure Seas" (accepted for publication by Harpers in 1939 but never printed) seems to be an aesthetic theory in poetic form.[4] It lays out, rather programmatically, the mind's relation to nature that would eventually become a foundation of Bishop's aesthetics.

In *Art as Experience* (1934), Dewey argues for a philosophy that "accepts life and experience in all its uncertainty, mystery, doubt, and half-knowledge, and [in imagination and art] turns that experience upon itself to deepen and intensify its own qualities" (Dewey 41). In its understanding of meaning, Dewey's book comes close to Bishop's early prose theorizing and sharply contrasts Niebuhr's. Dewey says that meaning accumulates by the observer's successively taking in new observations and reinterpreting what has come before. In setting the foundation of art on "uncertainty" and "half-knowledge," Dewey would have given validity to that very "tentativeness" that Moore, in the same letter of May 1, 1938, had labeled a "danger" for Bishop's work.[5] And Dewey speaks explicitly about surface and depth in experience, offering a definition of "profundity of experience" that does not depend on Christian truth.

Dewey's definition of depth focuses on perception. Mere identification of phenomena is a kind of nodding off, a way of avoiding experience because one applies the previously known too imperiously to new phenomena ("not perception but recognition"; Dewey 58). In Dewey's terms, this imperiousness overemphasizes "doing" in contrast to "undergoing," which has the sense of "suffering" or "taking in" (47–48). If "doing" rather than "undergoing" is overemphasized, experience is "all on the surface" (51). In contrast to that skating over the surface, depth of experience is created by the reciprocal relationship between mind and nature or object: "What is done and what is undergone are thus reciprocally, cumulatively, and continuously instrumental to one another" (57). Depth occurs in the permeability of objects by emotion as well as by intellect: "There is, therefore, no such thing in perception as seeing or hearing *plus* emotion. The perceived object or scene is emotionally pervaded throughout. When an aroused emotion does not permeate the material that is perceived or thought of, it is either preliminary or pathological" (59). The mind is imagined as balanced between taking in and giving out: "Perception is an act of the going-out of energy in order to receive, not a withholding of energy. To steep ourselves in a subject-matter we have first to plunge into it. When we are only passive to a scene, it overwhelms us and, for lack of answering activity, we do not perceive that which bears us down. We must summon energy and pitch it at a responsive key in order to *take* in" (60, emphasis in original).

Depth of experience arises from the fluid reciprocal interaction between intellect, emotion, and material object. Dewey's *Art as Experience,* therefore, provided an alternative definition of *profundity of experience* based in the integrity of sensory, perceptual, and intellectual interaction with nature, a theory ready to hand for a poet who needed to create depth without grounding her work in moral pronouncements. In fact, Dewey's descriptions of depth allowed Bishop to defy Moore's parenthetical "since no one admits profundity of experience" (Moore 1997, 391). Dewey *did* allow for depth of experience and showed the way to escape from the demand to reach depth of utterance by moving toward the Christian, the political, or the moral.

Dewey drew on Meyer Schapiro's ideas about Impressionism when composing his theory of art (in the preface to *Art as Experience,* Dewey thanks Schapiro for reading and revising the book). In the mid-1930s and 1940s, Schapiro had a galvanizing effect on the art community in New York City. He achieved almost cultlike status, and Moore herself had been swept up by him. In a letter to Bishop, Moore described hearing Schapiro lecture on Merovingian art as "an almost capsizing experience for me" (February 28, 1937, VSC). Many years later, Bishop mentioned Schapiro as "just about our very best art critic" (letter to Kit and Ilse Barker, March 23, 1956, PUL). Perhaps even more significantly, Margaret Miller admired Schapiro and chose him as the director of her master's thesis on an eleventh-century British psalter. Although Schapiro left New York University to take up a position at

Columbia before Miller finished her thesis, it is Schapiro, rather than her official advisor, who Miller felt had been the more profound influence on her work. She writes that Schapiro had "suggested the manuscript as a subject for study" and says that she is "endebted [to Schapiro] not only for much helpful criticism in the course of the preparation of this paper, but also for my general conception of Romanesque art, an obligation which exceeds footnote acknowledgement" (Miller 1941, 2). Although in the 1930s Schapiro worked mostly in the field of medieval art, he had become well known also for essays on modern art. An early essay had become integrated into the textbook for Columbia University's core curriculum and a long essay reviewing the Matisse exhibit at MoMA in 1931 had become equally well known. Miller may have become familiar with these articles at Vassar (especially given that she wrote the review of the extensive modern art exhibition held at Vassar in 1934), and she would certainly have become aware of the articles when she took a course at New York University from Schapiro on illuminated medieval manuscripts and then chose him as her thesis director. Given Schapiro's popularity among the artistic community (a popularity based partially on the circulation of his manuscripts), Miller's enthusiasm for Schapiro, Bishop's attendance at some of Schapiro's classes with Miller, and Bishop's interest in visual art, it is probable that Miller shared these publications with Bishop.

Schapiro's essays on impressionism and on Matisse's relationship to impressionism contain much of the thematic program for "Pleasure Seas." In impressionism, nature is "presented as a field for direct and immediate enjoyment"; impressionism takes as its subject matter "aspects of nature like sky, water, vistas, light, atmosphere, moving objects, which we enjoy for their own sake" (Schapiro 1932, 23). So, "Pleasure Seas," a poem that treats sky, water, vistas, light, and atmosphere in the key of pleasure, locates itself in the arena of impressionist painting. The setting of a sequence of colors that "expand the range of color"; the inclusion of "the most unusual coloring of objects"; the move toward "vibrant" high-keyed tones; the change of colors over time; contours and lines that lose "their definiteness"; and "restlessness of surface," broken surfaces, irregular surfaces—all these elements of impressionism described by Schapiro appear in Bishop's poem (Schapiro 1932, 24, 25, 35, 36). Yet, Bishop does not merely draw Schapiro's theory of impressionism into the medium of poetry. In his essays, Schapiro makes clear that tentativeness and lack of depth were charges brought against the impressionists, so Bishop would naturally have been interested in the means by which Matisse and other postimpressionists emerged from their encounter with nature having recovered from the formlessness, flux, and dissolution of line reveled in by the impressionists.

In setting out Matisse's relationship to impressionism, Schapiro made clear that impressionism had come to stand "at the opposite pole of form" (Schapiro 1932, 22). According to Schapiro, for the impressionists, "shape" and the renaissance imposition of "preconceived design," like Dewey's preconceived ideas, prohibited a fresh true rendering of nature. In impressionism, "form was almost completely disintegrated" (Schapiro 1930, 277). Impressionists embedded objects "in a continuous atmospheric or luminous field," where they were "rendered by minute, vibrant, overlapping particles which hardly resembled in their flecked or dotted character the original constituents of the object" (Schapiro 1932, 24). Schapiro explains, "Impressionists destroyed drawing in the classical sense. There ceased to be such a thing as correct drawing, or any linear drawing, for that matter, since contours had lost their definiteness" (1932, 25). But, he argues, postimpressionists, such as Paul Cezanne, Seurat, and Henri Matisse, all experimented with the reintroduction of form, depth, and shape. Bishop chose the *post*impressionist Seurat as the painter named in "Pleasure Seas," and she made the landscape move into and out of form, depth, line, and meaning. She took this discussion of line, definiteness, and fluidity and translated it into her own attempt to see and render nature. The poem moves from boundaries and lines and hard edges to spaces of increased fluidity and back again. Schapiro claims that impressionism used "shapes and colors without respect to their meanings" (1932, 23), but he suggests that postimpressionism leaves the space of pure tentativeness and flux and moves partway toward certainty, distinctness of outline, articulation of shape, and the reintroduction of depth. As if entering the space of impressionism and also leaving it, Bishop arranged to have the speaker of the poem go beyond the flat surface, through the dots, and enter first a bas-relief and then a three-dimensional space. If impressionism provided a means of recording the individual mind's responsiveness to nature, postimpressionism more nearly resembled the kind of perception that Dewey had described, one that included ideas brought to the encounter and arising from the encounter. In "Pleasure Seas," Bishop experimented with the intellectual, allowing conceptual language and meaning to enter into and arise out of the scene of perception.[6]

In the process, she invented for Dewey's philosophy of experience a new set of images. The poem tells the story of a deep experience, such as Dewey had described, rendering the experience in a series of reflections on thematics that Dewey had considered: depth, absorption, permeability, "doing," and "undergoing." Bishop also brought into the poem, as Dewey had discussed, the past of other perceptual experiences (looking at the sea from a boat and from a plane). "Pleasure Seas" provides an answer to Moore's challenge, redefining the relationship between surface and depth so that "profundity of experience" becomes something other than moral judgment. The poem can be read as a meditation on surface and depth and shows us Bishop's working out a theory of intricate description that can attain "profundity of experience." It allows us to begin to unravel the story of the significance, for Bishop, of the complex dynamic between the two-dimensional and three-dimensional, a motif that appears more or less continuously throughout her career. The poem provides an early indication of the way that Bishop used the dynamics of form-flux and surface-depth relations in visual art as a means of conceptualizing those relations in verse.

Verse and Water

Scattered passages in notebooks, prose, and poetry reveal Bishop's imagining a metaphorical resemblance between the dynamics of water and those of the verse line and demonstrate that she imagined the surface of verse as the surface of water. These excerpts reveal that Bishop associated verse with water, especially with water's fluctuation between two and three dimensions so that verse becomes felt as a deep surface. One of the first descriptions of water in the notebooks shows Bishop's interest in the play between surface and depth: "the water so clear & pale that you are seeing *into* it at the same time you are looking *at* its surface. A *duplicity*—all the way through" (VSC 72A.3, 2, emphasis in original). Bishop's comment shows her to be intrigued by a medium that can be flat surface and open depth simultaneously. She seems especially alert to water's ability to hover between two and three dimensions. A note taken on Erwin Panofsky's New

York University course reinforces this impression. Although her notes for the course are almost entirely without personal comment, we find a marginal notation of a large question mark that indicates increased attentiveness or interest in Panofsky's remark about one feature of baroque art: "perspectival tension between two and three dimensions" (VSC 71.1, 21). Uncharacteristically for these class notes, Bishop wrote a phrase on the back of one of the nearby pages, "glassy water," suggesting that for Bishop "glassy water" exhibited that perspectival tension between two and three dimensions (VSC 71.1, 20).

In the later of Elizabeth Bishop's two Key West notebooks, we find an idiosyncratic conceptualization of water's play between two and three dimensions, one that I think is of long-term and broad significance for the way that Bishop imagined nature. A draft of a bitterly humorous, rather unpromising poem is entitled "The Sea, or, the Moderator Modulated" (VSC 75.3b, 197). *Moderator* is a nineteenth-century term for an oil lamp or the device on an oil lamp that controls the intensity and therefore the color of the flame ("the mechanism which regulates the flow of oil to the wick in a moderator lamp"; *Oxford English Dictionary [OED]* 8). Calling the sea a "moderator" imagines the water as a device for changing the quality, color, and intensity of the light that passes through it or touches its surface. Or it imagines the sea as the screen material or mantle of the lamp through which the light passes. Bishop's European travel diaries and the notes from both Provincetown and Key West record her fascination with the alteration of the surfaces of the world under differing conditions of light, weather, and time of day, but in the notebooks, the sea—even more than olive groves, fields, or buildings—appears as a particularly finely tuned instrument for displaying variegated and surprising beauty. The poem fragment's title, "The Sea or the Moderator Modulated," allows us to see that Bishop had a private term for the way that the sea worked as screen and projector of luminosity and color. We can feel the presence of that private association in the well-known line from Bishop's poem "The Bight," where water is "the color of the gas flame turned as low as possible" (*CP* 60).[7] As a moderator lamp, the surface of the sea becomes a glass on which the changes of light and weather become visible and are intensified or transformed, moving through the fullest range of modulations of tone, hue, brightness, shade, translucency, and opacity. The outside light, above the water, diffuses through the medium of water, recorded but also transformed and intensified on a new surface, one whose qualities arise partially from that surface having its own depths.

The poem fragment also explicitly reveals an association that Bishop frequently made implicitly—that the ever-modulating sea surface is comparable to the modulations available in lines of verse. The speaker of that fragment in the notebook claims to have promised "Always to live over water / & never to resist its verses" (VSC 75.3b, 197).[8] Clearly, the draft associates the sea and its waves with lines of verse that can move, moderate, or modulate the reader/viewer. Quite a few other passages in prose, notebooks, and poems show that Bishop associated the surface of the sea with verses. The most explicit linkage occurs in "Invitation to Miss Marianne Moore": "the waves are running in verses this fine morning" (CP 82). But, starting with her early essay on Gerard Manley Hopkins, we can see Bishop's thinking of lines of verse facing her on the page as a sea surface. She describes Hopkins's verse as "a fluid, detailed surface, made hesitant, lightened, slurred, weighed or feathered" and discusses the way that he can "blurr the edges with a kind of vibration and keep the atmosphere fresh and astir" (Bishop, "Gerard Manley Hopkins," 1934, 7). In the same brief essay, she compares a poem to a volume of water and compares the dynamics of emotion in the poem to the "drawing off" and "filling up" of that volume of water (6). In an isolated note on the bottom of a page of notes taken in 1934–1935 at the New York Public Library, Bishop conceived of the rhythmic lines of verse as a kind of "surface"; she wrote, "meter is a tangible surface of rhythm" (VSC 72A.2, 18). In "Over 2000 Illustrations and a Complete Concordance," to move into the sea is to move into or between "the lines / the burin made, the lines that move apart," which are also the verse lines of the poem that move apart to create the stanza break as the speaker travels from the page of an engraving to "real" sea (CP 57). So, lines of verse simultaneously act as lines of sea.

All of these passages, scattered over more than a decade, reveal that Bishop habitually imagined the sea as lines of verse and, conversely, imagined verse as a kind of liquid, contained by "walls." The walls can be the edge of the line, the use of rhyme, or the shape of couplet or stanza—"In this manner the boundaries of the poem are set free, and the whole thing is loosened up; the motion is kept going without the more or less strong checks customary at the end of lines," she writes about Hopkins's verse (Bishop 1934, "Gerard Manley Hopkins," 7). The lines are "wavy" with motion and momentum but also fixed in place on the page in their stanzaic or sentence-unit forms. Bishop is drawn to imagining verse lines as simultaneously but ever-variously wavy *and* stable. In an undated (probably 1930s) fragment, Bishop wondered whether "the sound of vowel goes *back & forth* between walls of consonant?" (VSC 68.3, emphasis in original).

The verse lines can run in waves, hold up objects, glitter, and become charged or magnetic. The sound and duration of syllables and words, their weight and duration according to sense, the resonance of a metaphor—all release in the liquid verse differing "charges" that create various kinds of force or movement and that interact with one another. Of Hopkins, Bishop writes, "Syllables, the words in their actual duration and their duration according to sense value, set up among themselves a rhythm, which continues to flow over them" (Bishop 1934, "Gerard Manley Hopkins," 5). Of Moore, Bishop writes: "metaphor, when used, carries a long way, reverberates, like her [Moore's] 'pulsation of lighthouse and noise of bellbuoys'" (Bishop 1948, 132). The verse line and its variations are an instrument for setting into activity this diverse array of kinds of materials and movements, touching one another.

It is clear that Bishop thought about these rhythmic interactions inside the waviness of the lines in relation to the dynamics of emotion in poems. We have already seen that she constructs the metaphor of verse as water to talk about the dynamics of emotion in her early essay on Hopkins. In her notebooks, we see that Bishop carefully recorded the variety of interactions between sea and light. But while the sea acted as a moderator for light, it was also a surface that could act as a moderator for the emotions, a device that could key them up or down. Frequently, we see in her travel diaries and observation notebooks that the sea's variousness of color, light, and movement gave rise to delight. But, as we can see in "The Bight," the moderator could also modulate "down," to "the color of the gas flame turned as low as possible," the key of a dangerous, almost final despair (*CP* 60). The surface of verse, like the surface of the sea, became a moderator for the emotions; the verse line, as instrument for setting into activity its diverse array of kinds of materials and movements, touching one another and moving one another, therefore opened into the materials in the mind, moving, condensing, diffusing. The materials of the mind become touched and can then participate in these fluid interactions.[9] The surface of verse, like the surface of water, becomes a threshold that registers but also intensifies, transforms, and refracts the variety of the mind's as well as nature's materials.

Because Bishop's notebooks often record her perceptions of the environment, the passages can provide a close-up view of the way that Bishop experienced the mind crossing over into the "intricate density" of nature's diverse materials, and it is instructive to watch that interface more closely, even when the presence of a surface of water or verse is not involved. Some of Bishop's more strangely charged passages show that space "opens" or "closes." These passages enact a spectator being "pulled" into a more intimate encounter with the space and then retreating into a more distanced look. Bishop recorded the look, feel, and sound of night from inside her closed and shuttered bedroom in Key West: "All night the closed shutters make me feel like Jonah in the whales belly, looking out the gills [. . . .] The stars slide slowly across the slits—stars on an abacus. When it is windy the palm trees moving between the street lamp & the shutter make them cast dense . . . shadows on the opposite walls—a heart fluttering among them" (VSC 77.3, 3). Here we sense the density of experience that results when Bishop plays against one another the different kinds of extensions or fields of attention. A dimensional space is created between or among the three kinds of movement occurring at their different paces (slowly gliding stars, stationary shutters, and swaying palm trees that produce shadows). The consciousness of the observer hovers among these spaces—"a heart fluttering among them" not located inside the body but outside, among the objects that draw her.[10] The consciousness at times feels withdrawn inward, condensed, hiding ("like Jonah in the whale's belly"), and at other times it seems expansive, extended or spread out among the objects of attention (stars, palm trees, and shadows).

Other passages that record observations made from inside the house produce an even more complex "pull" related to kinds of extensions of dimensions for attentiveness: "The rain has stopped a quarter of an hour ago, but the last drops are still falling around the house,— differently timed, at different points, some loud, some soft. Now there is one left—drop, drop. Drop. Oldest inhabitant" (VSC 77.3, 13). The outdoors, imagined from indoors, acquires spatial depth arising from the intricacy of detail about sounds and the timing of sounds. Raindrops falling at different rates create a kind of delay, or waiting, inside of which the consciousness of the observer "hangs" along with the drop. Raindrops are located at various distances from the house, stretching the location of the consciousness of the observer so that, in addition to time, space opens up and acquires a dimension of near-nesses and deep recesses. The variety of weight of the raindrops opens up still another extendable field, a range from light to heavy. Another possible field of extension and variation, temperature, appears in a brief note: "In the icy shadow of the lime-tree. Is the shadow of a large tree colder than the shadow of a small one?" (VSC 75.4b, 136). The landscape emerges, in imagination, as tones of combined shadow and coolness, from low to greater intensity. The depth of the land-scape (whether created by a variable field of spatial recess, weight, coolness, or delay) hovers in relation to the mind, which is suspended in attentiveness and alert to flickers of alteration in these fields. The depth of the experience is created by setting different kinds of dimen-sionality in relation to one another. Depth is created by a pulled atten-tion and multiple dimensions layered against one another so that what is out there becomes "thick" or "crisscrossed" with various kinds of extension. It is as if space is opened and the mind can move into it more intimately.

Bishop's sense of nature's "intricacy of density" or "interview" with itself shows that she thought of nature as having these kinds of grada-tions or modulations, as nature touched itself, crisscrossing different materials and registers (VSC 75.2; CP 28). She recorded her mind mov-ing into nature, suspended or projecting among these intricate mate-rials. Consciousness is pulled into the dimensions crisscrossing one another: stars slowly sliding, palm trees swaying, shadows on a wall; coolness of space below the variable size of the shadows of lime trees; and different weights of raindrops that have different lengths of time between their falls and are located at different distances from the ob-server. The notebooks show the opening and closing of space, the surface of the world opening. The surface itself becomes "thick" with variations and has depth. The observer's consciousness is stretched out as it encounters these variations. This is in no way a blurred merg-ing of the subject with the environment but, rather, a field of uneven and differently paced condensations, diffusions, and cross-registered identifications. The notebook passages render the experience of subjectivity in its mobility between extending itself to absorb the world and condensing into the feeling of self located inside the body, inside the mind. Like the child's consciousness in the passages about the child "hiding" in her grandparents' house quoted in the introduction, the mind "hides," closed in on itself within its own sense of circumference and sways out to see feelingly other materials in the periphery that become other skins, other circumferences. This tactile empathy that spatially locates consciousness inside the diverse materials of the surround diffuses the sense of the "I" so that it is stretched among the atmospheres, textures, and objects of the surround.

Yet these perceptual experiences locate the screen on which consciousness is temporarily held all over the place. The in and out movement of consciousness, therefore, becomes as various (in kinds of experience, in place) as the world that is perceived. Only by imagining a single surface—verse or water—capable of registering, reflecting, absorbing the materials of mind and nature, a surface on which they could then meet and interact, could the subject prevent itself from becoming scattered by its multiple and shifting sensations. In "Pleasure Seas," Bishop imagines the surface of water and the surface of verse—like the surface of a painting for the impressionists—as providing such a screen. In imagining both verse and the sea as surfaces that could record encounters between mind and nature, Bishop was maneuvering in the territory opened up by the discourse about impressionism and postimpressionism, where the surface of the painting became the screen or boundary that recorded the active encounter between responding sensibility and the exterior world. Like the surface of a painting, verse is a surface that faces both ways: toward an exterior nature, which it refracts and records, and toward an interior subjectivity, which it also refracts and records.

"Pleasure Seas"

"Pleasure Seas" works out a set of encounters between the mind and nature. The poem offers a sequence of spaces opening, one after the other. Water acts as a screen much like the moderator lamp, recording, refracting, and transforming light from above and below. It is a flat surface that also opens both upward and downward, so it is a flat surface that acts as a threshold open to deep spaces. In its sequence of glassy surfaces, "Pleasure Seas" launches a complex set of images that posit verse as a kind of deep threshold open in two directions: to nature and to the interior of the poet.[11]

In the first section of "Pleasure Seas," we encounter a bounded space in which the water is "perfectly flat" and the qualities of surface are explored in detail:

> In the walled off swimming-pool the water is perfectly flat.
> The pink Seurat bathers are dipping themselves in and out
> Through a pane of bluish glass.
> The cloud reflections pass
> Huge amoeba-motions directly through
> The beds of bathing caps: white, lavender, and blue.
> If the sky turns gray, the water turns opaque,
> Pistachio green and Mermaid Milk. (CP 195)

This opening passage locates the poem within the discourses about visual art, not only by naming Seurat but also by recalling Alfred H. Barr's famous formulation that "the shape of the square confronts the silhouette of the amoeba" (1935, 19). In Bishop's poem, the fluidity of the natural world, in its amoeba-like biomorphic shapes, crosses through the square of the pool and neither predominates. The poem thereby announces itself as a both-and construction, a work of art that will not adhere to the dichotomy announced by Barr. Likewise, refusing to settle into a flat or deep space, the poem instead opens passages or interfaces between them. The first verse line conveys a flatness or stillness, stolid in its lack of rhythmic interest and in its perfectly flat, dead-stop end of the sentence. The flat "walled off swimming-pool" is opened to a new (but not visible) depth as the bathers step in and out through the flat surface. The rhythmic flatness does not modulate until Bishop gets to the phrase "dipping themselves," with its brief downward stress ("dip-") produced by the two unstressed syllables that precede it. The stress sinks heavier than the rest of the line and then lifts up as the bathers go down and up, "in and out" of the flat surface of the pool. The surface of the water and the surface of the verse line are thus shown to have dimension as flat planes are shown to be capable of depth (the water has its depth in space; the verse line has its depth in weightedness of syllable).

So, the first plane has already become a threshold. It opens downward. Next, Bishop reveals that the threshold can be open in one direction and closed in another. The surface of the water, in its perfect stability that cannot pass beyond the walls of the pool, is completely still. Yet this still plane can "receive" both motion and color. On the surface of the "glass," and leaving the pane of glass completely still, "cloud reflections pass / Huge amoeba-motions" across the surface of the pool. The perfect stability (the still surface of the water being unmoved) includes in another dimension (color) a perfectly responsive being moved because the clouds change the color of the water as they move across its surface. The flat surface has thus been opened upward; the color of that surface (whether its previous "bluish" color or the current shadows of moving clouds) is produced by the sky. When the sky alters from moving clouds to all gray, the surface of the pool receives the color and becomes "opaque." The entire surface of the water is shown to be completely responsive to the sky, even though the surface now looks closed, cannot be "seen through." The parts of the water dotted with bathing caps do not receive this motion or color. The bathing caps of the swimmers, their dots of "white, lavender, and blue," are not open to alterations of color in their environment and are unaware of and untouched by the larger phenomenon that is passing "through" them (*CP* 195). Likewise, the individual words, set off in a listing structure, are suspended as single units, seemingly oblivious to and rhythmically untouched by the larger structure of the rhyming-couplet sentence in which they are placed.

Bishop keeps multiplying the ways that surfaces can touch, move through, reflect, open to, or resist one another. The perfect responsiveness, the gray being "answered" by an opaque, also transforms that gray into a different shade of opacity, "Pistachio green and Mermaid Milk." So, the surface records but modulates the nature exterior to itself. Likewise, mind and water modulate when they encounter one another. The mind of the speaker/observer enters the plane of the poem obtrusively with the phrase "amoeba motions" and with outrageous color names ("Pistachio green and Mermaid Milk"), which draw attention to the human mind of the observer in the act of naming. "Mermaid Milk," a pure fantasy, becomes a category applied to the color of the surface of the water. Yet it is also a human category derived *from* that encounter—the color of the water needed a new name, so the already existent human invention mermaid becomes

"Mermaid Milk" through the process that Dewey calls the active encounter with nature. Throughout the poem, the verse becomes a kind of surface from which human language and categories jut out, or project, more or less obtrusively. Just as Dewey suggests in his *Art as Experience,* the mind of the speaker touches nature with different levels of openness or projection in a highly variegated mode of encounter.

This responsiveness or modification of one part of nature by another was Seurat's special study. His painting attempted to systematize the way that one color transformed neighboring colors. In "Pleasure Seas," color becomes a marker of the way that the dimensions cross one another because color is involved in issues of saturation; permeability; and shading into the next or neighboring form, diffusing—it is the boundary crosser par excellence. The poem moves from discrete dots of color that do not touch the neighboring material to more diffused colors that mingle or touch. But Bishop explores this phenomenon in multiple dimensions, not just with color. She uses words as another "color" that alter the material that it "touches." Words are brought to touch the surface of the water—first, "Pistachio green and Mermaid Milk," and later "ballroom" and "delight" (*CP* 195).

The range of colors serves as a kind of correlative, in another medium, of other aspects of experience that can touch, reflect, modulate, permeate, or absorb. The poem moves through a sequence of palettes, beginning with the Seurat-like pastel pink, white, lavender, and blue and the "pane of bluish glass"; moving later into the range of earthier tones ("clay-yellow," "purple," and "green"); and then "keying up the chromatic intensity" by allowing the more saturated tones of "vibrant," "neon-red, and "burning" to electrify the poem (*CP* 195).[12] Varieties of diffusion across and saturation of other spaces link color to the thematics of the range of reciprocal permeabilities (emotional and linguistic) of mind and nature. Bishop also imagined movement in various postures of permeability. Movement can sit "on the surface" (as we see when clouds move on the surface of the pool); movement can also be diffused across or through a neighboring space—it can penetrate other surfaces and create depth.

> But out among the keys
> Where the water goes its own way, the shallow pleasure seas

Drift this way and that mingling currents and tides
In most of the colors that swarm around the sides
Of soap-bubbles, poisonous and fabulous.
And the keys float lightly like rolls of green dust. (*CP* 195)

The first glassy threshold (the "bluish pane of glass" in the pool) is a flat, still, hard-edged plane through which the bathers' bodies pass without ruffling or moving the plane. The second threshold ("cloud reflections pass / Huge amoeba-motions") allows movement to skate over the surface, without any depth to the interaction. The third threshold (water colored by sky) becomes open to transformation (in color only) along its whole horizontal "edge." Here, the *but* that opens the second section of the poem points to increasing permeability across all these thresholds or edges. The surface opens or extends horizontally; there are no walls (only the extremely tenuous ones of the sides of soap bubbles and those only in a metaphor). The surface opens downward, a depth that is not underneath its reflective surface but is part of itself (the water is not flat with a depth underneath its "skin" but composed of "currents and tides"). The palette opens toward the widest possible range ("most of the colors that swarm around the sides / Of soap bubbles, poisonous and fabulous"). Movement is not merely on the skin of the surface (not just cloud reflections) but composed of "currents and tides." Objects are not isolated in the environment but drift ("the keys float lightly like rolls of green dust"). The land itself is not an edge but merely "dust," crumbled, granular, and open to diffusion or scattering. Likewise, the verse lines lose their firm edges, pick up a drifting rather than symmetrical balanced texture, and float unwieldy polysyllabic words in almost uncomfortably long-winded lines. And language now allows itself to place emotions in objects ("pleasure seas")—an alteration that extends later in the middle section of the poem when we see emotion (without the word naming it) go "inside" the water, saturating it. Losing "line" and "edge," keying up the palette, and increasing movement are all features of impressionism that Schapiro describes. But Bishop seems keenly interested in expanding the range of this impressionism to include a variety of experiences of depth.

After this introduction to surfaces that open (or become permeable) in multiple directions or dimensions, Bishop allows the reader to enter an increasingly deep space. The new landscape has a density of texture and weightedness that continues to increase as the next space opens between airplane, water surface, and underwater life. The pastel reflecting surface of the pool becomes a darker but also a more open surface, one that can be passed through, not by the bather's body but by the eye, looking from the plane above. Just as in the notebook passages, where the consciousness of the observer was pulled into nature and then retracted into its discrete location, so too the mind of the observer in "Pleasure Seas" sways back and forth, retracts to a discrete place of observation (the plane) and then goes out to diffuse itself, immersing in the materials of nature.

> From an airplane the water's heavy sheet
> Of glass above a bas-relief:
> Clay-yellow coral and purple dulces
> And long, leaning submerged green grass.
> Across it a wide shadow pulses. (*CP* 195)

Although the surface is again like glass, this time it is not reflective or opaque but allows the eye to enter. The "skin" of water now opens downward to include the depth "behind" it. The "shallow" "currents and tides," which were deeper than the pane of bluish glass, have yielded to an even deeper "surface," a "bas-relief"—not quite three dimensions but somewhere beyond two.

Depth of saturated color and density of materiality ("the water's heavy sheet") carries or opens toward depth of emotion. Beneath the surface, objects are saturated with emotion. The more saturated colors ("clay-yellow" and "purple") give a different kind of pleasure than the pastel pool, less light and airy, deeper. "And long, leaning, submerged green grass," with its swelling of forward motion, inclines with gentle insistence and desire. This movement is not just the mingling of currents and tides or the scrim of atmospherics of light and sky on water but pleasure in another key, slower, more languorous, the deeper pleasures of a denser materiality. The pleasure is conveyed also by the historical shadow of the word *dulces*, literally an edible seaweed but also linked to pleasure by its Romance meaning of "sweetness." The *OED* defines *dulce* as "sweetness, gentleness" (n.1) and as "sweet to the eye, ear, or feelings; pleasing, agreeable, soothing" (a.2), conveying sweetness and gentleness in the realm of both sense and emotion. The word caught Bishop's attention the previous summer in

Provincetown; she later wrote to Moore: "*dulces*—have you ever eaten it?—which is the most beautiful color of purple and green. Loren [MacIver] said a large Irish family used to come here to gather it every year, and the grandmother always referred to it as 'the lovely dulce'" (Bishop 1994, 77). The word's emotional weight of lovely and sweet seems to be carried within the word and the object, not applied to it from above (as in "pleasure seas" or, later, spray explicitly considered to be dancing "happily"). As the saturation of color and movement increases, Bishop alters the permeability of object by emotion. In these lines of the poem, objects are suffused by emotion rather than named by the words for emotions. The suppleness, ease, and amplitude of the verse's rhythm and the ease of the dulces's physical movement are saturated with one another. Like the tangible surface of verse that "floats" syllables, words, images, metaphors and that is acted on by them, the water "liquidly / Floats weeds, surrounds fish, supports a violently red bell-buoy." The different materials of verse and nature are here permeable to one another and to the mind's emotions.

By this point in the poem, it is clear that surface and depth are not opposites but on a continuum that keeps crossing itself in multiple dimensions. Surfaces have all kinds of "edges" that turn them into multidimensional thresholds. Now the surface/threshold between sky and depths becomes more open, and color, language, emotion, and line all "dissolve" in a crescendo of motility, restlessness, and permeability. Rather than the water's being merely colored by the sky, the dimensions of color and movement, held apart in the pool, come together as "across [the surface] a wide shadow pulses." With that dark pulse, the immobility of "the water's heavy sheet / Of glass above a bas-relief" is suddenly perfectly mobile, carrying inside itself, as the pool water did not, the movement of the clouds above. When, in the next line, "the water is a burning-glass / Turned to the sun," the intensity of the interactiveness of sky and water, again mobilized on the threshold/surface, increases dramatically. Intensity of feeling alters with intensity of color ("the water is a burning glass / Turned to the sun" modulates the gentler desire in "long, leaning, submerged green grass"). The emotional temperature rises along with the explosion of light and the burst of the trochee opening the line. The surface's horizontal "edge," which had increasingly gained depth, now has broken open into a many-faceted but liquid set of touchings.

. . . [the water] supports a violently red bell-buoy
Whose neon-color vibrates over it, whose bells vibrate
Through it. It glitters rhythmically
To shock after shock of electricity. (CP 195)

The height of emotional temperature coincides with the multiplication of "edges" and thresholds and the experience of saturation of one element by another. Set off by the neon color of the bell-buoy, the surface is so "open" or fractured that "touch" and "edge" are everywhere. The "violently red" neon color vibrates over the water while the sound of the bells of the buoy vibrate through the water. This is the kind of "painting" that Schapiro says "could alone record transient colors and reflections, and achieve a truth, brilliance, and vibration, unobtainable by conventional means" (1930, 271).

The threshold between the observing consciousness and world has also become an "everywhere" threshold, with no pane of bluish glass or heavy sheet of glass or burning glass in sight. The speaker/observer in this section has become immersed inside the water, no longer looking from poolside, plane, or shipboard. The consciousness of poet/observer has disappeared into the objects being described. It is not stretched from observer to object but surrounded by or inside the multiple edges of the object. Likewise, the verse's "tangible surface of rhythm" here becomes full of vibrating edges with forceful pulses and their vibrating aftereffects of feminine endings ("whose bells vibrate / Through it. It glitters rhythmically / To shock after shock of electricity"). This section illustrates the most intense interpermeation of mind, verse, and sea.

Pulling out from that immersion in experience, as Dewey described, the mind of the speaker now begins to launch interpretation, bringing to—but also out of—that depth of experience two single ideas. Bishop crosses, as starkly as possible, the realms of water and conceptual language ("the sea is delight. The sea means *room*."). She launches, as Dewey suggested, conceptual categories that arise from the depth of perceptual "undergoing." Immediately, Bishop alters the threshold again by replacing the conceptual moves ("is delight," "means *room*") with a set of visual images: "It is a dance-floor, a well ventilated ballroom." By means of this pun, Bishop's speaker actually moves inside the "dots" or "balls" of Seurat's painting, falling through the surface of the painting and experiencing the dots three-dimensionally as an airy space or "ballroom." She produces for the reader an experience of falling through a surface (of dots) into a three-dimensional space.

The threshold between the emoting human mind and the surface of the world then becomes the explicit subject of the poem, as first "Pleasures," then "Grief," and then "Love" approach that surface. Here Bishop seems to almost explicitly test Dewey's claims about emotions: "We are given to thinking of emotions as things as simple and compact as are the words by which we name them. Joy, sorrow, hope, fear, anger, curiosity, are treated as if each in itself were a sort of entity that enters full-made upon the scene. . . . Experience is emotional but there are no separate things called emotions in it" (Dewey 48). In each of the next three movements of the poem, the observer's mind brings to the act of encounter an already bounded emotion (pleasure, grief, and love). In each case, the surface of the sea becomes far more resistant than it had been earlier in the poem. Nothing gets through the "tinsel" surface. Instead of saturation, the surface becomes agitated, reflective, and it acts back toward the mind's emotions, causing them to hum, skip, float off, and disperse. One of the emotions, Love, is so bounded and so inattentive to any interaction with the surface/threshold of water, so focused on a single kind of walled edge, that in defeat at ever reaching its goal, the boundedness of the emotion ("one of his burning ideas in mind") "suffers refraction, / And comes back in shoals of distraction" (*CP* 195–96). (Here Bishop seems to bring in Dewey's own language, "suffers.")

Refraction has, in a sense, been the subject of the poem all along. It is "the action of breaking open or breaking up" (*OED* 1a); it is also "the fact or phenomenon of a ray of light or heat being diverted or deflected from its previous course in passing obliquely out of one medium into another of different density" (*OED* 2a). The poem tracks light, color, movement, emotion, and language as it moves across media of different densities, entering at different angles or modes of intensity, agitation, or receptivity. The poem closes with a quick review of the mind pulled out into the landscape and then the mind pulled in, viewing from a distance:

> Lightly, lightly whitening in the air
> An acre of cold white spray is there. (*CP* 196)

The first line in the couplet has the looseness and rising rhythm that enacts the excitement of the mass of tiny explosive metamorphoses as water turns to air. The perceiver has no separate location from the natural phenomena but is immersed in it, suspended within the airy and flying quality of the dynamics of the verse line. The second line of the couplet, in its march of divided knifelike syllables ("An acre of cold white spray is there") records the same scene perceived from the distant discrete location of the airplane. The observer glances down and, way off in the vast expanse of water, notes the "acre" of spray. The materiality of the verse lines enacts first the mind suspended among the scattered phenomena of natural objects (the tiny droplets of white water turning into air) and then the mind pulled into itself, withdrawn, viewing nature from its discrete and distant viewing station as an observer in a plane, looking at the surface of a "closed" phenomenon with clear square boundaries. Bishop ends the poem with the opposite kind of surface with which she began—particulate three-dimensional diffusion ("lightly, lightly, whitening in the air") in contrast to the sleek flat plane of the pool. In between, using the metaphorical correlatives of the surface of verse, the surface of water, and the plane of a postimpressionist painting, Bishop produced a systematic exhibition of her theory of verse as a surface that acts as mobile thick threshold, the arena for the encounter between the interior of the self and nature.

In "Pleasure Seas," the "screen" of a painting's surface, like the surface of water or the surface of verse, is imagined as a site of "thick reciprocity" that hosts "oddly angled" encounters between mind and nature. The mind moves "in and out"—from a distanced perspective to total immersion—but it does so by itself fluctuating between condensed and diffused, distant and "overwhelmed." Bishop's interest in capturing the dynamics of such a labile encounter made the dynamics of surface and depth in the visual arts a richly productive correlative for her own subject matter. The surfaces of the mind and world can be "remote," glinting or glancing off one another, but they can also be almost without boundary in their reciprocity or saturation. The rhetorical level shifts throughout the poem; the description moves on a continuum from sheer sensation to sensation with emotion to implied conceptual categories to the explicit pronouncement of the meaning of an object.

Like the sea, verse itself is a glassy surface that acts as threshold, open to the world on one side and the mind of the writer/reader on the other. The surface of verse, like the surface of the sea, can be just surface, open on to a shallow or deep depth, move into "meaning," and become saturated with or merely carry as "name" the emotion of the speaker. The surface of verse can open to various kinds of depth and with its varying kinds of movement, density, opacity, and translucence, becomes a medium through which the world's modulations are refracted into the mind and vice versa. The flat surface of verse, like the flat plane of the surface of a painting, can record the opening into and encounter between mind and nature.

The poem stands not only as Bishop's response to Moore's challenge to produce "profundity of experience" but also as Bishop's solution to the early Wallace Stevens's meditations on the mind meeting the surfaces of nature. In his volume of poetry *Harmonium* (which Bishop had "almost by heart"; Millier 1993, 51) and in his two subsequent volumes, Stevens, too, presented Bishop with the problem of depth. He situated himself intensely in the divorce between the lovely surfaces of the world and the equally intricate interior depths of the consciousness that projects its own dramas and desires on to that world. Stevens was troubled by nature as a kind of impenetrable surface, the skin of the world that was alien to the mind or could merely be projected on to or imitated by the mind. Stevens's poem "Sea Surface Full of Clouds" shows that language and mind can project any color, mood, or idea on to the changing colors of the sea (from "paradisal" "calm" to "radiance" to crass "chop-house" stridings and "gongs" to precious and "polished" to a fluency full of "dank stratagem[s]" to a fluency more circus-like and filled with "conjuring" (Stevens 1997, 82–85). Stevens's poem is a *cri de coeur*—the mobility of language and the mind feel imposed on the sea's surface, even though the sea has its own spectacular mobility. For Stevens, so much choice and contingency in the poet's choice of mood and language is felt as an epistemological problem and also a problem of loneliness, no matter how he turns to embrace it in the close of the poem. Stevens loves the variety of the world and the variety of his mind's response to it, but, especially in his earlier work, he is ever anxious about his mind's inventiveness while it interacts with the landscape. But in Bishop the variousness of landscape and of human mood is keyed down, less anxious, softer, and more reflectively catalogued in order to go inside the variety of interactions between mind and nature, not choosing between them or feeling guilty that they are imposed.

We can tell that Bishop is responding to this feature of Stevens not only because she answers his poem about the sea's surface but also because her awkward emphasis on the word *sides* makes a reference to Stevens's "Nomad Exquisite" likely ("beholding all these green sides / And gold sides of green sides"; Stevens 1997, 77). In "Nomad Exquisite," Stevens emphasizes the vibrancy and dynamism of the world's variety and the vitality and variety of the mind's response to it. Still, in that poem too, the mind and nature meet one another in a violent clash of "flinging / forms" (Stevens 1997, 77). In contrast, Bishop represents the encounter differently; sometimes the mind is a passive receptive surface, and sometimes the mind crosses out into the landscape to "move" or "color" it. There is a lot of space for interaction, a large middle zone of in-betweenness, consonant with the way that Dewey had imagined it. Bishop multiplied the variability of the textured mind's relation to the surface. Surface is not always flat and not always opaque; it has so many variations of tangibility, reflectiveness, flatness, recession, and projection that it comes to have depth, whereas the mind that comes to "meet" it arrives in a variety of postures of resistance, imitation, and permeability. Unlike Stevens's hard-edged clashing of mind against surface, Bishop invents a less aggressive, softer, more multilayered means of moving between the surface of the world and mind's elaborations.

"Pleasure Seas," in its careful depiction of the variousness of color, luminosity, and movement of water, seems to be the poem in which Bishop most thoroughly explored the sea as the metaphorical equivalent for verse. At a time when Moore was critiquing Bishop's lack of depth, Bishop redefined the whole question of surface and depth, making possible the "long sweet edge" of a dynamic threshold experience (VSC 73.7, 44). Surface and depth cannot be dichotomous because their multiple kinds of extent and dimension open and close in too many different modes of interaction. The "next to—against" of saturation, whether airy and well-ventilated or dense like "clay-yellow coral," whether still and open to the color of the sky or moving in "mingling currents and tides," provides a richly textured way of imagining a project for poetry's encounters between the mind of the poet and nature's "thick" surfaces. Verse, mind, and nature are all imagined as "glassy water." They are skins or skeins that act as polished, two-dimensional, resistant surfaces. But they each have depths—they can become porous, three-dimensional, and open to saturation by one another. The image of this mobile threshold becomes Bishop's contribution to the postmodern reconception of surface-depth relations, and the poems in *A Cold Spring* become poems of threshold, edge, surface opening out to depth. The surface of a painting, as theorized by the impressionists—a screen that records the encounter between nature and the responding sensibility of an individual temperament—became Bishop's image for the surface of verse. Painters' experiments with the relations of surface and depth, with tactile empathy, and with the relation between the subjectivity of the viewer and the "surface" of the painting became a rich field of imagining for Bishop. In "Pleasure Seas," Bishop pushed her exploration of "the bright skin of Impressionism" (Hughes 215) to explore depth in a way not possible for the impressionists. Later, she continued to be attracted to visual artists who opened up the relation between surface and depth and invented ways to position subjectivity in relation to deep space.

TWO

INFILTRATION AND SUSPENSION

Klee, Notebook Poems, "Faustina," and "The Shampoo"

In "Pleasure Seas," Bishop imagines the speaker of the poem dropping through the surface of a Seurat painting. She places the painter's mode of representation on top of the landscape of the sea and then enters its particular rendition of depth, creating a complex of correlations between the surface of verse and the surfaces of painting and water. These surfaces act as thresholds as well as edges, "facing" in both directions by opening inward and outward. Bishop's second volume of poems, *A Cold Spring* (published in 1955 but written almost entirely during the 1940s) shows that visual art continued to be a lively and productive site for her working out novel solutions for her own poetics. By 1937, Bishop had become intrigued by the painter Paul Klee, whose work, as described by critics at mid-century, demanded that viewers step over a threshold and hang, float, or drift in a fluid deep space.[1] Bishop began to use Klee's work to reimagine the positioning of the lyric speaker. Her unusual positioning of the speaker can partly be explained by her use of Klee's writings and his paintings—particularly those paintings that located the beholder suspended among floating motifs or that used the concepts of a "fish swimming in all directions" and an eye in a landscape.[2] Drawing on Klee's innovative use of a fluid deep space, Bishop located the eye/"I" deeply, extensively, and expressively within the complex relations of a mobile environment of other motifs, bodies, and textures that carried multisensory and emotional experiences. The eye/"I" almost without skin becomes witness to and host of the "events" of the environment in which it hangs.

Bishop's correspondence reveals that some of Klee's paintings moved her because of their ability to express the dismemberment caused by the invasion of a force from outside that enters the self and severs its integrity. In these paintings, subjectivity became catastrophically open to the surround that violently encroaches across the membrane of skin or consciousness. But Bishop also used Klee's experiments with deep space to protest that invasion and to redress it. Drawing on the aesthetics of Klee (as made available to an American audience through the 1945 MoMA publication edited by Margaret Miller), Bishop created poetic structures that allowed the relation to external forces to be held at a distance, where differences in scale and speed do not threaten the self but are ranged around it in a variety of shapes or orbits. Contemporary criticism on Klee described an alternative structure for the engagement with forces outside the self, stressing the suspension of the subject in relation to floating motifs and the variety of colors and textures that cross into but do not threaten the self. In this mode, openness allows for a genial capaciousness, gentle emotional warmth, and response to the surprise of encountering motifs and textures that emerge in the environment. Such poems as "Faustina, or Rock Roses" combine the two responses to Klee's work, holding subjectivity suspended among and viscerally open to textures and motifs in an environment that also carries a potential sense of threat.

Klee in Bishop's Correspondence

Three moments in Bishop's letters suggest that Klee was of particular importance to Bishop and begin to characterize the nature of her interest in his work. In the famous October 17, 1940, letter in which Bishop managed to hold her own against Marianne Moore's suggested revisions to "Roosters," Bishop referred to the feeling that arose in her when she viewed Klee's painting *The Man of Confusion* (figure 1), arguing that her own antiwar poem sought to recreate a similar feeling. In response to Moore's critique of the crudeness of triple rhymes, Bishop tells Moore, "I can't bring myself to sacrifice what (I think) is a very important 'violence' of tone—which I feel to be helped by what *you* must feel to be just a bad case of the *Threes*. It makes me feel like a wonderful Klee picture I saw at his show the

Figure 1. Paul Klee, *Der Mann der Verwechslung* (*The Man of Confusion*). 1939. Oil on canvas. 26 1/4×19 7/8 inches (66.7×50.5 cm). Saint Louis Art Museum, Gift of Mr. and Mrs. Joseph Pulitzer Jr. © 2009 Artists Rights Society (ARS), New York/ VG Bild-Kunst, Bonn.

other day, *The Man of Confusion*" (Bishop 1994, 96–97). The painting derives from the last period of Klee's life when he was dying from scleroderma, which subjected him to "progressive hardening of the skin, a stiffening of the features to those of a 'mummy face,' and immobility of the hands" (Glaesemer 307). *The Man of Confusion* displays the severed sections of a disintegrated human body, literally fallen apart and scattered over the surface of the canvas. The figure is ambiguously also a woman given that the separated pearls of a necklace, without a string, are arrayed under the detached head. The features of the woman's face have also begun to "fall out" of the face; the mouth has migrated over toward the edge of the face and one of the eyes has begun to widen and become detached, yet the other eye maintains its normal position, giving the uncanny effect of a person trying to hold on to normalcy and ignore the loss of her own body. The normal eye creates a consciousness inside the picture that watches as a distanced observer while its own body is subjected to violence. Bishop's invocation of Klee's painting to explain her use of triplets reveals her intention to replicate this "severing" through the triple rhymes that harshly break up the sentences and return with crude overinsistence to the same sound, drawing undue attention to and therefore detaching each item so that it stands isolated at the end of the line. Each end rhyme is spit out: the cock's cry "grates like a wet match / from the broccoli patch, / flares, and all over town begins to catch" (CP 35). The brevity of Bishop's remark makes it difficult to determine whether she was referring to only the rhymes or to also the content of the poem, which contains two startling dismemberments. Either way, the remark does suggest that Bishop thought the "severed" nature of the rhymes and their crude violence was expressive of the position of the speaker, who is torn apart by the rooster's calls. The roosters, who "planned to command and terrorize the rest," enforce "deep from raw throats / a senseless order" by "active / displacement in perspective; / each screaming; 'This is where I live!'" (CP 35–36) and thus tear apart the just-wakened sleeper by pulling her attention harshly and forcefully in many different directions. This violence to the "I" becomes the psychological equivalent of the second dismemberment, which occurs in the "falling apart" of the roosters'/ soldiers' bodies as, in their dying fall, feathers and then eyes "detach" from the bodies. Holding on to this "'tone' of violence," produced by rhymes, diction, and subject matter and legitimized by the Klee painting that so moved her, Bishop refused to alter the poem in accord with Moore's suggested revisions. Within the next month, Bishop twice invited Moore to see the Klee exhibit (at the Buchholz Gallery October 9–November 2, 1940), suggesting not only that Bishop wishes to make amends for her rebellion by inviting Moore on an outing but also that it would be of particular importance for the younger poet to see Klee's paintings with her mentor at her side (Bishop 1994, 97).

The second significant reference to Klee in Bishop's letters occurs when Robert Lowell sent Bishop the poems that eventually became part of *Life Studies*. Bishop responded enthusiastically to Lowell's new style. In her reply of January 29, 1958, she calls on Klee to get across the aesthetic that she is praising in Lowell's work:

> I bought that Webern you had before I left, and I'm listening to parts every day. I think I'm so smart, because when you played me one piece I immediately thought it seemed like the musical equivalent of Klee. Now, according to the notes, Webern was actually a member of the Blue Rider group. . . . I still can't take very much of the songs. For one thing, those voices aren't too good, even if accurate, but I am crazy about some of the short instrumental pieces. They seem exactly like what I'd always wanted, vaguely, to hear and never had, and really "contemporary." That strange kind of modesty that I think one feels in almost everything contemporary one really likes—Kafka, say, or Marianne, or even Eliot, and Klee and Kokoschka and Schwitters . . . Modesty, care, *space*, a sort of helplessness but determination at the same time. Well, maybe I'm hearing too much. (—and admission of final ignorance!) (Bishop 2008, 250)

Again, Klee's name appears at a moment when Bishop was struggling to get at a description of her aesthetic. Lowell's new poems and the Webern instrumental pieces allowed her to replace an inchoate vision ("what I'd always wanted, vaguely, to hear . . .") with the thing itself, but Klee's name still hovered, close to the unnamable indescribable ideal.

Writing to Lowell three years later, Bishop again struggled to articulate a possible way forward for poetry. Looking for an alternative to the Beats, she can only vaguely point Lowell (and herself) toward a not-yet-discovered mode of writing, one that she senses is possible because she saw it in Klee:

> What you say about Marianne is fine: 'terrible, private, and strange revolutionary poetry. There isn't the motive to do that

now.' But I wonder—isn't there? Isn't there even more—only it's terribly hard to find the exact and right and surprising enough, or un-surprising enough, point at which to revolt now? The Beats have just fallen back on an old corpse-strewn or monument-strewn battle-field—the real protest I suspect is something quite different. (If only I could find it. Klee's picture called FEAR seems close to it, I think.) (Bishop 2008, 364)

As in the letter to Moore and the previously quoted letter to Lowell, Klee stands here as an achieved mode, an aesthetic model, even though a poetic corollary remains difficult to invent. Bishop invokes Klee to explain, clarify, and more fully imagine the mode of writing that she herself finds desirable but not yet attainable. Bishop must have seen this painting more than ten years before writing the letter, in another Klee exhibit at the Buchholz gallery (May 2–27, 1950).[3] Composed using oil on burlap, *Fear* shows a person completely submerged in the fabric of the irregularly spherical shape of his/her own "body" (figure 2). Only the eye is visible, and even the eye is composed of the same burlap texture as the body in which the eye is embedded. The body itself is barely distinguishable from the surrounding environment, also composed of burlap in ochre and blue-tinted browns. The effect is an even more extreme version of Klee's earlier *Arab Song*, in which the subject clandestinely peers out from its "cover" to see what is "out there" but the "out there" has already infiltrated inside the subject. In both *Fear* and *Arab Song*, it is impossible to determine precisely where the body ends and the surroundings begin. In *Fear*, the "hiding" eye also bears a red slash mark, generating the sense that the eye has seen violence and is itself wounded. The painting produces the feeling of a person as composed only of an eye; the substance of the person is barely demarcated from its surroundings, which are in fact also the "inside" of the person. The eye is intensely diminished in power (it has no real body capable of action) and intensely private, but, in spite of its position of hiding or helplessness, the subject remains in revolt against an environment that contains a violence so powerful that it has entered the space of the self.

From Bishop's letters emerges, then, a more definite set of qualities that she associated with Klee: (1) an ability to invent an unconventional form to express visceral emotion, even if crude or raw, and particularly a means of producing the sensation of a subjectivity

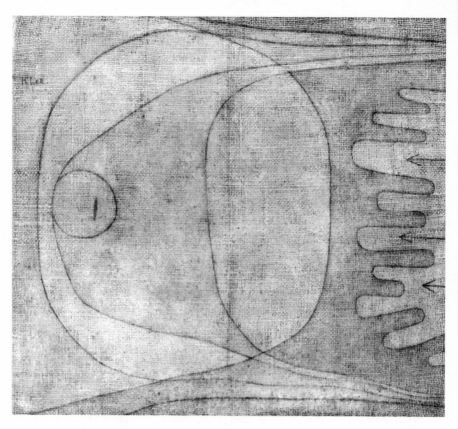

Figure 2. Paul Klee, *Angst (Fear)*. 1934. Oil on burlap. 49.9×60.0 cm. National Gallery of Canada, Ottawa. © 2009 Artists Rights Society (ARS), New York/ VG Bild-Kunst, Bonn.

dissevered by its environment (the "'violence' of tone" in *The Man of Confusion*, which in "Roosters" appears as crudely "severed" rhymes that correlate with the speaker's consciousness pulled apart by the environment); (2) qualities that she valued, such as "modesty, care," and "determination" in the face of an acknowledgment of "helplessness"; (3) a protest or private revolt that went beyond the protest of the Beats; and (4) "*space*," a category emphasized by Bishop's use of an underscore but remaining undefined by her in the letter. All four categories are apparent in both paintings that Bishop mentions by name as particularly affecting her. Both paintings are hugely emotional;

produce a subjectivity that is helpless and modest but "still there," determined although in "hiding"; and therefore produce a subjectivity in a position of private protest or revolt. Both paintings invent subjectivity beyond the usual idea of person, giving up the illusion of personhood by refusing to represent the body as an integral unit or as bounded by skin. Both produce a protest on another level than personal feeling by representing the situation of the eye/"I" (how the eye/"I" came to this state; its relation to its environment). Yet it is unlikely that these paintings can serve as complete models for Bishop's interest in Klee's invention of "space." To define that term, we must turn to the contemporary intellectual context for the reception of Klee in America in the late 1930s and 1940s.

Reception of Klee

The closest intellectual context for Bishop can be found in her former college roommate and close friend, Margaret Miller, a research associate and later an associate curator at MoMA. Miller made particular selections from Klee's writing for the MoMA publication on Klee that she edited in 1945. In addition, her correspondence with Christian Zervos, the editor of *Cahiers d'Art*, shows her enthusiasm for the special issue on Klee published by Zervos, which had several articles that rather lyrically rendered Klee's use of deep space. The discourse surrounding the reception of Klee's work, with particular attention to Miller, both reveals the general assessment of Klee as an artist working on an intimate scale and explores his further uses of "space" beyond the uncanny and frightening relation of the eye to its own body and environment already discussed.[4] Criticism of his paintings by John Thwaites, David Sylvester, and authors writing in *Cahiers d'Art* described the invention of a deep space that undoes the violence of a subjectivity open to the environment. Such critics emphasized Klee's situating of the viewer as an eye or ear wandering among a landscape of floating colors, textures, and shape motifs. As in the paintings already described, the psycho-physical forces in the environment serve to infiltrate the viewer, removing a sense of the boundaries or membrane of the body, but the fluidity occurs not only as a mode of anxiety or violence but also as pleasure and surprise. Colors and textures become mobile, infiltrating the somatic and emotional experience of a mobile self that floats, sometimes as only an eye, with its body composed of the surround. In a more structured vision of the subject's relation to its environment, the excerpts from Klee's writing that were chosen by Miller positioned a figure in relation to objects with disparate trajectories, sizes, and speeds. Unlike *Fear* and *The Man of Confusion*, the body in these paintings is not viewed solely as subject to unseen forces but is set in a more structured, distant, and controlled relation to those forces.

Among divergent critics, one point of agreement was a stress on Klee's intimacy. In the 1940 Buchholz catalogue for the show that Bishop visited, both James Johnson Sweeney and Herbert Read stress Klee's modesty and intimacy. "In an age that blasted privacy Paul Klee built a small but exquisite shrine to intimacy" writes Sweeney. And Read opens his remarks by declaring, "Art has to choose between being monumental and intimate. A destructive age can only erect valid monuments to destruction ([Pablo] Picasso's *Guernica*)" (Klee 1940). According to Alfred H. Barr, "Picasso's pictures often roar or stamp or pound; Klee's whisper a soliloquy—lyric, intimate, incalculably sensitive" (Klee 1945, 7). In the early and mid-1940s, critics distinguished Klee's work from the monumental egoism of Picasso; in the later 1940s, although the abstract expressionists developed ideas that they found in Klee, he was to be distinguished from their large-scale myth-making (Lanchner, 104–8).

Because small-scale intimist art, modesty, and determination in the face of an acknowledged helplessness are all qualities commonly associated with Bishop's own values and poetry, we can readily see the connection between these 1940s descriptions of Klee and Bishop's interest in his work.[5] Bishop's report of a dream to Lloyd Frankenberg in juxtaposition to a comment in a postcard to Loren MacIver shows that Bishop too poised Klee against the "big picture" artists:

> Last night I dreamed one of the living rooms was filled with huge abstract paintings, in sections set up like screens—absolutely terrifying, for some reason. We all had to paint them; they were "compulsory" and I was reassuring some stranger that he too could do it. "All you have to remember," I said "is to paint either a dyptich, a tryptich, or a styptich [sic]. (Letter to Lloyd Frankenberg, January 13, 1951, VSC)

Two days earlier, Bishop had written in a letter to Loren MacIver, "I love the Klee book—just the thing" (January 11, 1951, VSC). We might tentatively conclude that reading through the Klee book had given rise to the dream, the Klee paintings allowing her to acknowledge her resistance to the prevailing rules for creating "big" art. Also, Bishop's interview with Ashley Brown registers just this placement of Klee, intimately scaled against the "mythic" abstract expressionists. When Brown inquires whether Bishop thinks "it is necessary for a poet to have a 'myth'—Christian or otherwise—to sustain his work," Bishop replies, "Look at Paul Klee. . . . he didn't have a formulated myth to look to, apparently, and his accomplishment was very consider-able. . . . I'm not interested in big-scale work as such. Something needn't be large to be good" (Brown, 24). The response reveals Bishop's association of Klee with an alternative aesthetic to that of Christian myth as well as abstract expressionism, with its attraction to primitive myth and large-scale paintings. Because the abstract expres-sionists, with their huge-scale paintings, were understood to be paint-ing in response to the terrors of war and to the tragic knowledge of the human capacity for violence, we can see why Bishop associated Klee with an alternative kind of protest. Likewise, Barr's and Read's contrasting of Klee with Picasso, particularly in his monumental pro-test against war, sheds some light on the way that intimist art set itself in protest to a world of violence but in a quiet, private voice rather than in monumental gestures.

Many of Klee's paintings that include either an injured figure or a small vulnerable figure lost on the margins or hiding within a larger landscape could be considered as registering a protest. Yet critics also discussed many paintings by Klee that provided, rather, a use of space that allowed for a more genial openness to the environment. In these paintings, the subject matter of the painting seems to be the viewer himself who becomes relocated *in* the canvas, sometimes as a floating eye in the landscape (figure 3). The eye, a consciousness open to mul-tisensory experience, wanders in a landscape. The eye is bodiless but nevertheless is touched and moved by floating motifs (sticklike trees) where sheets of red and orange drift across the membrane of the (now missing) body. Klee's critics stressed especially his innovative con-struction of this new feel for space.

John Thwaites, who wrote at the time that Bishop first became inter-ested in Klee in 1937, taught his readers to experience Klee's innovative

Figure 3. Paul Klee, *Blick einer Landschaft* (*Glance of a Landscape*) (1926). Transparent and opaque watercolor sprayed over stencils and brush applied on laid paper, mounted on cardboard with gouache borders. 11 7/8×18 1/8 inches (30.2×46 cm). Philadelphia Museum of Art: The Louise and Walter Arensberg Collection, 1950. © 2009 Artists Rights Society (ARS), New York/VG Bild-Kunst, Bonn.

deep space by feeling their way inside it. The "eye" of the viewer wanders inside the space of the painting as if floating through a landscape where the parts of that landscape have the tactile feel of textures and atmospheres available to a body in motion. Thwaites emphasized Klee's interest in conveying the object not as the stilled cubist object, frozen in time, but as it existed in multiple sensory dimensions. Whereas Georges Braque, according to Thwaites, can deliver only a "strong way of seeing," Klee captures nonvisual perception in addition to the visual: "Klee is interested in movement because he is interested in the object in all its ways of being. The object in space or in time, in sight or in sound, in temperature or in touch, interest him equally" (Thwaites, "First Part," 11). Hence, Thwaites emphasizes Klee's use of texture to build in a more visceral, somatic element beyond the optical: "he learned to use texture, not as the cubists did for a plastic feeling of the object, but to give a psycho-physical reaction." Such a view clarifies the link between Klee's use of color ("the color is laid on in undefined areas like stains") and his production of a sense of movement: "the red-brown surfaces vary in intensity, letting your eye through to different depths as the Chinese sepia does. Then a fistful of blue breaks through the sky and is echoed in a blue border like Seurat's. That color relation makes the little landscape flame and shake." Thwaites emphasizes the way that Klee unfolds the colors and textures of objects into movements: "He brings a Greco-Roman fold out of an arabesque, but you feel it fall and settle" (Thwaites, "First Part," 8, 10). While the mood here has softened and has nothing to do with the vulnerability of the figure in *Fear*, colors and textures "touch" the body and the mind of the viewer, who has gone over the frame of the painting to float among colors and textures inside the landscape.

In the first issue of *The Tiger's Eye* (which a letter to Lowell shows that Bishop read), David Sylvester similarly describes Klee's invention of a new space filled with movement in contrast to cubist space, which held the object frozen: "the movement of the motifs themselves defines the fluid space they inhabit" (Bishop 1994, 153; Sylvester 35). Sylvester writes that the viewer must "feel into" the painting "to explore those perspectives already visible from outside. A late Klee is the face of a cliff. To 'feel into' it is to clamber over it" (Sylvester 37). Sylvester is even clearer in a 1951 essay about the late Klee:

While the spectator *may* project himself into any picture, he *must* project himself into a late Klee. . . . As the spectator moves between the signs of the Berne pictures, he feels, not that he is travelling on a surface, but that he is suspended in space and that the structure of the picture is three-dimensional. This is in spite of the fact that it contains none of the devices—linear or serial perspective, plastic colour, overlapping of forms—normally used to give an illusion of depth and space. And, indeed, no space is signified so long as the spectator confronts the picture. Yet when he projects himself into it and moves about in it, the signs situate themselves at different depths, thereby implying space. (Sylvester 41)

In Klee's space, the subject of the painting and the viewer himself are suspended or "swimming" (Sylvester) in a landscape of different textures, atmospheres, and motifs, many of which carry what Thwaites refers to as a "psycho-physical" effect. In some paintings, the eye in the landscape flips the viewer so that she is not merely traveling through the landscape but actually is the eye of the landscape's body (see figure 3). As Carolyn Lanchner later summarizes it: "The space . . . is organic weightless, and indeterminate . . . deeper [than cubist space] in that it has become metaphysical, iconic with the painter's and the viewer's interior space, both sensuous and ideographic" (Lanchner 89).

Several of the essays on Klee in the 1945–1946 issue of *Cahiers d'Art* (which Margaret Miller admired and would have shared with Bishop) emphasize that Klee's mode of seeing involved a visceral and somatic openness in a fluid space of floating motifs.[6] Roger Vitrac begins his essay "Le regard de Paul Klee" by emphasizing the receptiveness and clarity of Klee's vision: "au fond de l'oeil le plus limpide" (Vitrac 53). The eye, in its receptiveness, felt open and waiting, like an ear open at night. The body itself seemed open, operating with an extensive network of heightened sensory awareness based in the organic or botanical level of the body ("des sens et des passions les nervures grandissantes de la connaissance"). Vitrac describes a viewer encountering depths of anxiety, a vertiginous falling ("les vertiges") into realms usually forbidden to our view, dreams of despair, shame, and silence (Vitrac 53, 54). For Georges Duthuit, the viewer moved in the space of a Klee painting as if walking backward blindfolded at night, feeling traps underfoot and encountering small flashes of living things—eyes of trout, flowers glowing like nightlights at the bottom of a pond ("les yeux bandés, marcher á reculons: trop de pièges sous nos pas. . . . La scène s'éclaire des petits yeux de la truite et des fleurs en veilleuse, au fond de l'étang") (Duthuit 20). Christian Zervos writes that Klee "inserts us into the mystery of a world of shifting, fluctuating boundaries" ("a nous insinuer le mystère de ce monde aux frontièrs flotantes") (Zervos 16). Several of the *Cahiers d'Art* critics emphasized the paintings' immense silence, imagining both painter and viewer hanging in space, stretching out via the ear toward the world, consciousness open, and stretching beyond the boundary of the body so that colors, textures, and motifs seem to cross into the interior space of the self (Bousquet 50–51; Grohmann 1945–46, 63–65).

From these descriptions, we can derive something of Bishop's definition of *space* as she connects Webern and Klee in her letter to Lowell. The Webern instrumental pieces that felt so contemporary to Bishop are filled with tiny melodic motifs, modest attempts at movement or expression that do not go far. The motifs are very idiosyncratic, personal, and expressive, but they do not connect to any larger whole. They can be described as "all over the place," floating in an atmosphere that has no "edges" or boundaries or overall structure. At the end of her typed letter to Lowell, Bishop added a handwritten addendum to her list of qualities in these contemporaries (after "modesty, care, *space*, a sort of helplessness but determination at the same time,"): "and admission of final ignorance" (Bishop 2008, 250). To float among motifs in an undefined space, without orientation or ground, felt as if it expressed the epistemological tentativeness that characterized her move away from modernism toward postmodernism. Here was the equivalent in visual art to the kind of movement that Goldensohn describes in Bishop's poetry and painting, where "the depths and interrelations of space are characteristically resolved upon by groping from point to point in situ, and are fastened and probed by contiguity not by imperial overview" (Goldensohn 2001, 105).

Klee, himself, provides a kind of antidote to this floating without orientation in the organization of "space." Miller includes the relevant excerpts from Klee's writings in the 1945 MoMA publication. Miller mentioned the booklet twice in letters to Bishop (letters from Margaret Miller to Bishop, March 7 and May 6, 1945, VSC), and Bishop's interest in Klee and friendship with Miller makes it highly likely that the poet read these particular excerpts. In his remarks "On Creation," Klee reveals his interest in setting up relationships among various kinds of movements, shapes, lines, and times (opposing "forces") in the space of one painting. The subject, even while moving, is suspended among this array of other shapes and movements:

And now the experiences of the modern man striding across the deck of a steamer: 1. his own movement, 2. the course of the steamer, which could be contrary to his own, 3. the direction of the movement and the speed of the stream, 4. the rotation of the earth, 5, its orbit, 6. the orbits of the moon and stars around it.

The result: a complex of movements within the universe with the man on the steamer as the center.

. . . .

A sleeping person, the circulation of the blood, the measured breathing of the lungs, the delicate function of the kidneys and a head full of dreams related to the powers of fate.

A complex of functions unified in repose. (Klee 1945, 12–13)

In both passages, Klee jogs loose painting's adherence to the planar and resituates it so that both the subject of the painting and the viewer are oriented inside a wider world, filled with trajectories of different shapes, densities, and directions, moving at various paces and durations. These shape-motifs do not diffuse across the space of the self, the way that sheets of color cross into the eye in *Glance of a Landscape* or burlap texture crosses into the body in *Fear*. The figures in these excerpts are not imagined as open to the environment across a missing boundary or membrane; nevertheless, they retain an orientation toward motifs in the landscape that somehow "bound" or circle them. In the man on the steamer, the figure is not so much subjected to those outside trajectories and forces as held in relation to them. He moves in relation to their movements. Pacing on the deck, he has a certain degree of independence from the forces ranged around him, but he is nevertheless held within the relation of their disparate shapes and movements. In the passage about the sleeping person, the sleeping consciousness is held at a distance from but in relation to the movements of his own body (the circulation of the blood, the movement of the lungs, and so on) and then, at an even greater distance, the movements of his more amorphously shaped dreams and then his "fate." In both Klee excerpts, the figure is opened to and held by an environment located outside the direct control of the subject.

Bishop's Use of Klee's Aesthetic

Both unpublished and published poetry by Bishop from the mid-1940s demonstrates a widespread affinity between Bishop's developing aesthetic during this period and Klee's work. The positioning of the speaker in these lyrics experiences an openness to the environment, not always in the mode of bodily severance or invasion but in a milder aspect whereby fields of color and texture cross the boundary of a form or the speaker is placed within a "complex of movements" or suspended within different kinds of lines and shapes. At times, Bishop renders the crossing of those boundaries by submerging the body or subject in its environment or surround, effacing the subject and leaving only an "eye" that is itself variously saturated by an environment that is also, somehow, the eye's own body—resembling Klee's use of an "eye" floating bodiless in space, where the landscape becomes the "eye's" body.[7]

Bishop's unpublished and perhaps not fully achieved poem "On the *Prince of Fundy*" about Bishop's 1946 trip to Great Village allows us to watch the poet experiment with Klee's aesthetic. The poem creates a "complex of movements." Like the man on the steamer in Miller's excerpt of Klee's writing, which places a man walking forward on a steamer's deck in relation to the different pace and direction of the movement of the ship, the revolution of Earth, and the orbiting moon and stars, Bishop's poem suspends the speaker in relation to disparate speeds, directions, and circulating shapes in a "complex of movements."

ON THE *PRINCE OF FUNDY*

We must weigh tons and tons and tons
with all those cars & cars & trucks
stowed below.
The cabin is pitch-black.
We gently gently rock this way and that.
Someone has a heavy tread, above.
Someone else—a woman—is singing. Why?
And why does she sing so high?
Everything creaks. And someone taps the pipes.
We gently rock. WE *think* we rock because
there's nothing real to judge by.
I love you more today than I did yesterday.   apologetically
Isn't that nice?
[I thought I loved you. Now I know I do.]
Why are they walking around like that
and singing, too, at all hours of the night?
While we sway gently gently in the dark
(up, down and sometimes sidewise, too)   put it into 4's

(We shall be arriving at Yarmouth, Nova Scotia in
Approximately two hours and twenty-five minutes.) (Bishop
2006, 92)

Like Klee's positioning of the man on the steamer among a range of differently timed movements and shapes, "On the 'Prince of Fundy'" suspends the speaker amid opposing weights, movements, shapes, and lines. It opens with the sense of weight pulled downward (the "weight of tons and tons and tons" of "cars & cars & trucks / stowed below") and sets that weight in tension with the light airy high voice of a woman singing ("And why does she sing so high?"). Suspended between these poles, the cabin is a dark hole that introduces another kind of movement ("we gently rock") into the existing field, a movement in which situational instability is increased by the epistemological inability to "judge" against any firm stable horizon or marker ("WE *think* we rock because / there's nothing real to judge by"). Instability becomes the site where another kind of possibility opens. Inside that space of gentle rocking, suspended somewhere between weighty immobile depth and airy wavering height, emotion has altered, shifted into a more joyous affirmation ("I love you more today than I did yesterday. / Isn't that nice?"). The affirmation is without cause or motive, a free and gentle event that floats up inside of a matrix of other movements and events, a shift that could just as easily have been other. The shift comes without preparation, appearing inside of a field of other objects, movements, and events—some of long duration and others intermittent. Its own continuity cannot be known. (Will it be a long period of shared love or a brief sensation soon to dissipate?) After the emotional shift, the field continues, surrounding the event. A shape/movement of circling ("Why are they walking around like that") of fairly extensive duration ("at all hours of the night") holds inside and slightly below itself the cabin, still dark and gently swaying, "up, down and sometimes sidewise, too." Another "line" is introduced at the close, one in which the ship has a directness, moving unidirectionally, straight toward a named and stable destination for a named duration ("two hours and twenty-five minutes") with a minuscule uncertainty ("approximately" as spoken in the official voice of announcer of timetables and schedules). We can recognize Klee's "arrow" shape, discussed by Alfred H. Barr in the MoMA exhibition catalogue, in the unidirectional movement of steamer toward port (Klee 1945).

"On the 'Prince of Fundy'" can function as a particularly clear example of Bishop's situating a "complex of movements" in relation to one another and to an observer, comparable to the man on a steamer or the man in repose in the excerpts from Klee's writings on modern art. The closeness in the dates (the publication of Klee's writing in 1945 and the composition of this draft in 1946); the use of the same location (person on a steamer); and the use of orbits, directions, and speeds make it likely that here we are seeing Bishop experiment with Klee's means of orienting the human subject in a space that would otherwise be without boundaries or organization. Keeping in mind "On the 'Prince of Fundy,'" and Klee's writings, we can more fully comprehend the final poem in *A Cold Spring*, Bishop's tribute to her love for Lota de Macedo Soares in "The Shampoo," composed in 1952. Bishop herself was surprised when the *New Yorker* first rejected the poem and when readers did not seem to understand it because she considered it to be without difficulty (letter from Bishop to May Swenson, August 10, 1953, WUL). The poem becomes more accessible when set in the context of the excerpt about the man walking forward on the steamer. "The Shampoo" gently suspends the human figures in relation to the speed, scale, and shape of heavenly orbits and earthly objects. The poem is short enough to be quoted in full.

> The still explosions on the rocks,
> the lichens, grow
> by spreading, gray, concentric shocks.
> They have arranged
> to meet the rings around the moon, although
> within our memories they have not changed.
>
> And since the heavens will attend
> as long on us,
> you've been, dear friend,
> precipitate and pragmatical;
> and look what happens. For Time is
> nothing if not amenable.
>
> The shooting stars in your black hair
> in bright formation
> are flocking where,
> so straight, so soon?
> —Come let me wash it in this big tin basin,
> battered and shiny like the moon. (*CP* 84)

The speaker of "The Shampoo" and her lover are suspended among shapes and lines that also contain movements of varying speeds.

Lichens, as circles, will take much longer than our memories can hold to grow far enough "to meet the rings around the moon." These circles, slow and capacious, are poised against other shapes and speeds, such as Lota's white hairs that, like comets, shoot more precipitously toward the moon. The precipitous, precocious movement of shooting lines is contained by another shape—the circle of the tin basin where Lota's hair will be washed. In the middle stanza, poised or "hung" between these two kinds of time (imagined as shapes with variant speeds), there is the trajectory of the meeting of the lovers themselves. They too could have waited much longer to meet or to enter into a loving relationship (as "the heavens will attend / as long on us"), but Lota has been "precipitate and pragmatical" not only by growing gray hair but also by inviting Elizabeth to live with her sooner rather than later. "Time" is "amenable" to this arrangement; the warmth of that word *amenable,* with its shades of amiable and accommodating, and its softness against the harsher member of the rhymed pair, "pragmatical," creates a soft atmosphere, implying that the Time (and the stanza) in which the lovers reside is suspended amiably, unhurriedly amid the harsher "shocks," "rocks," "shooting stars," and "tin." The fact that the time of that second stanza is like the time of the first allows the interval in which they are suspended to be elongated beyond even human memory and makes the felt experience of their love more expansive than the little action of the shampoo. Their love then can hang inside of that expanded space, while also acknowledging its eventual limit (closed by the aging and death that are signaled by the white hairs that move too quickly and by the aging "battered" basin). The lovers are suspended amid motifs of circles and lines that vary in speeds and carry "psycho-physical" forces. The proliferative "spray" is played against more controlled "intact" forms: "still explosions on the rocks" are also rings ("concentric shocks"). The straight exploding lines of Lota's hair are contained, in the final stanza, by the circular shape of the "big tin basin." The proliferative lives of these two women, which could have gone anywhere and dispersed, are now inside a container of sorts since their growth has "arranged" to "meet the rings around the moon" and they meet inside the circle of the basin, the loving action of the shampoo, and their own room or space of living together (*CP* 84). The subjectivity of both speaker and lover has become dispersed or distributed in and among shapes other than themselves, shapes that are provided by the natural and human environments and that also provide containers for subjectivity.

For an equally clear demonstration of an above-mentioned technique of Klee's work, noted by both American and European critics—allowing fields of color and texture to cross the boundary of a form and the suspension of the "I" in a field of floating motifs—we can first turn to Bishop's own notebook observations that constitute her raw material for many poems. Bishop repeatedly shows an interest and takes pleasure in the dispersal of drops through a three-dimensional field, suspended in emulsion and then dissolving. Often she describes different textures or atmospheres of different densities touching or passing through one another. To select one of numerous examples, here is a note taken while staying in North Carolina:

> October. The nights of the full moon this month were beautiful. The mountains looked bluish, snowy, & wasted. Gay sparks from the little river floated through the black oak trees. Then a thin, high, silvery fog came through all the valleys, from different directions—watched it coming closer & closer until it came through the oak trees, hid them & then through the screens into the room which suddenly got very cold. (VSC 77.3, 52–53)

We can also see this interest in sparseness, diffusion, varying atmospheres and textures crossing one another in the short poem "Mimosas in Bloom" as well as in her painting "Graveyard with Fenced Graves" (Bishop 1996, 33). The poem shows Bishop's delight in textures meeting one another, their mode of touching or passing through.

> Dust from the floors of Heaven
> that makes one sneeze and then smell honey.
> What angels threw it out down here,
> the lovely, yellow, air-light litter?
>
> The gray-green leaves fold neatly back
> like kittens' ears. The hillside's gold.
> No, better than gold
> This fine, soft, unmixed pigment. (Bishop 2006, 132)

Fineness, softness, and gentleness occur in different registers: the less dense, "barely there" of the "air-light litter" in the petals or pollen from the trees next to/against the comparatively denser, more solid but still light in weight substance of the "gray-green leaves / . . . like kittens' ears." In another register, the diffused golden pollen crosses into the even more diffused realm of air as, by a tiny adjustment of weight and color, the pollen that filters over the hills becomes diffused like golden light.

A notebook entry renders the same subject and thematizes it: "the ground that would dry their [the mourners] tears like blotting paper—in the cemetery—or let it through, scarcely detaining it, to join the sea below" (VSC 75.3a, 14). Here tears gently dissolve into the earth of the graveyard, and their gentleness in this dissolution is associated with an acceptance of death. These notebook passages prepare us for textures and colors diffusing across the boundaries of other forms or across the membrane of the self in a mode other than fear and violence. In this brief poem, we can sense the way that any natural object, not just the sea surface, can work as the thick, mobile threshold, open to other spaces, that Bishop renders in such detail in "Pleasure Seas."

In another unpublished fragment, "Whitewashed," from this period, lovers are set as a barely distinguishable object (only the mouths visible) in a field of other objects, movements, atmospheres, and textures:

> In the most brightest sunshine I have ever seen
> we made the night again with our mouths
> at ten one morning
> The darkness [flowed]
> the fountain of night
> misplaced dreams that overpowered
> us ("mugging") from behind—
>
> Imagine restoring the night intact
> like that
> It grew dark
> & darker as we went upstairs
> into the (brilliant) white room
> with the palm trees swinging &

clashing like (taffeta) bright tin blue flowers
outside, & the   nine blue -flowers
the darkness we were enabled to
a gift
came down like   *Thunbergia*
    displaced night (Bishop 2006, n. 79, 288–89)

"Whitewashed," gathers power from its reversal of the aubade tradition, which managed only to wish the night prolonged and the sun
delayed. Here, the speaker and her lover bring back "the night intact"
when they kiss. Inside the "(brilliant) white room" they bring into
being and also receive as a "gift" an enabling darkness descending from
above. The darkness, imagined as a "fountain" or spray rising and
spreading or raining down also appears concentrated, not diffused, at
the place where the two mouths meet. The steady climbing movement
of a gradual darkening ("it grew dark / & darker as we went upstairs")
stands slightly ajar from the two poles of darkness imagined as "intact" and "fountain." Somewhere between the different densities of
darkness imagined as a concentrated whole ("intact") and imagined
as a diffusion or spray ("fountain"), the room itself "holds" the darkness in a less dense, airy way. The "space" of the brilliant white room
surrounding the lovers holds the darkness inside of its airy openness,
suspended in it, like an emulsion. The feeling of suspension derives
from the lovers' movement upward rather than downward and from
the way that the upstairs room is an enclosure open to the outdoors.
Outside of that space, but also inside because present in the speaker's
awareness is a different kind of diffusion of color or movement, "palm
trees swinging & / clashing like (taffeta) bright tin . . . blue flowers"
(not the movement of the gradual climbing upstairs nor the stopped
movement of the intactness of two mouths meeting). The taffeta and
the palm fronds both yield up an image of a diffused, netlike, or
ragged texture, becoming even more ragged when described as dotted with a multitude of "blue flowers." Textures "touch" or infiltrate
one another. Ragged fronds swaying and crashing, the stiff harsh
brushing of taffeta, tin, and blue flowers on a vine are all agitated
surfaces that stand apart from (but also serve to characterize the other
mood of) the more sedate shifting of planes in the thematics of a "displaced" night (Bishop 2006, n. 79, 288–89). In this case, one set of
images of excitement or agitation hovers like a penumbra around the

borders of the room and, because the poem is about two lovers' passionate return to one another in the daytime, the movement at the edges is implicitly also occurring in the unshown dark center where the two mouths meet.

In "Whitewashed," Bishop suspends the speaker in a field of shape motifs that, in Thwaites's terminology, have clearly become "psychophysical" fields of force. In these drafts and in "The Shampoo," as in Klee's paintings, movements, lines, speeds, shapes ("motifs") are in complex relation to one another and become the setting in which a speaker is suspended but also, simultaneously, expressive of that speaker. As in Klee's laying of transparent washes of color across one another or across the boundaries of a form in *Glance of a Landscape*, we see the crossing or infiltration of the speaker by atmospheres or textures from the environment. The boundary line around the subject becomes indistinct so that the speaker, while still holding the objects of the environment at a distance, experiences them somatically as simultaneously inside, as part of the interior feeling of the self. Whereas the paintings *Fear* and *The Man of Confusion* show the invasion of the violence of the environment across the boundary of skin, "Whitewashed" and "The Shampoo" situate the speaker in an openness to the shapes, movements, colors, and textures of a milder environment. The speaker and her lover are suspended among these shapes and textures, and the psycho-physical forces arranged around the speaker become the range of her interior experience.

This more genial relationship between environment and interior of the self, in which the interior of the subject becomes filled by or comes in intimate somatic relation to the environment, can also be seen in the postcard that Bishop sent to Margaret Miller in September 1950. Bishop tells Miller that she is sending her "next-to favorite card," a reproduction of Klee's painting *A Young Lady's Adventure* (1922) (September 19, 1950, VSC). The "open" boundary of the girl's body allows the elements of the cosmos—moon and night—inside the body. Her openness to the environment allows her to enter an intimate conversation with the animals and the bird around her. Her wide floating sleeves and her feet that do not touch the ground give her the sense that she is floating through the genial nightscape, open to and partially containing its elements.

A draft entitled "Gypsophilia," set in Samambaia after Bishop moved to Brazil in 1951, again suspends the speaker (as "we") in a deep fluid space amid a field of shape motifs of varying speeds and directionalities. Standing high on a mountain in a diffuse terrain where the "air is thinner" and the "blue / deteriorates," the speaker is crossed by the "hard and thin" sounds of a voice yelling "*Din-ner!*" and by the metallic clang of someone beating an iron bar in the orchid nursery below. The presumably sedentary speaker herself seems to be floating off: "The last clangs are / the last words of a bell-buoy out at sea" (VSC 66.5). Standing high on the mountain in her "cold sub-stratum of dew," she is also floating beneath a circling spray of white stars and so appears to be at the bottom of a deep space. When Manuelzinho's family appears on the road below, carrying burdens, the speaker is suspended among a different set of shape-motifs, resembling "the spiky things Klee loves, sprays of grass or reeds, fronds or fir twigs or the backbones of fishes" (Thwaites, "Second Part," 8). The family, carrying "a load of dead branches," and an "enormous sheaf" of "'Gypophilia [sic],' 'baby's breath,'" with Manuelzhino's wife possessing "hair hang[ing] down under . . . an old felt hat," is rendered as a series of short straight lines, not quite aligned, first lying sideways (the branches as they are carried), then pointing downward (the hair), and then pointing upward in a tiny set of explosions (the "baby's breath"). Later, the speaker imagines herself as a small, dark, condensed black seed carried or "borne" in the "minutely, whitely, blossoming sprays" of white stars above: "a dead black seed / caught somewhere / caught, somehow, and carried, carried / in those glimmering sprays about us" (VSC 66.5). She terms the spray a "fascicle," the exfoliated bursting shape of a flower's stamens. Invisible at the center of a circle of a white spray of stars, the lyric speaker is suspended, borne along, "carried." As in "Night Intact," the speaker of "Gypsophilia" hangs among floating motifs that are arrayed about the speaker and cross into the interior, felt as "psycho-physical" forces. Each object of attention resituates the consciousness of the speaker so that the "center" where the speaker is located "tips" in relation to another object or "moves off."

Again and again Bishop shows us surfaces that modulate in texture or tactility, that open and become airy or diffuse and allow infiltration by other colors, atmospheres, or textures. Resembling the painting *Fear*, this fascination with infiltration is not merely the aesthetics of placing color against color, shade against shade, texture against texture, but involves a particular kind of ontology that sees subjects as partially open, airy, crossed by the textures and movements of the environment, and modulated by the intricate density of that environment. Whereas in *Fear* the crossing into the boundary of the subject occurs in the mood of a deep anxiety about infiltration, other moods—as we see in "Whitewashed" and "Gypsophilia"—are possible. The boundary of the body can be dangerously open when unable to prevent frightening forces from crossing into it (the arrows at the right-hand edge of *Fear* emphasize this effect) or more pleasurably open when other kinds of "psycho-physical" fields cross its membrane. Like the bodiless eye floating among drifting reddish-orange diaphanous sheets of color in Klee's *Glance of a Landscape*, Bishop's speaker in "Gypsophilia" stands in an atmosphere where "blue deteriorates" or the sound of metal drifts away, like "the last word of a bell-buoy." The speaker hangs as eye or ear in that deep space, among objects that float toward or away. The release of the line from bounding the figure in Klee's work is closely related to the subject's perception that the surface of the body is incompletely and incoherently sensed from inside and so cannot properly "bound" the ego. Ultimately, Bishop's noting of an "I" comes closest to the mobility of Klee's staging of an "event" in which an object "appears" in a field that did not before contain it but that immediately rearranges itself, opening, to hold it. The self is not the center of that occurrence. The "I" is itself a kind of field, and its elements, variously remote or close, both inside and outside the skin, resituate the speaker as the environment changes. These lines, shapes, motifs, and orbits cause the registering of sensation in the perceiver, rearranging and creating anew the proprioceptive subject. As Henri Wallon defines it, *proprioceptivity* is the result of the "gathering together and unification of otherwise disparate and scattered sensations provided by the various sense organs, in all their different spaces and registers" (*Les Origenes du caractère chez l'enfant*, quoted in Silverman 16). The experience of sensation causes an identification-at-a-distance, as Kaja Silverman terms it, and diffuses the sense of the "I" so that it is "stretched" among the atmospheres, textures, and objects of the "surround" (Silverman 15).

One of Bishop's favorite poems in *A Cold Spring*, "Faustina, or Rock Roses," demonstrates most clearly the way that different textures and shapes infiltrating one another includes not merely a visual aesthetic but an ontology of the subject. In this poem, as in *Fear* and *Glance of a Landscape*, we become intensely conscious of eyes in bodies that are open to the atmosphere. Suspending the speaker in a deep fluid space of floating shapes and materials that open into or drift across that speaker, Bishop creates a dynamic sense of subjectivity intensely vulnerable to an environment that can diffuse across its boundaries and yet also be held in suspension among its objects. The poem, which is about Bishop's visit to an invalid under the care of Faustina, a Key West black woman, appears as a collage of variously textured whites. Inside the invalid's room, the various surfaces are layered across or next to one another: the white on white of the fine lines of hair on the white pillow, nightgown against undershirt, and the papery "pallid palm-leaf fan" that the papery pallid invalid is too weak to wield (CP 73). Textures vary from smooth to encrusted to opening: the white enamel of the bed frame with its surface crazed; the loosely dotted powder of talcum; the rough, more solidly meshed "pasteboard boxes"; and the condensed but ornamented spheres of pills with their encrusted surface "half-crystallized"—these are textures that open toward one another, varying in the diffuseness or "openness" of their surfaces. They will dissolve away, like the flags with their patterns and images "bleached" away. The field of whites occasionally moves through various kinds of luminosity and occasionally rises to a color, and Bishop orchestrates their emergence in the mode that Klee's critics described, as flashes encountered, floating up into view: dew that "glint[s]" on the mesh of the screen door, two glow-worms beyond the screen with their subdued light not quite emergent from a dark field ("burning a drowned green"), the harsh lighting from a bare bulb that suddenly makes tack heads glint, and the "wall-pocket, / violet-embossed, glistening / with mica flakes." The surfaces sometimes move or open or wilt: the bedposts that unfurl into "four vaguely roselike / flower-formations"; the undulating lines of the sagging floorboards; and the white sheets, with their undulating lines and dissolving enervated folds "like wilted roses" (CP 72–73). We should see these motifs in relation to Klee's insistence on the textures of objects that erupt into movement and that the viewer feels as "psycho-physical" effects.

The figures in the poem are suspended within this field of textures, and the human figures' interiors can open out extensively or toward various depths like the other materials in the room. Beyond, at the edges of the various whites, lurk several darks. A night deep and dark enough to semidrown the glow-worms' two green lights hangs beyond the room. The night is a hole that one could step out into and become lost in. Inside the white space, other "holes" appear. In the white room that constantly fluctuates between two and three dimensions, the visitor herself and the interaction between the visitor and the invalid woman remain shadowed, almost invisible, silent, effaced, like holes that are deeper than the rest of the space. The question of whether the women will "open out" to one another is central. No words are spoken between visitor and invalid. The visitor is only known as a figure that deviates from that white-on-white environment.

> The visitor is embarrassed
> not by pain nor age
> nor even nakedness,
> though perhaps by its reverse. (*CP* 73)

Full of a gentle "embarrassed" pathos, Bishop captures the shame of the still-living in the presence of the dying. The almost-effaced assertion, in that gentle "perhaps," marks the visitor as caught in the embarrassing situation of being embarrassed by living instead of dying. She is too ashamed to "show" in the picture. Her invisibility becomes a kind of hiding, a not-wanting to be so embarrassingly bright or alive. Because the next line is "by and by the whisper / says," we know that the speaker has been sitting in silence for some time, suspended inside the space of the collage of whites and hearing only the inaudible whispered words of the invalid. We do not see the invalid's face, which occurs only as the blank from which the whisper issues. We see/feel the visitor only as "perhaps the reverse" of "pain," "age," and "nakedness." Neither the face of the visitor nor the face of the invalid comes into focus (the invalid's surround has been shown but not her face). Both the invalid's face and the speaker's even less visible face sink (almost) into the environment so that only the eyes are visible—like the eye in *Fear* that hides in its body composed of the textured burlap of the environment.

As in Klee's *Glance of a Landscape*, which suspended the "eye" in a landscape of drifting sheets of color and spiky stick shapes, this poem suspends the speaker in a complex of shapes, lines, and textures of different densities moving across or through one another, opening into one another, closing to one another. Distinct from the white-on-white environment and these deeper "holes" in that environment, the

black face of the caretaker, Faustina, looms with an engulfing sudden-
ness as the focal point and is viewed, in a strange and "sickening" reversal, as if the visitor were in the sick bed looking up.

> She bends above the other.
> Her sinister kind face
> presents a cruel black
> coincident conundrum.
>   Oh, is it
>
> freedom at last, a lifelong
> dream of time and silence,
> dream of protection and rest?
>
> Or is it the very worst,
> the unimaginable nightmare
> that never before dared last
>   more than a second?
>
> The acuteness of the question
> forks instantly and starts
> a snake-tongue flickering;
> blurs further, blunts, softens,
> separates, falls, our problems
> becoming helplessly
>   proliferative. (*CP* 73–74)

The face is condensed in the two words "sinister kind" ("her sinister
kind face / presents a cruel black / coincident conundrum") so that opposed meanings and contrasting sounds cohere in a tight space juxtaposed to one another. The binary falls or collapses into itself in the
phrase "coincident conundrum," where the similarities of consonants
and vowels, their "nearness" to one another, make the binaries cohere
even more closely in a denser relationship, as if a pattern of contrasts
can become tighter and finally one part of each contrast can squeeze
into the same space as the other. Then contrast or pattern opens out,
briefly, for a second, with the light, airy, long-drawn, upward inflec-
tion of "Oh, is it / freedom at last, a lifelong / dream of time and
silence, / dream of protection and rest?" The two blank spaces between

stanzas—after "oh, is it" and "rest?"—provide intervals that are suspended, uplifted in hope. Just after that the line comes down sharply: "Or is it the very worst?" The horror is intensified by "rest" in slant rhyme with "worst," again pressing contrasts together in an uncomfortable embrace. Then, "shape" leaps out of the scene, which until now has been largely texture against texture of only slightly opening or unfolding whites (varied by the small glints and glows and the "holes" of the invisible faces and the dark night). As if leaping out of the deep space of Faustina's black face, "The acuteness of the question / forks instantly and starts / a snake-tongue flickering; / blurs further, blunts, softens, / separates, falls, our problems / becoming helplessly / proliferative." The sudden explosion of squiggly lines, uncontained, is unlike anything that has been seen in the poem thus far (meshes, textures, of white on white, or little squares—the wall pocket—or rounded forms that open out only as far as something like a rose). This little chaos of sharp sticklike propulsive lines (the question felt as a shape, "acuteness" experienced as shape) is then condensed into the two eyes. The proliferative questions are held inside two darkened unreadable circles: "the eyes say only either" (*CP* 73–74). At the close of the poem, the "proliferative" is carried over into the bunch of roses that the visitor hands the invalid, roses that have a "blurred" or infiltrated section of rust and that begin to disperse in a spray of petals. The interiors of the speaker, the invalid, and even Faustina open out, become opaque or unreadable, turn propulsive, cross over into one another, and reclose. Subjectivity, suspended in its fluid space of floating textures and motifs, can be infiltrated or invaded in a mood of geniality or fear.

Even more striking, Bishop seems to produce in this poem the kind of reversal of viewer/object that Klee produced through placing a floating eye in a landscape or an eye inside a body submerged in the surround. The viewer of Klee's *Glance of a Landscape*, when entering the painting in the way that Thwaites and Sylvester suggest, clambering over into it, finds him- or herself suddenly inside the painting and now located in the eye, looking out, with the painted landscape serving as the viewer's body. So, too, the speaker of "Faustina, or Rock Roses" flips from watching the invalid at the bedside to inhabiting the invalid's body, which is partly composed of the "body" of the room of whites surrounded by an unknown night. Both sets of eyes (the invalid's and the speaker's) then stare up into the downward-leaning eyes of Faustina, as, in fact, the reader of the poem is likewise forced to do.

As a viewer of Klee's paintings in the late 1930s and 1940s, Bishop would have been taught by critics such as John Thwaites, David Sylvester, and the critics in *Cahiers d'Art* to move past the two-dimensional surface of Klee's paintings and cross over into the deep space where the eye wanders among moving motifs and engages in intimate and quasi-physical encounters with a sequence of variously dense or diffuse materials that infiltrate the "body" of the subject. Positioned inside the picture, the viewer, like the speaker in these Bishop poems, drifts in a weightless deep space in relation to a complex of shapes and lines moving at various speeds, crossed by textures and atmospheres of variant densities, the empathic subject of a bedazzling variety of "psycho-physical" objects and environments. Textures or atmospheres lying against, infiltrating, passing through, falling into, or glancing off; undulating and dissolving planes; and spiky, circling, explosive lines—these sites for surfaces to sink into or reach out into depth become the subject of much of *A Cold Spring* (as well as the subject of "The Moose," which Bishop began in this period). The diffused and the dispersed, the open and the closed, and the proliferative and the contained become a political subject (in "View of the Capitol from the Library of Congress") or a deeply human one (in "Faustina" and "The Shampoo").

Finally, "The Shampoo," "On the 'Prince of Fundy,'" "White-washed," "Gypsophilia," and "Faustina" allow us to see the existential or ontological import of Bishop's interest in depicting a range of textures, kinds of concentration and diffusion, colors, and luminosities simultaneously "touching," crossing, and sometimes sharing one another's "spaces" or reflecting off and obstructing one another. "Faustina," especially, reveals the way that human relationships and human questions are felt as the opening and closing, appearance and disappearance of shapes or lines that project out or are introjected across the various materials of the environment and the self. Skin, as the drawn boundary around the subject, diminishes into near-invisibility as the space of the self becomes crossed by or suspended among other objects and textures and the artistic space becomes the arena for "fish swimming in all directions," where the positioning of the lyric subject moves in and out or floats among these other sensory objects. The paintings singled out by Bishop in her correspondence about

Klee picture the massive disintegration or near-effacement of the body, leaving an eye (or eyes) submerged in a field. Bishop's frequent use of a nearly effaced or submerged speaker, arising only gradually and gently to speak the "I" from within a multitude of acts of perception and relations with a landscape, becomes most visible to us when understood as the poetic corollary to Paul Klee's floating eyes submerged in landscape or surroundings, crossed by atmospheres and textures, and suspended within a "complex of movements." For Bishop, Klee's aesthetic provided a less intellectualized, more visceral and somatic understanding of depth that, like the concept of a "thick" mobile threshold articulated in "Pleasure Seas," could replace Moore's deep Christian metaphysics. Bishop located the eye/"I" deeply, extensively, somatically, and expressively within the complex relations of a mobile environment of other motifs, bodies, and textures folding into and across one another's surfaces. The speaker in Bishop's poems is like Klee's staging of an "event" in which an object "appears" in a field that did not contain it before and that immediately rearranges itself and opens to hold it. The self is not the center of that occurrence. The "I" is itself a kind of field. As in the paintings *Fear*, *The Man of Confusion*, and *Glance of a Landscape*, the eye/"I," almost without skin, becomes witness to and the host of the "events" of the environment in which it hangs. Even though tentativeness and an "admission of final ignorance" mark the speaker's mode of experience, an active field of feeling and relationship has opened and become available for exploration in poetry.

THREE

MODULATION

Disconnection and Meaninglessness: *Arts of the South Seas* and "Over 2000 Illustrations and a Complete Concordance"

Bishop had first become interested in Klee in 1937, when some of his work was included in the MoMA exhibit "Fantastic Art, Dada, and Surrealism," and her correspondence records that she continued to follow his work in galleries such as Buchholz and, later, in the 1949 MoMA exhibit on Klee that traveled to the Phillips Gallery in Washington D.C., which Bishop saw three times (letter from Bishop to Marianne Moore, January 5, 1937 (VSC); Bishop 1994, 96–97; letters from Bishop to Loren MacIver, March 2 and June 29, 1950, VSC). It was in this period, between the late 1930s and late 1940s, while she struggled to come into her own beyond the tutelage of Moore, that Bishop most intensively looked to the visual arts to nourish her own work. The 1946 and 1947 trips to Nova Scotia provided Bishop with material that she would take years to fully develop, and the visual art that she came across during this period played a central role in setting the course for that development. Bishop's correspondence with Margaret Miller during the mid-1940s reveals a continuing exchange about art, including their sharing of books by Erwin Panofsky, Joachim Gasquet on Cézanne, and Daniel-Henry Kahnweiler's biography of Juan Gris.[1] During the summer trips to Nova Scotia, Miller continued to introduce Bishop to works about the visual arts, sending her at least one MoMA publication during the 1946 trip, *Arts of the South Seas* (letters from Margaret Miller to Bishop, July 3 and July 21, 1946, VSC). While traveling, Bishop also recorded a few excerpts from and responses to Alfred Barr's book on Picasso (VSC 75.4b, 156). Ultimately, however, it was the German artist Kurt Schwitters, central to Miller's curatorial work at MoMA in 1946–1948, who became most interesting to Bishop during this period and who provided her with the means of translating her responses to Barr's book on Picasso and *Arts of the South Seas* into an aesthetics of her own.

Although there need be no originating cause other than Bishop's own travels and wandering trajectory in life for the genesis of "Over 2000 Illustrations and a Complete Concordance," it is likely that the problem of disconnection—the problem of "'and' and 'and'"—was intensified or even precipitated by Bishop's reading of *Arts of the South Seas*. Published by MoMA in conjunction with a large exhibition, *Arts of the South Seas* presented a rapid sequence of descriptions of Oceanic cultures, each with its own aesthetic practices, religion, and sociopolitical system. The rapid movement through descriptions of culture after culture gave an intensified experience of arbitrariness that was comparatively new in the 1940s (even though anthropology as a discipline had emerged in the early years of the century, the experience of reading thirty-five descriptions of different cultures—each inventing meaning systems, art objects, and rituals—would have been unusual). Moving through a book that presents the fantastic array of cultural inventiveness in "the desolation of god-forsaken specks of coral lost in a vast ocean," as the authors, Ralph Linton and Paul Wingert (7), put it, gives the inventiveness a sense of meaningless accumulation that occupies the central subject of "Over 2000 Illustrations and a Complete Concordance."[2]

The importance of *Arts of the South Seas* for "Over 2000 Illustrations and a Complete Concordance," however, goes beyond merely the intensified experience of "'and' and 'and.'" *Arts of the South Seas* starkly demonstrated not only the sheer arbitrariness in the construction of meaning and artistic forms but also revealed that most cultures organized themselves around a deeply recessed, sacred space. In each culture, a deep interior space—a niche in rock cleft or a carved shrine— held back the most meaningful object in the most sacred place. The description of Marquesan religion provides one example from the many presented in the book: "Marquesan religion was strictly a tribal affair.

Each tribe had one or more sacred places, usually a series of stone-faced platforms running up the crest of a steep ridge. The upper-most platform bore images of wood and stone, often of very large size, while on one of the lower platforms there was usually a small house with a very high roof used for the storage of sacred objects. The sacred place always stood in a grove" (Linton and Wingert 34). The production of such recesses, difficult of access, often elevated and orna-mented to enhance their value, were the typical premodern means of orienting people in the world (Summers 152–66).

Arts of the South Seas presented very clearly both the existential problem of disconnection and the potential (ultimately unavailable for Bishop) solution to that problem by the creation of a space of special depth that oriented the disconnected pieces around a sacred center. In this book, Bishop encountered starkly the way that premodern cultures typically construct sacred deep spaces to orient people in an otherwise pathless world without centers or boundaries. Bishop structures her poem as the movement toward such sacred spaces, which each appears as the hoped-for answer to the problem of disconnection. In the poem, the sarcophagus of the "poor prophet paynim" and the sacred objects of a "family with pets" hidden inside the rocks (and also inside a physical book) emerge as variant conclusions of the speaker's wanderings (*CP* 58–59).

Both spaces (the paynim's grave and the rocks) that hold the sacred deeply within them have close correlatives in *Arts of the South Seas*. In the New Hebrides culture, the object "held back," encased in a decorative cover and revered was the body of the leader: "At the death of an important man commemorative figures are made signifying his importance and decorated with symbols of his eminent social position. These figures are life-size . . . afterwards the effigy is stored in the men's house where it remains until it rots away" (Linton and Wingert 84). The revered cultural leader, his corpse rotted away beneath his decorations, underlies Bishop's creation of a "poor prophet paynim" now turned to dust in "Over 2000 Illustrations." *Arts of the South Seas* also provided the startling final image of the poem, where the object of reverence emerges not as a divine being or revered leader but as a "family with pets." Linton and Wingert briefly tell the story of a Hawaiian rebellion that replaced the divine figures of a priestly class with a simple family cult. The rebellion was staged against "the old state religion [that] imposed heavy burdens upon the common people and subjected women to many restrictions" (64). Linton and Wingert give a memorable insider's picture of a family under the oppressive rule of this priestly culture supported by the king:

> Each household also had a stone pounder for crushing taro. It is said that in some districts the pounders were made very small so that the meals could be prepared as quietly as possible. If a palace servant heard the sound of food pounding he would come and take the food away. At night the family slept under blankets made from several sheets of bark-cloth which were sewn together along one edge, like the pages of a book. (Linton and Wingert 61)

This oppressive religious system, which had its priestly class and temples located outside of the home, is overturned so that the object of reverence is located not in the temple but, instead, in the family:

> In 1819 two of the widows of Kamehameha I persuaded the then reigning king to break the religious taboos. The priests tried to reassert their authority, but their army was defeated and the common people destroyed the temples and their contents. The simple family and occupational cults [that replaced the priest's religion] survived until a much later time, being carried on to some extent long after the islands had become officially converted to Christianity. (Linton and Wingert 64)

The surprising ending of "Over 2000 Illustrations"—surprising even if we read it as a homely restatement of the Christian nativity—resembles the simple family cults of the new Hawaiian religion. Both Bishop's "family with pets" and the Hawaiian family cult replace reverence for images of a divine figure by reverence for the life of a simple family. And Linton and Wingert's suggestion at the end of the passage that the family cult became conflated with Christianity gives rise to an image closely resembling the closing image of Bishop's poem, where we find the overlapping of the two systems: the Christian divine family of the Nativity and the everyday human family refigured as divine.

The crucial point, however, is not that *Arts of the South Seas* provides a possible source for the swerve to a rather unpredictable cult at the end of "Over 2000 Illustrations" but that *Arts of the South Seas* presented the use of art to solve the problem of disconnection. Each culture artistically fashioned a sacred space that held meaning in a deep interior space. Because the book on Oceanic art showed such a long sequence of those sacred spaces, it vividly exhibited the insufficiency of escaping from the experience of "'and' and 'and'" by means of the artistic invention of a deeper interior where meaning is located. Each culture created a sacred site with a hidden interior that grounded that culture and provided a "there," toward which the subject could face rather than wander. But, by giving the reader the sense that human cultures could and would produce a potentially endless series of these deep interior spaces, *Arts of the South Seas* made clear that a deeply interior space could not solve the problem of disconnection but was itself only another version of "'and' and 'and.'" The sacred spaces and objects that proliferate in the survey of so many different cultures become hollowed out of validity. In her poem, Bishop reproduces this serialization of the experience of meaning locked in a deep interior by describing *both* the paynim's grave and the rocks (or the book) as breaking with light. Although the ending of "Over 2000 Illustrations" offers a locus of meaning in the "rocks breaking with light" and in its vision of a "family with pets," the sheer arbitrariness of the vision, its appearance as an unexpected and merely hypothetical solution, undercuts its ability to function as a viable answer to the interrelated problems of disconnection and lack of meaning. The problem that the poem addresses has its real-life corollary not only in the speaker's sequence of travels, which cannot locate a "behind" to the surface of the world, but in the *Arts of the South Seas*, where culture after culture invented meaning by hiding its sacred figurines "behind" the surface of the culture: inside a temple, a grove, or a ceremonial house or in the remote interior of the landscape. *Arts of the South Seas* showed that art was used to produce these deep spaces of revelation. Bishop's focus on a physical book that itself provides a deep recess harboring a sacred presence conflates her own art, the art of poetry, with the spatial art of Oceanic peoples. The poem casts suspicion on any use of poetry that creates a deeply recessed space that the reader would face to experience some sort of revelation. The very fact of multiple sites of depth—in Bishop's poem and in *Arts of the South Seas*—shows that art cannot serve modern culture the way it served premodern cultures.

Yet, if *Arts of the South Seas* presented the problem of disconnection, the arbitrariness and therefore lack of a center or of a deep space where meaning could be located, it also presented depth itself in a new kind of sequence. The descriptions of artistic practice in the book on Oceanic art set the relation between surface and depth on a complex continuum. The book surveyed a hugely various range of kinds of artistic carving. Partly because they are attuned to the 1940s controversies in Western art about geometric and biomorphic visual art and the production of flat surfaces for painting, Linton and Wingert organize their discussions partly by contrasting the various cultures' use of surface patterns that are ornamental and surface patterns that emerge from the shape of the object ("rhythmic organic curved surfaces" arising from the "exaggeration and distortion of natural forms"; Linton and Wingert 9). That is, Linton and Wingert present the Oceanic aesthetic traditions varying from culture to culture partly by contrasting surface decoration and the "deeper" carving of more organic forms. As we move through the book, we encounter various levels of decoration at different depths. The result of this survey, then, is an interrogation of the modern separation between flat painting and three-dimensional free-standing sculpture. This modern organization of aesthetic experience comes to seem only an arbitrary schematic division of the possibilities for visual art. Omitted from modern painting and sculpture are a whole range of artistic practices, practices that occupy some middle position between writing and drawing, between the two-dimensional and the three-dimensional, between painting and carving. In Linton and Wingert's book on Oceanic art, although the sacred site stands as the deepest most recessed space, the carvings and relief sculptures and drawings with raised designs and the carving/drawing on skin, all produce the movement from surface to depth as a sequence of modulations across different kinds of materials and different levels of representation so that art keeps "crossing over" into the house, on to the body, on to a tool, or on to a natural object. Moreover, meaning (associated with depth) kept crossing over into design (associated with surface).

All the examples of artistic objects in the book wavered between surface and depth, the purely aesthetic and the real. In central Polynesia (Samoa and Tonga), "the usual method was to spread the cloth over a surface bearing raised designs, then rub it [the cloth] with red earth or soot, thus transferring the design to it" (Linton and Wingert

28) so that a design was not entirely flat, as in a drawing or painting but, instead, had some "body" because "earth or soot" lay on the surface of the cloth. In the Easter Islands, "wooden tablets [were] inscribed with characters incised to make pictographs" (46) so that art lay in an intermediate zone between the written and the drawn, and existed as relief rather than either flat or fully carved. Among the Maori in Australia, "gable, door and window frames and sometimes the entire house front were decorated with elaborate carvings" (50) so that a real object (the house) became simultaneously an art object, decoration excessively "covering" function. In contrast, in the Admiralty Islands, there was "complete integration of geometric pattern and representative sculpture into one harmonious unit" so that the surface decoration never pulled away from the form (174). Among the Maori, "tattooing was really flesh carving" (50). On Easter Island, the body became a kind of paper or surface that art was written on: "clothing was scanty, but both sexes were elaborately tattooed with large curvilinear designs" (43). In the Marquesas, tattoo artists first carved a design on a wooden limb (three-dimensional) and then transferred the design to the human skin so that the three-dimensional carving became a drawing laid or wrapped over a three-dimensional form (34). These pictures on the skin also became a form of writing among the Maori: "no two face tattooings were identical, and in early days chiefs drew details of their face tattoo on treaties with the whites by way of signature" (51).

Why does this matter for Bishop's poem? I suggest that *Arts of the South Seas* allowed Bishop to reimagine the art of poetry as part of what David Summers calls "real space." That is, writing became more visible to Bishop as taking place in a physical space in a particular format, inside a series of human artistic practices that included carving, inscribing, drawing, and patterning on a range of materials from monumental stone to human flesh.[3] The intensification of this insight was significant enough to her that she used the entire first section of "Over 2000 Illustrations" to undertake a minute description of the issue that Summers calls format. It is worth taking a moment to understand Summers's argument, which hinges on our paying attention to the cardinality of the human body:

[T]he cardinal structure of the human body—its normative uprightness, symmetry (including the asymmetry of handedness) and facing—is reiterated in much of the basic and assumed meaning we take as given in the world round us. Things "stand" (or do not stand) in relation to our standing, "face" in being faced by us, just as they are large in relation to our size, heavy or immovable in relation to our strength, resistant, blunt or sharp in relation to our touch and vulnerability. (Summers 37)

Format takes account of this cardinality in thinking about art. Summers defines *format* by setting up a lengthy comparison. He describes a human being facing an 8-foot Aztec sculpture of volcanic rock set in a sacred temple precinct and used to orient people's movements in a city as well as in the temple. He then contrasts that experience of art, in that real space, with a landscape drawing by Rembrandt, also set in real space:

> . . . the drawing is small, portable and possessable; it is in relation to our facing that it faces, has a back and front, a top and bottom, a left and right, and it is in relation to our verticality that the horizontality of the landscape is meaningful and that the rectangle of paper has been cropped. . . . When hung vertically for modern museum display the marks therefore seem suspended, free from gravity, which helps to make the landscape seem hovering, distant, available only to sight . . . the evident hand and handedness of Rembrandt give the drawing "personality" and intimacy, qualities enhanced by the fragility, even the ephemerality, of the paper itself. The intimate scale of the marks complements the close viewing distance demanded by the small size; and for all its dazzling virtuoso illusionism, which seems at once to seize the eye, the drawing must be closely examined, like a signature so often repeated that it is not at once legible. (Summers 51–52)

Summers's description focuses our attention on the physicality of the art object in relation to the physical world in which it is placed, emphasizing that the experience of the art object is in some intimate and powerful way related to the scale, weight, fragility, directionality, and cardinality of the human body. In emphasizing the physical properties of the drawing, Summers places the art object and us in the same real space, removing the object from its isolation as framed-off in a purely aesthetic realm. Likewise, *Arts of the South Seas* places writing, drawing, and carving in real space.

For Bishop, the range of art objects presented in *Arts of the South Seas*—carvings on stone, houses, sticks, bark, and skin; drawings that were also writing; and writing that is also carving—brought the physicality of the format for poetry, typed on its piece of paper, into relation with all such practices. Typed on paper and bound in a book, lines of verse were also black ink on a material object, a physical body. The book on Oceanic art revealed that the separation between the two-dimensional page and three-dimensional life—the separation between poetry and life, between book and travel—was not a vast uncrossable distance. There were small steps of degree between flat writing and real three-dimensional space. A sense of the physicality of verse begins with envisioning type on paper, but it can move on to the weight of syllables, the physicality of a line that "moves" heavily or lightly, and the condensed or diffused feel of a line that opens to the world. The book on Oceanic art made it clear that the problem of the disconnection between the flatness of poetry—its existential entrapment in the space of "surface"—and a three-dimensional real space is actually an illusion created by our blindness to the issue of format. Just as we can shift our focus and see Rembrandt's drawing as a real physical object, with real physical properties, rather than merely as depicting a scene, so too we can shift our focus and see writing as a real physical practice that manipulates the material properties of words on paper: weight, solidity, density, fragility, movement, emptiness, and space.

So, in a poem that focuses on the disconnection between book and life, Bishop presents the physicality of the book as central. She makes three-dimensional "life" (in the travel section of the poem) come toward two-dimensional design; and she makes two-dimensional design (in the engraving section of the poem) come toward three-dimensional life. She describes the pages of the Bible with its "serious" engravings in continuous movement out of and back into surface decoration. The three-dimensionality of the "branches of the date-palms" modulate back into two-dimensional pattern when they "look like files," so they modulate from "real" to artistic pattern (*CP* 57). Likewise, the slightly less-three-dimensional cobbled courtyard (a flat surface with some depth, like a relief) becomes flattened into two dimensions when it looks "like a diagram." The representation of a "real" "human figure far gone in history or theology" retreats into a vast desert, without markings of any sort, as if disappearing into the blankness of the paper page. By having the "real" figures of human and camel disappear into the materiality of paper, Bishop focuses our attention on the slight wobble in our perception that transforms the blankness of paper into a desert (or, vice versa, the desert into the knowledge that it is just paper). So, too, by using the word *speck* in "specks of birds," she creates a wobble of meta-reflection so that we focus on the medium (a blot of ink) while seeing "bird." The "smoke" that we see "rising solemnly" is pulled by "invisible threads" that are lines of ink (*CP* 57). Bishop's language focuses our attention on the cusp between a visible image (smoke) and the materiality of the engraving (lines) that is producing that sensation of smoke. The experience of the passage makes us travel in small steps that tip over into another kind of materiality or another level of representation and, therefore, another kind of depth. The verse enacts modulation: from blank piece of paper to desert; from airy nothingness, the invisible, the insubstantial, to the "barely there" of "real" smoke; from a line of flat ink to a line of thinly three-dimensional thread.

Lifting our attention "up" and "out" of the minutely considered multileveled experience of the engraving that wobbles between inked medium and "real" visual representation, Bishop then focuses us on the format that "holds" the whole experience itself—the frames that hold the separate engravings in place, the paper of the page of the book on which they are held (and, later, the gilt edges of the book and the fingers that hold the book). The modulations now simply move to a different register—still focused on materiality but this time not so much on ink and paper as on the other materials that make up the structure of the book. The "surface" of the engraving becomes both deeper (at a greater remove) and less real when it is understood to be located on the page of a book with decorated "lunettes" and decorative type. The "stippled gray" of the lunette, the "toils of an initial letter" of the type, and the "cattycornered rectangles" in their ornateness rise up to the surface of the picture plane and make the "scenes" drop down into a deeper space, where the "eye" eventually follows them. In this way, the eye that "drops, weighted through the lines / the burin made" serves as only the last move in a series begun at the opening of the poem, a series that involves moving between different registers of experience (*CP* 57). There is a dizzying sensation as Bishop first raises us up to notice the level of printed book, then drops us down through the level of engraved lines, and then moves up again to notice the similarity of lines of poetic verse to lines of an engraving, which by resemblance then move through multiple registers, multiple levels of reality. They are ripples in sand (as drawn or engraved), then the more illusory ripples of heat above sand, which now lift even further into the realm of ideas rather than material, becoming the lines of God's fingerprint impressed on the world, and then modulate back from idea or metaphor into real ripples of waves in water.

Just at the moment that Bishop leaves the book of illustrations—with its dizzying modulations between registers of materiality and representation—she makes us "wobble" in perception so that we become aware of the physical typed verse lines of her poem on the page as located on a kind of cusp, sharing or wobbling between the qualities of lines of an engraving and lines of sea. As we move into the real, from book to world, we experience a startling transition into a new format, where writing, drawing, and engraving leave the boundary of the traditional format of the book and are seen as features of the actual world.

> The eye drops, weighted, through the lines
> the burin made, the lines that move apart
> like ripples above sand,
> dispersing storms, God's spreading fingerprint,
> and painfully, finally, that ignite
> in watery prismatic white-and-blue.
>
> Entering the Narrows at St. Johns
> the touching bleat of goats reached to the ship. (*CP* 57)

The physical white space between the two stanzas draws our attention to format, to the physicality of the lines of verse on the white page. The reader's eye moving downward on the page of the real book physically enacts the dropping of the eye through the lines of an engraving into the "real" world with its "lines" of sea. The sequence of increasing materiality culminates in the addition of new dimensions of sensory experience. The black-and-white engraving enters into color. And, in "the touching bleat of goats reached to the ship," Bishop's phrasing humorously mingles touch, sound, and pity, emphasizing that we have entered the real, where touch and emotion become three-dimensional (*CP* 57–58).

But, rather than serving as only a stark contrast to the experience of the book, the experience of the "real" continues to be one of modulation from two to three dimensions. Bishop repeats the sensation of wobbling, but this time it is one level up. Before, we were modulating between lines of ink and representations of date palms, courtyards, humans, and camels; now, we wobble between the real world seen as flat two-dimensional geometric patterns and the real world seen as lively three-dimensional biomorphic shapes. The more that Bishop locates us in the register of real sensation (color, sound, and touch), the more all this sensory and human world are imagined as the fluctuation of pattern and nonpattern, two-dimensional design and three-dimensional design. Bishop's draft of the poem makes it clear that she was thinking about the thematics of design—writing "obvious in design," where later she decided on "the brickwork conduits / are vast and obvious" (VSC 56.9; *CP* 57). Collegians, when looked at differently, tip over into black lines and then black dots. The mosaics with their geometric designs are poised against the sagging, soft, biomorphic shape of the "fat old guide." The "real" dead man lies next to the clear, colorful geometric shape of the "blue arcade." The dim and triangular "dead volcanoes" are poised against the fragrant bright and biomorphic "Easter lilies" (*CP* 58). The "real" travel merely repeats the fluctuation between the two-dimensional and the three-dimensional levels experienced in the engraving.

The question is why a poem about disconnection takes the trouble to focus so much on this kind of wobbling between representational levels. The effect is certainly that the major binary oppositions of the poem—between "text and world," between "Christian archetype" and the "raucous vitality" of "excursive vision" and "history"—break down in a fundamental way (Costello 1991, 132–38). The poem goes far beyond having the world of travel provide parodic scriptural scenes so that doubt is cast on the inherited Christian stories. Bishop's energies seem to be directed toward a redefinition of the existential status of writing so that drawing or writing lines is seen inside a continuum of human experience of seeing and living.

During the course of the poem, lines of poetry modulate out of lines of an engraving and into lines of the sea and then into lines of collegians crossing a square, and then they appear as lines of exhortation incised on stone. Poem, engraving, sea, collegians, and epigraph on stone are separate realms, but they are also realms that modulate into one another by acts of shifted attention. The poem performs a sinuosity in which writing, drawing, and lines in real space keep turning into one another. The significance of such a sinuosity is that it provides an "all over" movement between surface and depth, life and art (as in the range of aesthetic practices among the Oceanic cultures) rather than the use of art to provide only a deep space that stands at a kind of vanishing point toward which the "pilgrim" directs her movements and that is ultimately not able, itself, to withstand dispersal or disintegration.

The dispersal at the paynim's grave that frightens the speaker "most of all" is merely an intensification of the movement out of geometric hard-edged design into something less shapely. During the course of the poem, the movement from two-dimensional to three-dimensional, one material opening out into another, has both the danger of dispersal and the excitement of an explosion. The two-dimensional engraving moving to the three-dimensional sea produces a tiny explosion (lines burst, they "ignite / in watery and prismatic white-and-blue"), so too the geometric patterns all seem to eventually explode into squiggliness: the mad vivacity of the "jukebox [which] went on playing 'Ay, Jalisco!'"; the "rotting hulks" with their "dripping plush"; the respectable pouring of tea that becomes immediately fertile and obscene, giving rise to a baby and then a prostitute; the flinging of the belly-dancers; and the ferocity and wildness of the touch of nakedness that reaches farther than the touch of the goats' bleating and is mixed with giggling and begging at close quarters. Writing itself is merely another part of the continuum between two dimensions and three, between geometric patterns of lines and three-dimensional dispersals and explosions. The march of heavy isolated monosyllables ("marched in lines") is poised against the increased vitality of "rapidly, purposefully." The sequence of isolated and rigid words, almost all monosyllables—"the dead man lay / in a blue arcade"—is poised against the slippery vitality of "glistened" and "Easter lilies." "Dripping plush" with its sloppy, slushy sounds and "Volubilis" with its soft saggy interior work against the hard-tile geometric patterning of mosaics. The extrusions of sexual desire (the leering sexuality of "made eyes") and the popping sound of the word "poppies," the colorful flowers breaking the geometric container of the patterned mosaics, occur also as a semantic flowing over when "dripping plush" becomes the "pouring" of tea, which becomes prostitutes pouring (flinging) themselves on to the knees of the speaker and her companion. Suddenly, the squiggliness of words such as "giggling" feel as ungovernable as the giggling girls themselves, who reach over into the speaker's space, fall on the speaker's and her companion's knees, and beg for cigarettes (*CP* 57–58). Geometric shape cannot contain this mad vivacity, and neither the art of writing nor the art of building deeply recessed spaces can stop such dispersal into disconnection and meaninglessness.

Deep writing (incised in stone) is imagined as the extreme opposite of such squiggliness. It is the ornament for and corollary to deep visual art (the real stone that makes a deep recess for the deep experience of the paynim's presence). The opening line of the poem—"Thus should have been our travels: / serious, engravable"—links the idea of meaning (seriousness) to the idea of a deeper writing as engraving, a deeper incision, worthy of permanence and stability. But the carving on the surface of the stone baldaquin, meant to deliver not only wisdom but a wisdom that would tell one how to live (an "exhortation"), is itself akin to "scattered cattle-teeth" rather than letters that would form a message. The actual incised writing (writing in stone), meant to be serious, important, and deeply meaningful, scatters without delivering any revelation. The grittiness and deterioration of the solid marble enact, in the sensory register of real objects, the scattering of letters in a sentence so that they cannot hold together as line or as legible meaning. Neither the deep visual space of tomb, pit, and sepulcher nor the deeply incised writing of exhortation in stone that would mark that space as deeply meaningful stands apart from the continuum of modulation from art to world, two-dimension to three-dimension, that the poem has paraded in front of us. Rather than becoming closed or ended by the geometric and solid "keyhole-arched stone baldaquin," the ferocity of dispersal (the ferocity of "'and' and 'and'") culminates in a container that is itself both empty and the marker for a more desperate kind of dispersal. The paynim's grave is an icon of stability, but it is unable either to hold or to keep still. With Bishop's line "But what frightened me most of all," the sheer openness, emptiness, and dispersal arrive as the summation of the previous experience, an intensification of the "frightening" dispersal and squiggliness, profusion, and shapelessness of other scenes of the pilgrimage (*CP* 57–58).

The ending image of the poem performs the wish for yet another explosive crossing between media that could take dispersal and make it into something more illuminating and stable. This explosion would move from the heaviest and densest materiality ("rocks") to the airiest material ("light") and from the completely scattered and dispersed ("straw") to the completely divisionless and uniform: "an undisturbed, unbreathing flame, / colorless, sparkless." Likewise the book, understood as a correlative to the deeply recessed shrine that holds the sacred presence, is imagined as being able to pass its substance into the world, scattering it not as frightening dust but as gilt that crosses from the realm of text to the physical world: "The gilt rubs off the edges / of the pages and pollinates the fingertips" (*CP* 58–59).

In spite of the frightening paynim's grave or the impossibility of the final vision, the book is part of the world, a physical object that can pass its materials into the world because its materials resemble that world. The poem enacts dispersal. It presents a clear "no," as in searching in books or in the world for a place of depth will not work; it is not locatable. We will find only the "tipping" from one register to another. Both text and world are composed of the movement across different registers, from two-dimensional design to three-dimensional vivacity. Writing organizes lines and dots, condenses and scatters, and ignites into "life" and falls back into design. The three-dimensional space of the world also modulates between registers; it can look like a stable geometric flat diagrammatic pattern, but can move into color, rapid movement, sound, touch, death, sex, birth, and desperate human need. The details of the poem—the focus on passing from two to three dimensions across different representational levels from representational figures of humans to ink or paper and back again, from actions in the world to pattern—provide a kind of counterstory to the narrative of disconnection. The art work in *Art of the South Seas* and the image of a visual engraving allowed Bishop to link lines of verse to lines of the world. The details of the poem reimagine disconnection in the form of a sinuosity of continual transitions across different materials and different registers of representation, many tiny movements up and down levels.

In "Over 2000 Illustrations and a Complete Concordance," such modulation is understood in the modes mostly of fear ("most frightening of all") or impossible wish ("why couldn't we have seen"); the later poems in *A Cold Spring* begin to shift the emotional timbre of ceaseless modulation into the key of pleasure. Bishop's instructor in such pleasure seems to have been Kurt Schwitters, whose work in collage often focused on modulation.

Collage as Modulation and Connection:
Margaret Miller and Kurt Schwitters

Collage is an art form that solves the problem of disconnection. It concerns itself with "disintegration, fragmentation and integration," serving to collect and contain difference so that it is rearranged to touch rather than to fly apart (Hoffman 3). Instead of bringing the viewer to face a deeply recessed space, collage orients the viewer in the midst of disconnection by bringing the disparate registers of experience and of representation into extensive relation with one another. Marianne Moore brings into the space of the poem quotations and texts from disparate realms to set them into conflict and to ironize or interrogate them (Costello 1991, 211–14; Miller 1995, 5–6, 33–39, 77–92). In contrast, Bishop arranges for the different registers of experience to "meet" one another through modulation across intricate layers of sameness and difference. A clear example of this movement across registers can be seen in her late poem "Sestina," in which Bishop unfolds a sequence of modulation across realms of lived and aesthetic experience: a grandmother's tears, rain on the roof of the house, a "teakettle's small hard tears" that "dance like mad on the hot black stove," and "little moons" that "fall down like tears / from between the pages of the almanac" and land in the flowerbed of a child's drawing (*CP* 123–24). The material and shape of tears move gently across the layers of the natural, human, and domestic object and across the layers of different styles of representation, from a stylized almanac to a stylized child's drawing held inside the more sophisticated but "stylized" form of the poet's sestina.[4] As used by Kurt Schwitters, the collage artist of most interest to both Margaret Miller and Elizabeth Bishop, collage arranges those kinds of sequences of modulation across different papers and fabrics and across different orders of reality to produce connection and relation. In Schwitters's work, not only are the real objects of the culture brought inside the frame of art—a feature common to most twentieth-century collage—but also the materials of art are sequenced in tiny intervals toward the real. Transparent fragile materials "gain" color, density, and weight, and line spreads out to become surface and then thickens into three-dimensional object, "crossing over" into the real by increasing in density, opacity, and saturation of color. In organizing modulations from art to life and across representational levels, Schwitters became a significant conceptual model for the poetics of *A Cold Spring* and some of the poetry that followed in later years. Bishop transforms Schwitters's fabrics into the materials of verse.

Again, Margaret Miller supplied the mediating context for Bishop's use of a visual artist. Between 1946 and 1948, Miller was hard at work curating an exhibit at MoMA for which she had sole responsibility.[5] The aim of the exhibit was to survey the art of collage, at the time a comparatively little-studied aspect of modern art. In a letter to Louis Carré, a Parisian gallery owner and potential donor, Miller described the scope and purpose of the exhibit: "The show will consist of some sixty or seventy works arranged to show the mutations of collage from the cubist *papiers collés* through Dada and Surrealism to the present, something in the manner of the Museum's *Cubism and Abstract Art* exhibition though on a much smaller scale" (August 21, 1947, Reg. Ex. #385, MoMA Archives, NY). Bishop and Miller's correspondence shows that, while traveling in Nova Scotia in 1946, Bishop participated in Miller's project to think through the history of collage. Bishop mentioned a collage and a photomontage to Miller, and Miller asked for a copy of the photomontage for possible inclusion in the catalogue (letter from Margaret Miller to Bishop, July 21, 1946; postcard from Miller, undated [1946], VSC). Miller shared with Bishop some of her excitement in putting together the show, telling of her triumph in arranging for a cartoon of a Picasso tapestry, for example, and describing it in detail to Bishop (letter from Margaret Miller to Bishop, July 26, 1946, VSC). For her part, Bishop asked permission to include notes about collage in her review article on the poetry of Marianne Moore (although the published piece did not mention collage). Miller answered:

> If the *collage* notion suggests anything to you in the way of an opening or particular way of discussing any one work don't hesitate to make use of it. If I use it at all in the catalog it would be only a sentence, along with a mention of Pound and Eliot. (Did

I tell you that Frani has asked someone to write a piece for *Modern Music* on quotation in modern music. She hadn't thought of it in connection with collage, but she had thought of the relation to Eliot.) (Letter from Margaret Miller to Bishop, August 11, 1946, VSC)

We do not have access to an extended, sustained account of collage by either Bishop or Miller. Although Miller worked extensively on preparing an exhibition catalogue, in summer 1946 she lost her notes on the subway (Margaret Miller to Bishop, July 21, 1946, VSC). At first she convinced herself that the project could be reconstructed, but she eventually abandoned the effort and no catalogue was ever produced.[6] Her passion for the project becomes evident when, after leaving MoMA in 1958, Miller mentions to Bishop that she is going to finish the book about collage, about which she has been thinking for many years (letter from Margaret Miller to Bishop, March 10, 1959, VSC). In spite of the loss of the catalogue notes, some of Miller's thoughts about collage can be gleaned from her correspondence with the collectors who loaned works for the exhibition and from a letter to Bishop.

At the time that Miller was working on collage, its importance for the development of twentieth-century art had not been extensively treated by art historians. Reviews of the show betray a general lack of comprehension of the significance of collage. Clement Greenberg vindicates Miller from what he calls the "scandal" of this "reception given by the general run of art reviewers" and calls the show "one of the most beautiful shows of modern art ever held in this country" (Nov. 27, 1948, 612). Miller's correspondence with those who loaned items contained flashes of the excitement of discovery as she worked on the basic significance of collage for early-twentieth-century visual artists. She corresponded with Daniel-Henry Kahnweiler, who reminded her to read the section in his biography of Juan Gris on collage for her show (letter from Daniel-Henry Kahnweiler to Margaret Miller, February 18, 1947; letters from Margaret Miller to Daniel-Henry Kahnweiler, October 30, 1946, and February 3, 1947, Reg. Exh. #385, MoMA Archives, NY). (Miller probably conveyed her enthusiasm for the book not only to Kahnweiler himself but also to Bishop because in July 1948 we find Bishop raving about the book to Lowell.)[7] Miller's excitement is evident when she received a response from Georges Braque that confirmed some of her own insights about the early cubist use of collage. Her inquiry to him reveals the kinds of questions with which she was wrestling:

> What I would like to know is the character of the first pasted element in a cubist work. I wonder if it served as a sample of the substance of the object, that is to say, if it represents the abstraction of an aspect of that substance, or if it was originally a real object, such as a poster or a piece of colored paper, used as a painted surface.
>
> Ce que je voudrais savoir c'est le caractère du premier élément collé dans une oeuvre cubiste. Je me demande s'il a servi comme échantillon d'une substance d'un object, c'est-à-dire s'il représente "l'abstraction d'un aspect," ou si c'etait un object réel, comme une affiche, ou bien un morceau de papier coloré, jouant le rôle d'une surface peinte. (Letter from Margaret Miller to Georges Braque, September 25, 1947, Reg. Exh. #385, MoMA Archives, NY)

Miller was delighted when Braque's answer matched her own conclusion. In a letter to Kahnweiler, she wrote:

> I was extremely interested in M. Braque's remarks about Le Compotier and his first p.c.s [papier collés]. The answers were exactly what I needed. I was happy that he placed the emphasis upon "dissociation"—"La forme et la couleur ne se confondent pas". I had already written in the provisional draft of the catalog text that 'the first pasted materials used by Braque and Picasso made the surface of the object separable from its shape. (October 20, 1947, Reg. Exh. #385, MoMA Archives, NY)

Miller's interest focused on Braque's peeling off one aspect of an object, one register of our experience of an object, and detaching it from the whole so as to make it able to be seen more starkly.

More than a year before, Miller's report of this insight about the crucial role of dissociation appeared in a letter to Bishop during the first trip to Nova Scotia:

> Last night or early morning there was a real tropical rainstorm with strong winds. . . . It all provoked a dream about 'collage'

in which my dream was mad at me for not having realized that it was fundamentally a question of dissociating. This was all illustrated with closeups of collage, with all the elements moving away from each other. I had just admitted to the Dream that it was perfectly right when I woke up and forgot all the finer points of its argument.

Monday I took the book of M. Moores [sic] poems to the Museum to mail and put in an order for the South Sea book. (Letter from Margaret Miller to Bishop, July 3, 1946, VSC)

The dream logic here links the genre of collage with the theme of disconnection in the South Sea art book. The dispersal into "'and' and 'and'" occurs here in the mode of a violent "tropical" storm, with elements "moving away from each other." Yet, although Miller seemed passionate about the way "dissociation," the peeling off of surfaces, and dispersal can explain the genre of collage, she also understood that dissociation allowed for a means of collecting that dispersal into a new arrangement. Collage allowed the artist to incorporate pieces of reality into the picture and created a way for art and reality to cross over into one another. Miller emphasized this feature in her press release: "[Collage's] significance lies not in its technical eccentricity but in its relevance to two basic questions which have been raised by twentieth-century art: the nature of reality and the nature of painting itself. Collage has been the means through which the artist incorporates reality in the picture without imitating it" (1948, REG, Exh. # 385. MoMA Archives, NY). The genre opened a site for experimenting with the relationship between art and reality, for conceptualizing the range of modes of their encounter.

Although resituating the real in relation to art was a prominent feature of much collage art, Kurt Schwitters's use of dissociation for that purpose became most relevant for Bishop. Of the collage artists in the MoMA show, he seemed to have been the most interesting to Elizabeth Bishop, and in this interest she followed Miller's own inclination. According to a letter from Bishop to Ilse and Kit Barker, Miller was passionate about Schwitters ("my friend Margaret Miller, whose passion is collage & Schwitters") (November 6, 1954, PUL).[8] Of the 102 works in the collage show, fifteen were by Schwitters (Orchard 282).[9] Several years later, Bishop again wrote the Barkers, "I am not so fond of the Expressionists in general, but there were some lovely Klees, Schwitters, fine early Grosz, etc. Schwitters I'm crazy about—if I were rich I'd buy up all on the market, I think" (November 28, 1957, PUL). Bishop had also gently offered Schwitters (along with Klee) as replacements when preventing Anne Stevenson, her biographer, from pursuing a line of argument about Max Ernst as a significant influence on Bishop's poetry (letter from Elizabeth Bishop to Anne Stevenson, January 8, 1964, WUL). With the help of Miller, who selected a collage from a show at the Janis Gallery, Bishop purchased a Schwitters for Lota's birthday in March 1953 (letter from Elizabeth Bishop to Margaret Miller, undated [1953], VSC).[10] And in a letter to May Swenson describing the "little gallery" of art that she and Lota had collected at Samambaia, Bishop also singles out Schwitters for praise (September 19, 1953, WUL).

Given the slow recognition of Schwitters in the United States (only in the 1950s did he become more well known to a wider audience of collectors), Schwitters may have been in some sense a shared secret between Miller and Bishop in the 1940s.[11] Miller had become central in the MoMA's relationship with Schwitters. She created the memos that advocated giving him a fellowship to allow him to reconstruct the Merz building that had been destroyed by the Nazis, and Schwitters thanked her by sending her a collage titled "For Margaret Miller."[12] At the time of the preparation of the collage exhibit, Schwitters's circumstances were quite dire, and the correspondence reveals that he relied on Miller as a crucial human connection in a negotiation with a distant institution. In addition to advocating that Schwitters receive a fellowship grant, Miller also arranged for food parcels to be sent, at least one of which she paid for herself (letters from Margaret Miller to Kurt Schwitters, July 17 and June 16, 1947, Cur. Exh. #1400, MoMA Archives, NY). In 1946, Miller received thirty-nine works from Schwitters, and because of the delay in the exhibition, she was therefore in possession of a considerable number of pieces that were seen only by the MoMA staff or people whom Miller invited to see the works.[13] In the late 1940s, there was very little criticism of Schwitters in English (Orchard 281).[14] Even in 1954, Bishop was still "trying & trying to get a book about him" and had found only one in German, which she would have trouble accessing (Bishop did not read German) (letter to Kit and Ilse Barker, November 6, 1954, PUL). Given the lack of art criticism on Schwitters, Miller would have constituted the closest mediating source for Bishop's understanding of his work.

In Miller's first published piece on visual art, a short review of an extensive modern art exhibit held at Vassar in 1934 (the year that she and Bishop graduated), Miller chose two and three dimensions, the relation of art to the real, and the issues of tactility as the central issues that defined the emergence of modernism, so she would have been poised to see in Schwitters's work his novel solutions to these central issues. In the review of the 1934 Vassar show, Miller describes the exhibition as "particularly rich in the abstractions of Picasso, Braque, and Juan Gris . . . [during] the point at which painting was subjected to the highest possible discipline, when the objects of the physical world were completely disrupted and painting was restricted to two dimensional effects, with a third suggested." Miller then calls this "pictorial stratosphere" a kind of "puritism" and clearly leans toward the "tactile excitation," which she calls "the only stimulants admitted in the austerity of the abstractionist's program and practiced so ingratiatingly by Juan Gris in his collation of blotting paper, newsprint, wall-paper, and sanded paints." In addition to championing tactility, Miller also writes approvingly of the return of "the third dimension, denounced as impure by the abstractionists" (Miller 1934, 8).

The correspondence related to the collage exhibition and Miller's selection among Schwitters's collages gives us some sense of Miller's understanding of Schwitters. Miller sent Schwitters a gift of some books, including the 1945 book on Klee that she had edited for Alfred H. Barr, and Schwitters replied, emphasizing his personal connection to Klee (letter from Kurt Schwitters to Margaret Miller, January 22, 1947, Reg. Exh. #385, MoMA, NY).[15] He then drew her attention to Herbert Read's remark in a catalogue for an exhibition in London: "I want to know, whether you know what *Herbert Read* wrote *in my catalogue of the London Exhibition. I sent it to Dr. Barr and Dr. Sweeney.* He writes about the mystic very very good. *Please read it!*" (letter from Schwitters to Miller, January 22, 1947, Reg. Exh. #385, MoMA Archive, NY). Read had explained that there was a "philosophical, even a mystical justification for taking up the stones which the builders rejected and making something of them, even the headstones of the corner" (quoted in Elderfield 93). Miller, however, warned Schwitters not to use the term *mystic,* which she explained had associations among Americans that made the word unusable (letter from Miller to Schwitters, February 10, 1947, CUR Exh. #1400, MoMA Archives, NY).

Later art historians have used the remark and other prominent features of Schwitters's collages to align Schwitters with a collage style that conceptually grew out of Expressionism as opposed to French Cubism (Dietrich 47). Although Schwitters was not interested in the expressionists' merging of all beings in a unified cosmos, he did very much concern himself with the expressionist passion for the "life" of inanimate objects (Elderfield 92). Schwitters endowed the individual collage fragments as objects with the power of expression. He "declared repeatedly that his collage materials lost their *Eigengift*, their particular characteristics of origin, when taken out of their original context and brought into the new context of the collage" (Dietrich 61). This form of disassociation allowed the object in the collage to retain its expressiveness and also to have features of itself "lift off" and come to meet or make unities with other pieces in the collage. For example, the wavy blue ink lines of a cancelled stamp would seem to lift off the original fragment and come to "meet" comparable colors or patterns inside the frame of the collage. This feature of his work corresponds to the feature that Miller noted so excitedly in her correspondence with Braque.

Although Schwitters sent Miller recent collages from 1946 as well as earlier collages from the late 1910s and 1920s, Miller chose to exhibit mostly the earlier ones.[16] Many of the collages from the earlier period arrange delicate relations among fabrics or materials. Schwitters's attentiveness to tactility and texture cannot be adequately conveyed in a reproduction. The collages' tiny size, often just a few inches wide (many are 4×6 or 5×7 inches) engage the viewer in an intensely intimate experience with the worn and fragile fabrics. Schwitters creates a sense of floating or drifting but not disorder (see, for example, Santa Claus, 1922, which was in the exhibit). In many works from this period, the papers are going to wear away—or are wearing away. One sees, for example, a beautiful faded washed-out turquoise emerging from a field of browns, beiges, soft reds, red on blacks, and grays (Mz 1600, 1923).[17] Color, as a substance, appears contained in a pattern and then released; for example, he builds a sequence of reds in a checkerboard and then red freed from that pattern, appearing as a splotch of color or amorphous shape and then as red type, red inside the type—so that a sense of binding and loosening occurs. The black in houndstooth cloth hovers next to a pool of denser painted black (MZ 150

Oskar). Tiny movements in depth occur in a descending sequence, for example, from a raised cardboard down to a surface that is only the "height" of a fragment of wallpaper, thin paper tissue, a thin layer of paint directly on the surface, and bare surface (Tearose, 1924).

Although it is a later work, the collage that Miller herself purchased from the exhibit, Like Marmor (1946), conveys a powerful and intimate tactile feel of the layering and arranged meeting of lighter and heavier papers: a thin Japanese tissue paper, wrinkled and nearing translucency, layered over or near black construction paper, gray (almost colorless) heavier cardboard strip, a range of handmade and machine-made papers, and a small fragment of linen textile. The writing on the papers ranges from printed type-set numbers on commercial ticket stubs to elegant cursive handwriting. The loosening and binding of materials by edge or line occurs by arranging four items: a paper with a patch of charcoal uncontained by edge or drawn boundary line, a reproduction of a drawing of a building in heavy dark graphite pencil, the reproduction of the wavy lines of an engraving of a landscape, and a piece of a box top printed with a geometric hard-edged blue shape. The sequence therefore moves from unbounded to firmly bound and from pure material (blotch of charcoal) toward figures (a drawn building; a landscape that, because it is cut off, becomes less legible as landscape and becomes just lines). A portion of the front of an envelope near the center of the collage has been torn off in such a way as to arrange the meeting of the word AIR; the personal name Mr. K Schwitt[ers]; and part of the address, the local geographical place, where this person resides—three "registers" of experience are brought to encounter one another and make a new whole.[18]

Miller's first extensive knowledge of Schwitters's aesthetic philosophy came from an article in *Der Ararat*, written in 1920 and, so, approximately contemporaneous with the earliest period of collages that Miller preferred.[19] In this article, Schwitters composes a comprehensive explanation of disassociation, the peeling off of surfaces and the "meeting" of disparate materials. With his characteristic mixture of seriousness and humor, he excitedly describes his plans for a Merz theater that would bring into his art the materials and cultural detritus from the world: "Take in short everything from the hairnet of the high class lady to the propeller of the S.S. Leviathan" (Schwitters 63). The clash of items produced the éclat of conflict, but Schwitters also passionately believed that the clash of objects, brought into tensile relations inside the "frame" of the artwork, produced new relations among the items: "Now begin to wed your materials to one another. For example, you marry the oilcloth table cover to the home owners' loan association, you bring the lamp cleaner into a relationship with the marriage between Anna Blume and A natural-concert pitch" (Schwitters 63). The things of the world, brought into the Merz theater or collage are made to meet one another. The letter "A" in relation to "A natural-concert pitch" involves Schwitters's customary removal of a component of an item, in this case a word, a proper name, and his lifting up or "peeling off" that small component, the typed letter "A," to bring into view its relationship with a different "A" in a different modality or different register, the "A" of the musical scale.

To grasp the features of Schwitters's work that are used most prominently in Bishop's poetry, we need to look more closely at the kinds of relations that are set up among the objects inside the collage. In the article that Miller read, Schwitters glosses his own work by explaining, "I have taken a step in advance of mere oil painting, for in addition to playing off color against color, line against line, form against form, etc., I play off material against material, for example, wood against sackcloth" (Schwitters 59). Sackcloth is a textile that in its heft, weight, durability, and coarseness can approach wood. Still pliant but having the quality of stiffness, the sackcloth grows close to wood, modulates toward it. The pairing, like notes in-between the half-notes on the harmonic scale, draws attention to the way one thing bends toward or closes toward another. In choosing as his examples wood and sackcloth, Schwitters reveals his obsession with the modulation of solidity to pliable texture and beyond, to more airy or light materials and vice versa.

So, unlike the photomontages of Max Ernst or the cubist collages of Picasso, Braque, and Gris, some of Schwitters collages focus on arranging sequences of modulations across the different components of the collage. Often the collages sequence materials from transparent to semitransparent to opaque, from light to heavy, and from diffuse to dense. To lay material against material involves resemblance in tones or texture. Some features of the fabrics will call out to one another in shared qualities, whether by color, pattern, weight, or extension. Schwitters arranges sequences of the like and unlike by small degrees of alteration. In this way, dense materiality can gradually segue into airy nothingness, as if reality can be made and unmade by degrees. *Mz 169 Formen im Raum* (*Shapes in Space*, 1920) (color plate

1) arranges a sequence of materials: whitish-blue-tinged gauzy tissue paper next to a deep marine blue heavier course-grained paper, above a twined-thread net with large squares, and across from a smaller gauged net of finer mesh; a light or airy diffuse blue segues into a denser, more deeply saturated blue; and the coarse grains of paper segue into a net of denser threads and then a net of even denser wire.[20] In his interest in modulation and difference, Schwitters does far more than merely bring pieces of "reality" inside the frame of his art; he produces a range of continuity, composed of many different degrees of modulation, across the boundaries of different materials and across the multiple boundaries between the world and art. The modulation from two to three dimensions becomes part of a sequence that moves from art (flat pattern) to life (actual object). In Schwitters, therefore, Bishop found a modern correlative to the extensive range of two- to three-dimensional forms that she saw in *Art of the South Seas*.

Unlike an art that understands itself as illusion, holding itself apart from reality to mirror it, Schwitters reproduces the supple pliancy of the world of things that can by tiny intervals cross over into the aesthetic realm. The redness of a cloth becomes perceptible as a quality, an essence, a beautiful object, when placed in a sequence that brings out that redness either in a close sequence of modulation or by contrast. The redness of the object seems to lift off the object and become another sort of object, unreal but intensely perceptible—an art object. Thus, modulation and the transformation into new orders of reality are produced by the sensation of one aspect of a material or pattern lifting off the substance in which it is enmeshed and becoming permeable to or perceptible as alike in relation to another material or set inside of a new set of relations. This technique maximizes the feature of cubist collage that interested Miller—the lifting of the surface of an object off that object—it peels off qualities one by one from different materials and thereby brings them in relation to one another.

To think about modulation in this way is to imagine it as permeability. It is a kind of connection by likeness, but a likeness that still preserves difference and partial distance. Schwitters makes objects seem permeable to one another. They share qualities across the boundaries of their edges. They seem to partly, but incompletely, go inside or across one another. In *Hansi Drawing* (1918), which Miller had planned

Color Plate I. Kurt Schwitters, *Mz 169. Formem im Raum (Mz 169. Shapes in Space)*. 1920. Collage auf Karton, 18 ´ 14.3 cm. Kuntsammlung Nordrhein-Westfalen, Düsseldorf. Photograph by Walter Klein. © 2009 Artists Rights Society (ARS), New York/VG Bild-Kunst, Bonn.

Color Plate 2. Kurt Schwitters, *C35 Papierwolken (C35 Paper Clouds)*. 1946. Collage of pasted paper on corrugated cardboard. 24.6 ′ 21.1 cm. Gift of Lily Auchincloss. Museum of Modern Art, New York. © The Museum of Modern Art/Licensed by SCALA/Art Resource, NY. © 2009 Artists Rights Society (ARS), New York/VG Bild-Kunst, Bonn.

to reproduce in color in the catalogue, a trapezoidal paper that has a mottled texture of orange, brown, and taupe shares qualities of color and shape with three nearby surfaces: a rectangular bright-orange strip, the extensive rectangle of the brown background, and the narrower rectangular strip of taupe (letter from Margaret Miller to Kurt Schwitters, December 16, 1946, Reg. Exh. #385, MoMA Archives, NY). Schwitters was interested in displaying not just the range of surfaces but also a surface's disintegration or dissolution and thereby "approach" to the other. In one sense, such a feature captured the "wear" of items and thus brought forth their beauty. "It is through wear, he [Schwitters] wrote, that things become wonderful and beautiful," reports Carola Giedion-Welcker, one of Miller's correspondents, in the only full-length contemporary critical article on Schwitters in the American press (Giedion-Welcker 221). This "wear" was part of Schwitters's sense of the mystical nature of objects taken out of their original contexts, the aura of their original context that they carry with them or can be disassociated from. But wear also functioned as a special form of permeability. The surface of something wears away and becomes other. Objects or surfaces can turn into one another or into nothingness. Schwitters calls this transformation "interpermeating surfaces seep away" (Schwitters 63). The fabrics and papers begin to "dissolve" when placed in sequences of modulation with other like but different surfaces. Wear is only a special case of the usual breaking-up of an object as it comes close to other objects that share some but not all of its qualities. Each object modulates toward and away from the others by nuanced degrees of difference.

Among these sequences of tiny intervals of modulation in tactile surfaces, Schwitters creates a series from line to thread to net. This sequence about nets is prominent in his prose description and can be seen clearly in *Revolving* (1919), in which Schwitters creates a sequence from string to wire to wire mesh to metal plate. He also begins the sequence from "before" a fine thread: drawn pencil line, thin single-ply thread, three-ply thread, thin twine, wide-gauge net, coarsely spun linen, fine cloth. Through that sequence, Schwitters transforms line into surface; drawing turns into "the real." Put in series, understood as a sequence of modulation, drawn line becomes a net, plane, or surface, which can then begin to undulate and thereby gain depth, gradually turning into a "real" three-dimensional object; art crosses over into nature by small steps. In his rowdy experimental prose,

Schwitters describes the sequence that he produces in his collages: "Wire lines movement, real movement rises real tow-rope of a wire mesh. . . . Make lines pulling sketch a net ultramarining" (Schwitters 62–63). Drawn lines with a sense of "pulling" become a sketch of a net that then transforms into an actual net, floating on or in the sea. He thought of lines as able to become things: "Let a line rush by, tangible in wire" (Schwitters 63). Lines had variability in thickness or density or varieties of energy and movement: "flaming lines, creeping lines, surfacing lines" (Schwitters 62). The lines interact violently or meld softly: "make lines fight together and caress one another in generous tenderness" (Schwitters 62–63). Schwitters runs the sequence backward and forward, from surface to line and back into surface: "Use is made of compressible surfaces, or surfaces capable of dissolving into meshes; surfaces that fold like curtains, expand or shrink. Objects will be allowed to move and revolve, and lines will be allowed to broaden into surfaces. . . . Make nets firewave and run off into lines, thicken into surfaces" (Schwitters 62–63). The collage then becomes the site of metamorphosis, where lines thicken into extendable surfaces and then those surfaces fold and ripple to have a depth in three dimensions.

Although it is typical of collage artists to juxtapose incongruous elements (art and everyday items; high culture and popular culture; trash and finished products), Schwitters did not merely juxtapose them to set up contrasts and relations among them. He orchestrated their convergence to emphasize their metamorphoses into one another. The modulation from line to surface to object also occurs in Schwitters's orchestrating the movement from sheer sensory materials to a cultural level of experience. From a "bare" sensory level, the materials in Schwitters's collages begin to cross over into the cultural realm or into the realm of idea and then fall back into mere pattern or material. In *Mz Elikan* (1925) (figure 4), Schwitters arranges typed words from sheer sensory material, through pattern, to legibility and language. Sparse words unreadably situated in cursive handwriting on the back of a piece of brittle vellum appear next to a repeated pattern of a nonsense word in lines of modern type like stripes—these words become close to sheer ornament or pattern. A readable but fragmentary piece of printed text using early modern type wavers (incompletely) toward legibility. A fragment with lines printed over each other modulates further toward both illegibility and sheer material;

in its density of overprinting it approaches the color black by bending toward resemblance to the condition of sheer sensory material in the (wordless) saturated black papers nearby. Thus, words, too, appear in a sequence of modulation from ancient to modern, from handwritten to machine-made, from sparse to dense. Words modulate from aesthetic pattern to marks that carry semantic significance to sheer material. In *Merz 19* (1920) (figure 5), Schwitters distributes similar patterns that condense, fade out, and "turn" from bureaucratic to homemade to natural. A black and white repeating pattern of irregular, labyrinthine, amoeboid shapes modulates to a tighter curl of a black and white swirl motif on a printed ticket, which modulates to the curvy typescript of letters on a bureaucratic form, which modulates to the black and white letters of a cursive hand—and floating behind, the irregular curve of white torn papers against a black background on the lower right edge resemble and modulate to natural cloud shapes in the upper right. Aesthetic pattern turns into bureaucratic tool and then turns back into a material soaked in human expressiveness which then turns toward the realm of the purely natural.

Last, Schwitters's collages also contain sequences of modulation through levels of representation, from a nonrepresentational emptiness (the bare surface of wood or canvas) to painted material to stylized image to photograph to artistic rendering. As he worked with the kind of visual rhymes that painters often used, Schwitters focused on the change of registers as the "rhyme" moved from one level of reality to another ("oilcloth table cover to home owners' loan association" certificate—a mere object with simple social relations as its nexus held next to an object at a different "level" of culture, imbricated in a much more complex set of social relations). Differing levels of representation not only coexist in the same work but are arranged in sequences, so that, for example, a series of papers shift by degrees from wallpaper with a stylized flower motif into an advertisement that has a photo of a flower, the painting of a flower, and then a three-dimensional "actual" flower made crudely out of wooden petals. Again, Schwitters sets up as a sequence of modulation different kinds of aesthetic experience, from the mere sensation of "bare" color to aesthetic pattern to stylized commercially produced representation to material object to cultural object with meaning provided from the culture outside the piece.

Figure 4. Kurt, Schwitters, Untitled (Mz ELIKAN ELIKAN ELIKAN). (c. 1925).
Cut-and-pasted colored and printed papers on paper with cardstock border,
17 1/8×14 1/4 inches (43.5×36.2 cm). Katherine S. Dreier Bequest. (208.1953).
The Museum of Modern Art, New York, NY. © The Museum of Modern Art/
Licensed by SCALA / Art Resource, NY. © 2009 Artists Rights Society (ARS),
New York/VG Bild-Kunst, Bonn.

In all these various modes of modulation—resemblance and difference peeling off and approaching one another in degrees of permeability,
the line thickening toward surface, the sensory gradually shifting toward culture, and levels of representation set in sequence—Schwitters's
work provided an aesthetic solution to the problem of disconnection,
a solution that did not depend on the illusion of depth and did not

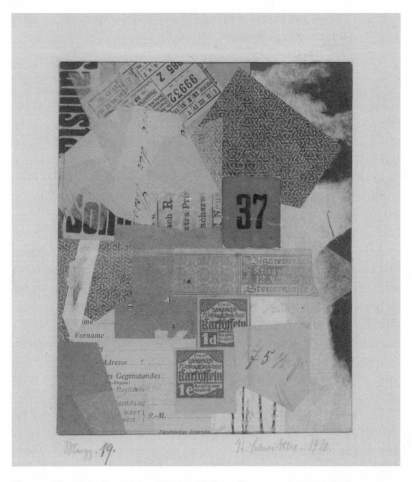

Figure 5. Kurt Schwitters, *Merz 19*. 1920. Collage. Sheet: 15 15/16×11 1/4 inches (40.5×28.5 cm); image: 7 5/16×5 7/8 inches (18.5×15 cm). Gift of Collection Société Anonyme. 1941.681. Yale University Art Gallery, New Haven, CT. Yale University Art Gallery/Art Resource, NY. © 2009 Artists Rights Society (ARS), New York/VG Bild-Kunst, Bonn.

become "mere" surface. By taking "surface" seriously, Schwitters created an intricate modulation by degrees between two and three dimensions and between "purely" aesthetic objects and objects of the world. The intricacy and density of modulation made for a multidimensional experience that continuously folds and unfolds across, up, and down through layers of sensory, emotional, aesthetic, and cultural experience.

Wholes and Layers, Peeling Off and Interpermeating Surfaces: "Cape Breton," "At the Fishhouses," Barr, and Panofsky

In some ways Schwitters provided Elizabeth Bishop with a visual analogue for techniques that she had already used earlier in her career. She had already juxtaposed "real" objects with the flatter representations of those same objects. In "Roosters," Bishop includes actual roosters in the yards of Key West along with the rooster weathervanes and the cock carved in porphyry come to "stand for" Peter and for forgiveness. In "Luxembourg Gardens," Bishop presents real birds next to carved ones and shared colors across materials with different levels of solidity: "Doves on architecture, architecture/ Color of doves, and doves in air" (Bishop 2006, 27). In the mid-1940s, Bishop was setting up her own assemblage poems complete with different kinds of "papers" and figures posed at different levels of reality or representation. For example, in "Key West" pictorial representation stands next to the "real" thing—the lid of a cigar box displays a stylized illustration of a woman dancer ("roses in her hair / And tulle-draped bust") while actual dancers at the carnival are "guaranteed to wear nothing but feather fans and jewels" (Bishop 2006, 51).

Likewise, Bishop's own drawings and watercolors demonstrate that she was interested in using the frame of art to display the array of variant levels of representation. In 1942, her sketch of the scene from a rooftop in Merida arrays objects across a range of levels: functional (windmills), religious (crosses), natural (the palmetto plants), and aesthetic (the urn) (Bishop 1996, 27). The watercolor "contains" the dispersal across different levels of reality: natural plant, functional machine, simple geometric religious symbol, and shapely artistic urn. The levels of artistic representation are likewise arrayed across a spectrum of completion and saturation: penciled sketch with no color, the dark "real" line of an electrical cord, "colored-in" lines, and deeply saturated green painted plant. The small (undated) drawing of her room at the Murray Hill Hotel (Bishop 1996, 7) carefully arranges a sequence from freely drawn to printed commercial image, from aesthetic to functional in a palimpsest almost at the center of the room: the metal of the lampstand (flat geometric design), the three-dimensional looser drawing of the chair, and the stylized imprint of a visual icon (a mythical medieval dragon in blue ink) of the Murray Hill Hotel stationery on which the drawing is made. Bishop arranges the only color in the drawing, the blue ink of the printed dragon icon, so that it simultaneously draws attention to the physical foundation of paper on which the drawing is made and the surface of represented reality: she places the icon on top of or "in" the surface of the mirror on the bureau so that the dragon hovers both on top of the drawing ("out" from the mirror, between the mirrored surface and the metal lampstand that is drawn over it) and more deeply "in" the drawing (inside the mirrored surface on the paper itself).

But in all these cases, Bishop's use of the poem or picture to assemble and set in relation different orders of reality did not concern itself in any sustained way with modulation from one level to another or modulation of surfaces into depth, the feature that became of most interest to the poet in her volume *A Cold Spring*. Schwitters's interest in arranging textiles to interpermeate provided a means of moving beyond the mere juxtaposition of different levels of representation. The distinctiveness of Schwitters's aesthetic involved the use of modulation rather than mere juxtaposition, and Bishop's poems enact this modulation largely by means of attentiveness to textures that open toward one another.

The first indication that we have of Bishop's interest in the tactility of materials in relation to visual art comes from a few notes that she took on another art book, Alfred H. Barr's *Picasso: Forty Years of His Art* (1946). Bishop copied several times the following quotation from the section of the book in which Barr discusses the cubists' increased interest in textures in 1912–1914: "The sensuous tactile reality of the surface itself in contrast to painting in the past which through more or less realistic methods took the eye and mind past the surface of the canvas to represented objects such as figures or landscapes" (VSC 75.4b, 156).[21] Barr teaches his reader to attend to the surface of the painting and not to look past that surface as if it were a transparent window through which one saw the representation of an object.

Bishop's choice of that quotation from Alfred Barr and her writing the word *tactile* on the top of the same page indicate her interest in the "sensuous tactility" of the surface of painting. A later note gives us more information about the way that she modified Barr's discussion of tactility and the manipulation of surface and depth in her own poetry. In her only other note taken from *Picasso*, Bishop responded to and critiqued Barr's discussion of the cubists' attempt to achieve the wholeness of an object by presenting it as if seen from various perspectives simultaneously. Bishop wrote about "one's capabilities to form the idea of the WHOLE of anything," defining the whole as "the simultaneous picture, or feeling, or even word, or physical sensation, or reminiscence" (VSC 75.4b, 141). In this crucial remark, Bishop critiqued cubism for overemphasizing the visual in the attempt to capture the whole. It is in this critique that we can see her transformation of cubism, revising it for her own purposes to create her own aesthetic, an aesthetic that was closer to Schwitters's focus on layering and modulation from bare sensory experience to cultural image. She begins to imagine the poem as a site of assemblage, where the layers of human experience—visual, personal reminiscence, a physical feeling, an emotion, an idea, a word—are brought together to interact as layers opening on to or into one another. The poem becomes a place where these layers can fold into or over one another and interpenetrate and where they can grow dense or thin out. Weight and density—sinking down into and rising up out of—become part of the story of the layers' interaction. As Schwitters had done in his collages, Bishop arranges materials in sequences of modulation from the dense to the less dense, from the material to the conceptual, and from the natural to the cultural. She also began to conceptualize layers peeling off or attaching themselves to other layers. In Bishop's poetics, this "peeling off" of one aspect of a material, performed originally by Braque as the peeling off of a visual surface from shape, becomes a fruitful means of conceptualizing the peeling off of other components—concept from sensory object, cultural meaning from image, emotion from image, memory from object, and so on.

In "Cape Breton," tactile materials are arranged next to/against one another and fall on to or into one another by becoming less dense. The textures and contrasting densities of water, mist, firs, and, later, rocks constitute a large part of the subject of the poem:

> The silken water is weaving and weaving,
> disappearing under the mist equally in all directions,
> lifted and penetrated now and then
> by one shag's dripping serpent-neck,
> and somewhere the mist incorporates the pulse,
> rapid but unurgent, of a motorboat.

The same mist hangs in thin layers
among the valleys and gorges of the mainland
like rotting snow-ice sucked away
almost to spirit; the ghosts of glaciers drift
among those folds and folds of fir: spruce and hackmatack—
dull, dead, deep peacock-colors,
each riser distinguished from the next
by an irregular nervous saw-tooth edge,
alike, but certain as a stereoscopic view. (*CP* 67)

The airy lightness of mist hovers over a larger denser material, the extension in space of the water as a flat plane extending outward. Like the rectangle of transparent tracing paper that hovers over heavier strips of paper in so many of Schwitters's collages or the white tissue paper that is suspended above denser papers in *C35 Paper Clouds* (1946) (color plate 2), surfaces in Bishop's poem occur in layers of variant densities that move across one another. The layers move under or over one another at different speeds: "the silken water is weaving and weaving, / disappearing under the mist equally in all directions." The density and movement of the layer of mist thins out as it moves over the different texture and shape of material in the next stanza, the land with its valleys and gorges. In this section, the mist gains a kind of three-dimensionality as its layers move both "among" and "over" the land beneath it. The fabric of mist both resembles and differentiates itself by tiny degrees from the materials that it neighbors. "Like rotting snow-ice," the mist resembles, in some aspects—whiteness and dispersal—the snow-covered land beneath it, but modulates that likeness to something other, something more conceptual, "like spirit" (*CP* 67). While "interpermeating surfaces seep away," they metamorphose into other materials along the continuum from solid matter to cultural idea.

Within the array of materials and textures, Bishop also orchestrates an array of kinds of edges and lines:

Out on the high "bird islands," Ciboux and Hertford,
the razorbill auks and the silly-looking puffins all stand
with their backs to the mainland
in solemn, uneven lines along the cliff's brown grass-frayed edge,
. . . .

each riser distinguished from the next
by an irregular nervous saw-tooth edge,
alike, but certain as a stereoscopic view.
. . . .
The wild road clambers along the brink of the coast . . . (CP 67)

The "solemn, uneven lines" of standing birds, the "cliff's brown grass-frayed edge," the "irregular nervous saw-tooth edge" of the firs, and later the scratches on the rocks are all kinds of lines, some furry, some serrated, some incised. When "the wild road clambers along the brink of the coast," two lines—road and coast—wobble toward and away from one another, tightly but not quite completely mirroring one another's movements. Some lines gradually turn into surfaces—the coast is also a kind of edge, and the road is a kind of surface. Each "turns over" on itself and extends as a plane. Other lines begin to expand into meshes or nets. The songs floating upward criss-cross one another so that they "[mesh] / in brown-wet, fine, torn fish-nets" (CP 68). Some of the surfaces turn into nets of lines ("water . . . weaving and weaving") so that a flat plane seeps away, becoming netlike.

In this way, lyric becomes the site where materials from different registers of experience "open" toward one another. A visual landscape "opens" to "incorporate sound ("the mist incorporates the pulse, / rapid but unurgent, of a motorboat"). A natural landscape "opens" to accommodate human machines and cultural ideas (bulldozers and churches). Dense materiality of rock ("mountains of rock") can accommodate writing ("scriptures made on stones by stones"). A strong diagonal ("a small steep meadow") softens and becomes less dense (appearing as "a snowfall of daisies") to accommodate the entrance of the human figure ("a man carrying a baby"). The entry is like material dropped into material, "little white churches . . . dropped into the matted hills / like lost quartz arrowheads"). Proper names from the linguistic realm ("spruce and hackmatack") are layered over and next to the visual ("folds and folds of fir" and "dull, dead, deep peacock-colors"). Symbolic and cultural materials (a "frock coat") are layered over a hanger or a human body (CP 67–68). The poem enacts "inter-permeating" (to use Schwitters's term), the complex layering over and through of different materials and levels of reality: tactile, visual, cultural, and linguistic.

Like "Over 2000 Illustrations and a Complete Concordance," the poem poses the question of depth.

> Whatever the landscape had of meaning appears to have been abandoned
> unless the road is holding it back, in the interior,
> where we cannot see
> where deep lakes are reputed to be,
> and disused trails and mountains of rock
> and miles of burnt forests standing in gray scratches
> like the admirable scriptures made on stones by stones—
> (CP 67–68)

In contrast to "Over 2000 Illustrations," however, there is neither the motif of a sequence of disconnected scenes nor the invention of a sacred space behind the others that promises (however unsuccessfully or hypothetically) to hold meaning and reveal it. Instead, the theme of revelation occurs, in the term "admirable scriptures," but the term appears now in a sequence of modulation rather than held separately and apart. Meaning, itself, becomes one of the elements that is subjected to modulation, but it does so inside a sequence of other materials. The word *scratches* turns from one meaning to another, across the sequence of those two lines of verse. *Scratches* first appear as a material surface, patches of gray stone, bare rock exposed because of the burning of the forests that used to stand above them. In the next verse line, the scratches have become the marks of stone on stone made by layers of glacial rock as they move across one another. This image of one layer moving across another—modulating in a different key, in a different density, the movement of the layers of mist over water—here becomes a kind of writing. The use of the word *scratches* and the tweaking of that word to bring out its associations with writing ("scriptures") allow that scratching of stone on stone, produced by the slowest, most long-lived, and heaviest features of earth moving across itself in layers, to hang "suspended" in some relation to the "mesh" of song birds, the weaving of water, and the human activity of writing. Unlike the deeply incised writing of "exhortation" that scattered into an irrecoverable disparate dust in "Over 2000 Illustrations and a Complete Concordance," the "admirable scriptures" here are "held" in suspension in relation to both natural and human activity.

In suspending these objects in relation to one another, Bishop creates the kind of depth that she had written about in her notebook entry about "wholes." Depth is created by producing a "whole," where "whole" emerges from the multidimensional modulation among visual images, words, physical objects, physical sensations, emotions, and ideas. One surface is laid on top of another and then sinks in, becoming absorbed, or layers drift across one another, merely touching lightly. Natural objects, writing, emotions, and cultural objects "touch" one another with different densities of interpenetration. In her own medium, Bishop renders Schwitters's attentiveness to the variance in fragility and solidity, weight and lightness, and diffusion and condensation of fabrics and materials.

In Schwitters's *Der Ararat* article, meaning itself occurs as one component only in a broader continuum from bare sensory material to "high" cultural concepts. Just as purely material color could move from red cloth to a stylized image of a cherry on a card used for primary education (in *Merzbild 32A. Das Kirschbild, The Cherry Picture,* 1921), so sound could move from material to cultural meaning: "And now begins the fire of musical saturation. Organs backstage sing and say: 'Futt, futt.' The sewing machine rattles along in the lead. A man in the wings says: 'Bah.' Another suddenly enters and says: 'I am stupid.' . . . Between them a clergyman kneels upside down and cries out and prays in a loud voice. . . . A water pipe drips with uninhibited monotony" (Schwitters 63). Crying borders on and falls over into praying. Repetitive notes from an organ leave the realm of music and approach the repetitive strokes of the sewing machine. Human imitation of an animal sound crosses over into a "meaningful" sentence. The monotony of ritualized sounds in liturgical formulae cross over into the monotony of dripping water. In Bishop's "Cape Breton," disparate realms can clash in a destructive encounter: sheep "frightened by aeroplanes . . . stampede / and fall over into the sea or onto the rocks." Conversely, the sounds of machinery (and mechanical life) can be incorporated more unobtrusively, as in the "unurgent" sound and feel of the motor or, later, in the trio of bird song, bawl of calf, and sound of the engine of a bus, a sequence, although not interpermeating, still presents a less violent "wedding" than sheep and the sound of the aeroplane that opens the poem (*CP* 67–68). Like their mechanical devices, humans are "incorporated" or "enmeshed" in the landscape. They are of a different texture, solidity, speed, directionality, but they do enter. The landscape opens for them, like the stile—a "spray" of "snowfall of daisies" splashing up and opening in a less dense material so that they can slip in. The differences between humans and landscape are far more extreme but still on a continuum with other differences.

Bishop "slips in or on" the order of reality that is culture—not only the mechanical inventions of humans (motorboat, aeroplane, and spare automobile parts) but also "the little white churches . . . dropped into the matted hills / like lost quartz arrowheads" (*CP* 67). Even with their difference from the hosting texture (shiny hard "quartz" into the duller softer "matte"), they too can be accommodated into the landscape. Religion and its "house" with its different mode of materiality can be dropped into the hills and a preacher's frock can, like a piece of surface, be deattached from a hanger and hung on a body, either to cling there as merely a layer on a layer or to penetrate more deeply.

As layers are laid over or slip into one another, some of the modulations are so close to one another that they are barely perceptible (mist to rotting snow-ice, and, even closer, fir trees next to fir trees), whereas others are vast degrees of likeness away from one another (scratches on rock to sparrow song). The closeness of modulation and its relation to resemblance becomes partly the subject of the poem. When folds and folds of firs, material on material, touch one another, they do not meet across some difference of density and color but in a closer interpenetration. The trees are all the same color, "dull, dead, deep peacock colors," and are seen as materially the same across their slight difference in species "spruce and hackmatack." Here, in this passage, Bishop becomes explicit about the concept of likeness. The rows of firs line up against one another in lines that Bishop calls "alike, but certain as a stereoscopic view" (*CP* 67). In this strange phrase, Bishop links the ideas of difference and depth. What is certain is that each of the two lines of trees is an edge, that each line marks a boundary of one row from another, and that there is depth between them because there is unlikeness. These trees have gone as far toward resemblance as it is possible to go; nevertheless, there is still a boundary line between them, and there is a depth as certain as we get in a stereoscopic view that lifts one layer "off" another so that visual experience widens out from two dimensions to three. The "edge" appears out of a field. For Bishop, knowledge (certainty) and distinction (an edge) are linked categories. Certainty derives from distinguishing, from precisely noting difference in the context of even extreme similarity. Certainty has to do with the perception of a line or edge that can somehow mark distinction within a field that is close to sameness. Depth arises from distinguishing, from noting layers of difference.

Looking at "Cape Breton" in these terms makes it possible to understand Bishop's quip in "At the Fishhouses" that she is a "believer in total immersion." In "Cape Breton," the lyric speaker has no interior subjectivity that is not filled by or immersed in the perception of the landscape. But this immersion is not a merging into some kind of vague feeling of oneness. The kind of immersion that the speaker claims to be an adherent of can only be an immersion of one differentiated materiality into another. And "At the Fishhouses" once again lays these materialities over one another, allowing them to interpenetrate. Again, as in "Cape Breton," we see the fascination with surfaces, the play of tactile materialities with different densities and opacities. In "At the Fishhouses," there is a greater emphasis on surfaces that peel off and attach themselves to other bodies; nets that begin to undulate, transforming into deeper surfaces; and there is the bringing together of unlike elements in a kind of "lucky strike" (*CP* 64). In "At the Fishhouses," Bishop includes more emphatically the relation of culture to this collage of lines and surfaces and is more explicit about the relation of the lyric speaker to this layering.

Her notes on reading the art historian Erwin Panofsky show that Bishop was ready to take advantage of Schwitters's layering of cultural meanings on sensory objects and to transform it fruitfully into an even more powerful method for her own poetry. Bishop would have heard some of Panofsky's methods of interpretation in his New York University lectures, which she audited in 1935.[22] Her reading notes on *Studies in Iconology*, which appear in the beginning of the later Key West notebook, show her partly recording images from Panofsky's text that have a particular *frisson* for her (e.g., "an hourglass with a bird's wing & a bat's wing to express day & night"), and in these cases she may simply be recording images for later use in poems (VSC 75.3a, 15). In addition, the notes record Bishop's comprehension of and interest in Panofsky's main thesis—that, transformed by medieval people with their different emotional capacities and ideological interests, the classical visual motifs accrued new thematic meanings. Bishop quoted Panofsky on "the emotional disparity between the Christian Middle Ages & pagan Antiquity" and copied down the example of a miniature from *Ovide Moralisé*, "'The Rape of Europa,' [in which] Europa, clad in late medieval costume sits on her inoffensive little bull like a young lady taking a morning ride, & her companions . . . form a quiet little group of spectators . . . —the illuminator was neither able nor inclined to visualize animal passions" (VSC 75.3a, 15–16). In recording this passage, Bishop captured Panofsky's point that in the transition from antiquity to medieval manuscript there occurred a leaching out of emotion from the scene. A particular visual image could collect or lose emotional timbre. The meaning of the visual image, given to contemporary artists from the past, drifts away from the original use and picks up other emotional timbres, ideas, and meanings. "Apollo [could be] copied as Christ" or Saturn could collect the emotions associated with Death and Time or Europa could shed her former traumatic story and become merely a daily genre scene. Bishop copied down Panofsky's phrase "ironclad arrangements of meanings," which referred to the display of allegorical meanings that medieval artists arranged on the page, the locking together of meaning and image as akin to a visual diagram (VSC 75.3a, 15–16). But the thrust of Panofsky's book shows that these ironclad arrangements shifted over time, as new meanings were inserted for older images. To some extent, then, the artist's work becomes a participation in this process of ongoing modulation, as images handed down from the past and images culled from the contemporary scene are accorded new meanings and begin to carry new emotional charges. It is clear that Bishop self-consciously participates in this kind of cultural revision by proposing a new meaning for the cock in "Roosters." To read Panofsky, and to take his course at New York University at the time that he was working out the ideas that later appeared in *Studies in Iconology*, is to become comfortable with meanings attaching and detaching themselves to visual images or objects, and this is just what we see happening in "At the Fishhouses."[23] Panofsky, however, had very little to say about tactility, textures, the materiality of nature, or personal human reminiscence—all arenas in which Schwitters focused his attentiveness. Like Schwitters, Bishop grounds the phenomenon of cultural meanings attaching and detaching from the visual (Panofsky's focus) in the more sensory experience of physical materials.

"At the Fishhouses" opens with a focus on tactility and materiality of surfaces. Human-made materials (lobster pots, benches, and masts) are scattered and partly incorporated into the natural rocks, whose own materiality and shape ("jagged") are able to accommodate or meet them in a semilikeness. Bishop displays two silver surfaces—one "opaque" and the other "of an apparent translucence"—next to other kinds of alike but distinct surfaces: the "creamy iridescence" of herring scales and flies that approach one another in their material surfaces of rainbow-like iridescence. The "sparse bright sprinkle of grass" resembles the herring scales and flies in luminescence ("bright"), but modulates into difference by being less dense (only a "sprinkle"); the stain of dried blood on top of the wood of the capstan resembles the grass in that it acts as an intensification of sparseness (there are only a few stains), but modulates away from brightness and iridescence to a duller color, which is then made to modulate more deeply in the "rusted" color of the ironwork (*CP* 64).

In the poem, surfaces peel off and attach themselves to other surfaces. Silver from the sea—the shine of the water at twilight and the herring scales—cross from one material to another, from the surface of the sea to the tools for fishing to the vest and thumb of the old man.[24] The encounters make the objects alike in some respects because some of their layers have slipped over the bodies of the other materials and objects. In the process, they have recorded one another's passing. Time is understood as becoming visible by means of the deposits left on things, in a texture or pattern. Heaviness, density, and speed of movement alter the arrangement left, the marks by which one could tell not the whole story of the past but, at least, gain some knowledge of what had been before one's arrival. Like Schwitters with his faded and degraded materials that give evidence of their trajectory through the world, the surfaces of the materials in Bishop's poem become torn, worn away, or spattered on because of their encounters. Like the natural elements that cross over one another's surfaces, leaving layers and deposits, there is the crossing of the speaker with the old man and, by association, with her own grandfather, with whom the fisherman had been friendly. The lyric speaker and the fisherman cross in their shared smoking of cigarettes, in the back and forth of conversation, and in the speaker's brief use of *we*; they modulate apart in that he is waiting there for a herring boat to come in while she is merely passing through, a tourist.

The cultural uses and associations of objects likewise cross, leave a deposit, and part:

Back behind us,
the dignified tall firs begin.
Bluish, associating with their shadows,
a million Christmas trees stand
waiting for Christmas. (*CP* 65)

The fir trees are bluish, as if their color could come off of them in layers, and that color will certainly vary as the light changes and darkness arrives. Just as their color and their shadows are only temporarily associating with them, their cultural association with Christmas is like a property that comes near to them, a layer that is close to them but not completely in them. The cultural association with Christmas has been deposited on the trees by some encounter in the past and remains there, hovering, detachable but still present. The seal, so humorously associated and dissociated with the singing of Baptist hymns, presents the layers of culture and nature at their most distant. The sea suspended and swinging over the stones is merely a more intense and "looser" instance of all of the layers moving over, across, and brushing against, sometimes leaving parts of themselves on other objects and surfaces; in this case, the sea and the layer beneath it do not touch or cross or leave any deposit.

As if to contrast the layering over and immersion into an undulating surface in "Cape Breton" and "At the Fishhouses," "The Bight" presents water as impenetrable surface. Water is "sheer," the "marl protrude[s]," and "pelicans crash / into this peculiar gas unnecessarily hard, / it seems to me, like pickaxes." The over-size crude "jaw" of the dredge contrasts with the delicacy of the undulating immersible net in "At the Fishhouses." The pliable net in "The Bight" has actually hardened into a fence of chicken wire. The stiffness is accentuated by the fence's inability to hold anything in a supple embrace; instead, the sharp objects with their undertone of violence are stuck into the holes in the wire: "glinting like little plowshares, / the blue-gray shark tails are hung up to dry" (*CP* 60). This inability of materials to delicately "cross" one another, resembling one another through sequences of modulation, is linked in Bishop's view with the use of metaphors at too great a distance from their "home." Bishop's mid-1940s list of Baudelaire's poems mentioned "Le Cygne," a poem in which Baudelaire creates an extended conceit, comparing the speaker lost and wandering in an urban landscape with a swan that also wanders there.[25] "Le

Cygne" serves as a good example of Baudelaire's creating a correspondence between two distinct objects that previously had no connection: the swan and the "exiled" man. Like the feat of turning the smell of gas in the harbor to the sound of "marimba music," these pieces of the world are brought together across a great distance. These correspondences do not gradually tilt or turn toward one another. They see one another across a great divide (and, of course, in Baudelaire, they ultimately point to some other realm).

In contrast, in "Cape Breton" and "At the Fishhouses," inside the net of verse, metaphor acts as a nodal point that turns the surface of verse and gives it depth. Thinking back to Bishop's commentary about "wholes" as composed of layers of different kinds of experience (visual image, physical sensation, emotion, word, and reminiscence), we can think of certain words as turning one of the layers of the "whole" into another layer. We have seen that in "Cape Breton" the word *scratches* modulates its meaning, turns from one meaning to another, across the sequence of two lines of verse. The material surface, a patch of gray stone, becomes in the next line of verse the scratches of stone on stone made by layers of glacial rock as they moved across one another. The word *scratches* that then is modulated to *scriptures* acts as a nodal point, releasing the theme of writing and so dropping the poem into another arena of meaning, creating depth by creating layers of meaning over one another, one emerging out from beneath the former.

In "At the Fishhouses," the word *immersion* works as one of these nodal points, where layers "touch" and then turn away from one another. Layers of the poem—the almost silly story of a seal coming to the surface of the water to hear hymns sung to him, the "heavier" question of whether humans can enter more deeply into the world, whether a "baptism" in the world is possible—slide past one another on the pivot point of the word *immersion*. Visual images, too, provide these kinds of nodal points, where layers of the poem and world can slide on to one another and then tilt away from one another. The seal who "stood up in the water," in his insistent verticality, becomes a visual rhyme for the concept of a religious idea so separated from the world (a monotheistic God, heavy and vertical as a fortress, completely unlike the surface of the world and sticking out from it rather than being immersed in it). The tactile quality of the verse is closely "netted" to the subject of the poem here, where Bishop's gentle, modest, and soft "I also sang" suddenly turns to a megaphone, "standing up" out of the gentle rhythms of the preceding phrases: "so I used to sing him Baptist hymns. / I also sang 'A Mighty Fortress Is Our God.'" The retention of the capital letters for the hymn's title emphasizes solidity, rigidity, and verticality. The layers of Bishop's idea of a "whole" slide on to and over one another: visual image (the seal standing up), religious idea (the monotheistic and monolithic vertical God), and the tactile quality of the verse "standing up." The verse stanza then slides away from this meeting of monotheism, Baptist hymn, and seal standing upright and subsides back into natural description, into the natural gesture of the seal: "Then he would disappear, then suddenly emerge / almost in the same spot, with a sort of shrug." The gesture pulls away from the theological questions or, perhaps, comments on them, lightly and irreverently (as if both the contemplation of theological mysteries and the encounter with this human other "were against his better judgment"). In this sequence we can feel the turn toward interpretation and philosophical investigation that Bishop's linguistic medium allows as she translates Schwitters's sequencing of fabrics into lyric. She sets the colloquial "against his better judgment" next to/against the questions of monotheism, releasing and then letting go of the question of a grander sort of Judgment that belongs to Christian myth. Likewise, a moment later, the fir trees are attached to and then dissociated from the themes of Christmas: "back, behind us, / the dignified tall firs begin. / Bluish, associating with their shadows, / a million Christmas trees stand / waiting for Christmas" (CP 65). The linguistic fabric with its words that "face" two ways (*scratches, immersion, judgment*), operates like the visual fabric of the world, with its images that "face" or can subside into the merely sensory or "turn" toward idea or cultural concept.

The surface of verse as a fabric that "turns"—as in the "grammar that suddenly turns and shines" in "Invitation to Miss Marianne Moore"—becomes the crucial ruling motif of Bishop's poetic practice in the volume *A Cold Spring*. The many variable fabrics of verse can be "netted" on to the world, undulate with it, and "turn" at nodal points such as metaphors or visual images so that layers can cross into one another or surfaces can unfold outward from other surfaces or drop into depths. These layers do not become stable but slip onward, tipping in new directions.

The same mist hangs in thin layers
among the valleys and gorges of the mainland
like rotting snow-ice sucked away
almost to spirit; the ghosts of glaciers drift
among those folds and folds of fir. [CP 67]

The surface of verse tilts and an interpretive or intellectual or meta-phorical register of experience gently rises into view. From "mist," which is physically insubstantial, emerges a quiet close likeness of the almost-not-physical "rotting snow-ice sucked away," and from this substance, an even-less-physical substance emerges in the quiet close likeness of "spirit." The verse gently "turns" toward idea, toward metaphor, and then can just as easily subside back into merely sensory experience. From "almost to spirit" to "the ghosts of glaciers drift," Bishop has turned the verse back toward the sensory, physical earth. In some poems, the tipping toward metaphor occurs as a momentary flash (*CP* 67). For example, "great shades" in "View of the Capital from the Library of Congress" shines out with a momentary implica-tion that the hovering heroic dead ("great shades") from previous wars prevent listening to and admiring the military's "boom-boom" (*CP* 69). In other poems, the tipping occurs in a sequence, for exam-ple, the almanac in "Sestina," with its open pages that "[hover] half open above the child," "birdlike" but also like the shelter of a schemati-cally drawn house (*CP* 123). An object tilts to become caught in an-other layer of representation, another register of experience. Meaning is not something arrived at as a conclusion but something crossed through (into/out of) in varying degrees of intensity and sustained for different durations. A metaphor opens out toward a new layer of experience and becomes a place where one register "touches" another. The almanac, which "bird-like" hovers above the grandmother and child, foretelling the tragic "future" that also constitutes their present and past, is also the (rooflike) space under which they are sheltered. Schwitters's sequences of closely woven paper to coarse netting have their linguistic equivalent in Bishop's unusually quiet movement into and out of metaphor that displays, self-consciously, the full range of degrees that metaphors float away from their sources—from the jar-ringly distant edge of a dogwood petal "burned" by a "cigarette butt" (in "A Cold Spring") to the gentle closeness of "mist" and "ghost" (in "Cape Breton") (*CP* 55, 56).

This conception of lyric, turning toward meaning or subsiding into the sensory, also allows the sequencing of the degrees (gentle, sharp, long-lasting, or fleeting) of the incorporation of deposits (cultural meanings and personal reminiscences) from history. On her trip to Mexico (1942), Bishop recorded her visit to a natural site that demonstrated the opposite of "peeling away," where time leaves a deposit of its encounters. The varying density of layers, their heaviness as they carry the memory of materials deposited by the past, comes across forcefully in this passage:

> We started out with hang-overs, having been to Pablo Neruda's birthday-party the night before (very "Villagey" I'm afraid) & as I said to Marjorie, walking around over fields of encrusted caustic soda, with a hangover, was my idea of hell—but actually it was *marvelous*. The spiral (*caracol* in Sp.,—which also means *snail* or *spiral-shell*) is over a mile across. I suppose—the water comes in from the lakes at the outside, & by gravity, moves very slowly towards the middle, it takes it about a year to get there. The sun evaporates it as it goes & the solution of salts gets stronger & stronger—at different stages different forms of animal-life live in it, & that is what makes it all different colors.—dark red on one side of you, pale tan on the other, etc. As the water gets heavier & heavier with the salts, it won't make waves or ripples— there was quite a wind yesterday, & the outside spirals were very rough, while the inside were dead calm & reflected everything just like a mirror. . . . Everything was crusted with crystals— your hand, in a minute, if you put it in the water—& the air smelled very salty, like boiled lobsters—I think you would have liked it. (Letter to Loren MacIver, July 14, 1942, VSC)

This passage lies behind some of the images in "At the Fishhouses"— particularly the air's smelling like salt and the hand placed in the water and immediately transformed by it. The water ranges in its degree of fluidity—from too heavy to be stirred to light and able to be flurried—corresponding to the different degrees of heaviness of materials suspended within it. This experience in Mexico linked the images of natural deposits left in layers with the concept of time leaving its deposits, producing the sensible feel of history as layers of materiality deposited or suspended in other materials.

At the close of the poem, Bishop shows that to move deeply inside another material—across too great a distance between orders of reality—is to experience pain and burning.

> If you should dip your hand in,
> your wrist would ache immediately,
> your bones would begin to ache and your hand would burn
> as if the water were a transmutation of fire
> that feeds on stones and burns with a dark gray flame. (*CP* 65–66)

The human body could be immersible in the body of water, but the lack of modulation, in color and texture and density and temperature makes the encounter fierce: water to bone, ice to human warmth, nature to mind. The water, miraculously, "approaches" or transmutes stone and fire, but in doing so it seems even more distant, impenetrable, dangerous, and unable to incorporate the human. To imagine that knowledge is left as a deposit in this flowing and in this kind of encounter is to imagine the layers left deposited inside the human mind and body as a kind of nourishing that burns with the intensity of its difference.

> It is like what we imagine knowledge to be:
> dark, salt, clear, moving, utterly free,
> drawn from the cold hard mouth
> of the world, derived from the rocky breasts
> forever, flowing and drawn, and since
> our knowledge is historical, flowing, and flown. (*CP* 66)

The modulation from rock to water to human knowledge separates the layers of human experience, placing them at a greater distance from one another than those closely set modulations earlier in the poem. The closing image sharply contrasts with the immersible net of the opening, where the "dark purple-brown" of the fisherman's net was almost "invisible" in the "gloaming" of a night air almost, but not exactly, the same "purple-brown." Immersion across surfaces, even in the opening of the poem, when smells run over the boundary areas of their "objects" and penetrate new objects, is not without its pain and burning: "The air smells so strong of codfish / it makes one's nose run and one's eyes water" (*CP* 64). Emotion is associated with this kind of crossing (the tears or pain implied in eyes that "water" is held next to/against the salty ocean water that has already crossed into the other medium of air). The peeling off of surfaces (the herring scales stripped from fish) has its aura of both beauty and violence. Likewise, the modulation across the vastly different registers of fire, stone, and water are associated with both burning and beauty. As the flame fantastically participates in the color of the stone (a "dark gray flame"), it crosses materials, registering precisely the resemblance in color with difference in weight, density, and movement. The mind, like the hand that has been held in water, is unable to hold the full weight and movement of the world. The world's freely moving quality seems unlikely to allow the mind to be able to catch what is "historical, flowing, and flown." The slant rhyme—"drawn"/"flown"—expresses the brushing past of human and nature, mind and history, with difficulty, across huge distances, interpermeating surfaces that approach, touch, partially incorporate, and pass on (*CP* 64–66).

Yet the tone of the poem transmits a tranquility and accepts this passing of one material across and through another, partly because of the beauty generated. It is that tranquility or resignation, and the sensation of both sorrow and beauty, in this narrative of interpermeating surfaces that allows one to link the poems to the emotion that Bishop names in her own experience of the Schwitters collage that she bought for Lota. In describing that Schwitters collage to the Barkers, Bishop first listed its colors and materials, "darkish, reds and browns and hennas—one piece of ink-blue fabric with spots—one yellowish piece of poster, etc. with what looks like a man's foot in a shoe on it." But, then, at the close of her description, Bishop wrote, "sad, tasteful,—*very* sad" (letter from Bishop to the Barkers, November 6, 1954, PUL). The deposit of materials and images detached from their origins in the Schwitters collage seems to produce the grief evident in "At the Fishhouses," where material can touch and resemble material but also must register the tension, beauty, and sorrow of difference and disconnection, especially the wearing away and leaving of deposits by the movement of time.

Something of this sadness comes across gently but powerfully in "Anjinhos" (Bishop 1996, 51), in which the bright almost fluorescent blue of the butterfly's wing tears at its edge and disintegrates and fades, first into the wings of the dead girl and then more fully, dispersing as the bluish sand between the repeated faces. The reprise of the blue in the lusterless condensed material form of an isolated plastic button can only intensify the sense of loss. Likewise, the yellow butterfly wings in their reprise as yellow angel wings and in the hair on the images of the drowned girl only emphasizes the associations with death as the immobilized wings of the butterfly cross over to mark the girl as similarly unable to fly. The collage orchestrates the modulation from life to death—the half of the bright blue butterfly shadowed by its other wing in a shade of brown that resembles the wood and leather of the sandal and the disintegration of the girl's face as it crumbles into or is crossed by brown sand and shadow.

FOUR

IMMERSIBLE NETS, LINES, FABRICS, AND ENTANGLEMENTS

"Insomnia," "Prodigal," "Argument" and "Four Poems"

Schwitters's aesthetic gave Bishop one way of conceptualizing the relationship among the layers of visual image, emotion, word, personal reminiscence, physical world, cultural history, and physical feeling. The "fabric" of verse was a supple and dynamic material that could become a particularly rich site for the interaction among these layers for differentiated kinds of absorption and modulation. In this chapter, I develop a preliminary survey of the ways in which Bishop imagined materials touching one another, with special attention to the way that interiority can be held by the materials of verse and environment. In so doing, I return to pick up more examples of Klee's situating figures open to the environment (building on the material presented in chapter 2). Schwitters's handling of materials and the thematics of absorption did not lend themselves easily to the kind of subjectivity that lyric allows, and Schwitters's collages were less able than Klee's drawings and paintings to provide a means of conceptualizing subjectivity. Here I suggest that, although Bishop translates the visual aesthetics of interpermeating fabrics into her own linguistic medium, it is ultimately Klee's situating of subjectivity in the materials of the environment and Klee's experiments with a loosely bounding line that provided Bishop with models for holding subjectivity in lyric. "Insomnia" and "The Prodigal" entangle subjectivity in the material environment, occasionally having the lyric speaker fall into various kinds of extents in that environment. In her sequence, "Four Poems," Bishop experiments radically with the lyric speaker held inside the materials of verse and landscape, exploring the questions of line, surface, and depth in the arena of lovers' touch and human intimacy.

Verse as Pliable Net: Lines That Hover, Sink, and Extend

In Schwitters's collages, the net serves an important role on the cusp between disintegration and coherence. When tightened, the lines in a net coalesce, becoming a surface, a thickly woven fabric. When loosened, an expanding net eventually frees the line to isolate itself from the fabric and the line begins to waver and wander. Because the sequence of lines in a poem coheres to a surface (the network of lines creates a plane that can feel tightly woven or loose), the surface of verse can appear as a net or fabric. In an early unpublished draft, "Full Moon, Key West," Bishop already creates a pliable net of verse that sinks over and into other surfaces and undulates with them. The poem imagines Key West itself as having a papery aspect, as if both the buildings and people had become as thin, flimsy, and two-dimensional as pages of paper. This papery quality of the material world allows the lines of poetry on paper to resemble the lines that occur in the landscape. A crossing of various kinds of papers and lines occurs.

> The island starts to hum
> like music in a dream.
> Paper-white, drunk,
> the sailors come
> stumbling, fighting,
> mumbling threats
> in children's voices,
> stopping, lighting
> cigarettes
> with pink dull fires,
> in groups like hands
> and fingers on
> the narrow sidewalks
> of cement
> that carry sounds
> like tampered wires,

                    —the long strings of
                    an instrument
                    laid on the stream,
                    a zither laid
                    upon the flood
                    of the glittering Gulf. (Bishop 2006, 59–60)

The narrow strip of the poem, which stretches itself in a string down the page, hovers over its white paper like one of the strings that stretches through the town and lies on top of the waves. In the prosody of the ending, two layers—verse and the surface of water—are layered over one another so closely that they undulate with one another. Shifting from the two-beat iambic line to the anapestic wavering of the final line ("upon the flood / of the glittering Gulf"), Bishop produces in the "string" of her verse the water's undulation, as if her line of verse becomes literally laid on the water and moves with it.

In "Cape Breton," too, the verse line is layered over the landscape in movements of undulation, hovering, and spreading. When the water spreads out as a flat plane in all directions under the mist, the verse line flattens out toward its edges in a more and more subdued barely accented line:

        The silken water is weaving and weaving,
        disappearing under the mist equally in all directions (*CP* 67)

Extension and flatness are enacted by a "flat" word (*equally*), in which accent is distributed flatly and equally over the length of the word, occurring in a line that also extends out in length. When the flat surface is interrupted by a cormorant, the verse line, too, is "penetrated":

        Lifted and penetrated now and then
        by one shag's dripping serpent-neck (*CP* 67)

The flatness of the line is "lifted" and "penetrated" by the head of the line's accent in "lifted" and the sharply accented "serpent-neck" that sticks out of the preceding series of flat, evenly unaccented slow syllables. When a different, more "all-over" and "shallower" penetration occurs ("And somewhere the mist incorporates the pulse, / rapid but unurgent, of a motorboat"), the verse line incorporates accent differently. The rapidity of the motor and its softness and lack of intensity in volume are captured in the quick trochaic opening ("rapid") and relaxed fluttering remainder of "but unurgent, of a motorboat." Bishop's layering of verse line on to material world can be felt in the lightness of "drift" hanging on the end of a line ("the ghosts of glaciers drift . . .") and in the subsequent voyage of that light word *over* the next line's "among those folds and folds of fir." The verse line becomes densely compact in the densely folded tactility of the word *hackmatack*, which lays itself next to or on the densely packed texture of firs. The irregularity and jagged quality of the verse layers itself on to the "irregular nervous saw-tooth edge" of those firs. Shifts in the density of the landscape are layered over by shifts in the heaviness, density, and lightness of verse:

> Except in thousands of light song-sparrow songs floating
> upward
> freely, dispassionately, through the mist, and meshing
> in brown-wet, fine, torn fish-nets. (*CP* 67)

The light and airy floating lines of song-sparrow songs gain solidity, weight, and density when they cross into mesh. These variable qualities of the verse make it a pliant, supple net of "strings" that lies over the world and undulates with it, condensing and diffusing, becoming heavy or tenuous when the world under it changes its tactile qualities.

In a strikingly original experiment in "At the Fishhouses," Bishop creates a net that enacts a crossing not only among verse lines, bird songs, and landscapes but also among the movement of human figures, the physical feelings of descent and ascent, and the movement of the reader's and the lyric speaker's eyes. When "At the Fishhouses" makes its transition to the experience of depth—to "Cold dark deep and absolutely clear"—Bishop draws unusual attention to the reader's physical movement of the eye down the page through lines of verse.

> Down at the water's edge, at the place
> where they haul up the boats, up the long ramp
> descending into the water, thin silver

tree trunks are laid horizontally
across the gray stones, down and down
at intervals of four or five feet. (*CP* 65)

The stanza provides evidence that Bishop was reinventing the "net" of Schwitters's journal article, using verse lines to constitute one kind of netting and "crossing" those fibers with other materials—in the physical world and even in the physical body of the reader. The stanza is a net of coarse criss-crossing elements laid across one another. The feeling of moving along the ramp, up and down, is produced by the movement of the verse lines—"they haul up the boats, up the long ramp," has a rising movement full of effort in a spondee and trochees. This upward movement of the physicality of the verse line then crosses a descending movement—"descending into the water," where the falling rhythm slips downward. That physical feel of the movement of the verse line upward and downward plays against (or makes a "net" with) the horizontal lines of type-set verse lines on the printed page. The verticals and horizontals in this passage occur in different registers of experience: the physical landscape of the horizontal "water's edge"; the physical feel of the eyes that move down the page; the visual spatial display of horizontal lines of print; the tension of horizontal movement stretching syntactically toward the end of the verse line; the visual image of the physical tree trunks "laid horizontally"; the vertical descent of the visual image of the ramp; the heavy feel of ascent when men "haul" heavy objects upward; and the imagined descent of the lyric speaker into water, "down and down / at intervals of four or five feet" (*CP* 65). In this passage, especially, Bishop makes her own immersible net, where physicality of the verse lines, visual images of the landscape, and the physical and visual experience of speaker and reader are netted together.

"Cold dark deep," the sequence of isolated "deep" monosyllabic syllables, each its own substance, produce, with the shock of their difference compared to the zigzag movement of the lines above them, the sensation of crossing into a completely other element. When the water is "suspended above the . . . stones," the net of verse shifts from enacting a heavy stability ("I have seen it over and over, the same sea, the same") to lightness and undulation: "slightly, indifferently swinging above the stones, / icily free above the stones" (*CP* 65). The caesura after *free* produces the uplift and suspension, the sense of the verse line hovering above. By these means, Bishop produces the sensations of hovering and sinking that Schwitters arranged in his collages of transparent and dense papers, sparse and saturated colors, supple and stiff fabrics, and loosely and tightly woven nets. She imagines the verse as a fabric that can hover over or sink into the world, where the material of verse can lay on top of the world and sometimes move into it or be netted with it. The pliable fabric of verse becomes the site where the incorporation of "real" materials and objects—landscape, boat ramps, and human activity—takes place. And, thematically, she understands human experience—knowledge in relation to world and human physical movement in relation to landscape—as structured by these relations of layers of different kinds of experience netted on to one another and hovering, sinking, brushing across, and fleeing.

Lines that Incorporate Objects and Hold Subjectivity

Bishop imagined the verse line as a pliable net capable of lying over, sinking into, or thickening into landscape, but she also imagined the verse line as incorporating objects. In *The Particulars of Rapture*, Charles Altieri writes that, "Poetry is an art that almost equals painting's interest in boundaries, if only because every line of verse faces several adventures in transition, culminating in decisions one makes about how one line will connect to the following one" (Altieri 2003, 243). Bishop's poems also often experiment with boundaries and "facing" by using the variety of rhythmic textures and their suppleness to vary which part of the world can be incorporated in or held by the line, as if the boundary of a line is not only at its end but in its openness to the world, all along its length. In "Song for the Rainy Season," Bishop thematizes the "holding" of different materials in an "open container" of verse, where the plane of verse becomes a kind of "house" for the objects named in the poem.

> Beneath the magnetic rock,
> rain-, rainbow-ridden,
> where blood-black
> bromelias, lichens,
> owls, and the lint
> of the waterfalls cling. (*CP* 101)

The visual similarity of the line of waterfall to the thin line of verse brings attention to the way that Bishop hangs objects inside the moving streamlike fabric of the verse. The streaming effect of the enjambed verse lines is held stable in its narrow stanza but holds the objects inside the stream.

> . . . vapor
> climbs up the thick growth
> effortlessly, turns back,
> holding them both,
> house and rock,
> in a private cloud. (*CP* 101)

Bishop emphasizes the way that the verse stream becomes a container, by placing "house and rock" on a single line, held together by the enveloping "atmosphere" of the verse stanza, the way that the "vapor" holds together "house and rock, / in a private cloud." Here, the verse stanza—turning and holding in "loose" embrace—becomes an open container, like the house itself: "house, open house / to the white dew / and the milk-white sunrise / kind to the eyes, / to membership" (*CP* 101–2).

In other poems, subjectivity becomes one of these objects held in or by the verse lines. Early poems, such as "The Imaginary Iceberg" and "The Monument" already contain some of Bishop's speculations about the way that verse can hold the subjectivity of the artist, although, in both those early poems, she emphasizes that the living artist cannot remain inside the construction: "The bones of the artist-prince may be inside / or far away on even drier soil" (*CP* 25). In some of the poems in *A Cold Spring*, Bishop goes much further in imagining the verse lines as mobile containers for subjectivity. In her imagining alternative ways in which verse lines can hold subjectivity, the prominence at mid-century of Klee's experiments with how line "held" the figure became of use. According to Andrew Kagan, "From 1935–1949 Klee's improvisatory drawing was tapped as a way beyond Cubism" (Kagan, "Paul Klee's Influence, Part I," 55). "As opposed to the essentially sculptural, static, fragmented piecework logic of Cubist figurative abstraction, Klee in his original realm posited the essentially graphic energy of the continuous, freely moving line as a basis of pictorial organization in two and three dimensions" (56). We can

Figure 6. Paul Klee, *Tiere bei Vollmond* (*Animals by Full Moon*). 1927. © 2009 Artists Rights Society (ARS) New York/VG Bild-Kunst, Bonn.

feel the line only loosely bounding a form, its improvisatory feel, and its ability to hold "tentatively" in Klee's drawing *Animals by Full Moon* (1927) (figure 6), a drawing available to Bishop in the popular Curt Valentin edition of Klee's drawings published in 1944.[1] Here, line wanders loosely as a free graphic trace before closing to bound a form. These animal figures could easily sink back into pure line; there's a gentle swell from wandering line to (partially) closed body and an implied ease of dissolving back into line.

Bishop's own amateur paintings sometimes play with this fluctuation between line as free graphic performance and line used to enclose form. Lorrie Goldensohn first drew attention to "Bishop's fascination with line" and notes that "in drawing and painting, Bishop's line is both an instrument of representation and a subject": "Line in this picture [*Olivia Street in Key West*]—as in *Interior with Extension Cord* and others that mix the pen and brush, the writer's and painter's instruments—is both representation, an abstraction contouring a plane, a device representing the thing, and also the thing itself" (Goldensohn 1999, 170).[2]

In some of Klee's drawings and watercolors, the looseness of the line contributes to an ambivalence or tentativeness about having made a contour at all and tends to open the contoured form to its background or environment; see, for example, Klee's *Lying as Snow* (1931) (figure 7). In this respect, Klee's figures can hover existentially on an edge between having a drawn boundary around (separating) and opening toward (connecting). Klee engaged in these experiments not only in drawing animals but in drawing the human subject, open to its environment and held tentatively as contour or shape that could dissolve or collapse. In *Lying as Snow*, exhibited at the Nierendorf Gallery in New York (October 1947), the loosely held contour line brings a man's shape into being while also enfolding the man in the "snow" "inside" of which he is lying. Contour delimits the body from and simultaneously connects the body to the landscape. The boundary is mobile, illusory, and subject to dissolution but also sustaining. The laxness of the line begins to feel as though human body and landscape are losing shape and becoming just graphic looping. Like the person in the painting *Fear* that Bishop had mentioned to Lowell, the man in *Lying as Snow* hides, fearful, isolated, and necessarily watchful for a means of escape or survival. This drawing, too, echoes Bishop's remark to Lowell about what she admired in Klee: "Modesty, care, space, a sort of helplessness but determination at the same time" (Bishop 2008, 250).

Bishop would have been able to see several of the Klee paintings that hold the human figure in and open to the landscape at the Buchholz in 1948 and in the major Klee retrospective that she visited three times (the traveling exhibit organized by MoMA came to the Phillips

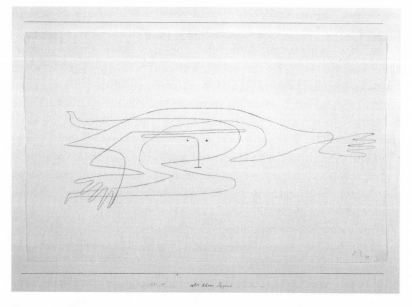

Figure 7. Paul Klee, *Als Schnee liegend* (*Lying as Snow*). 1931. Ink on paper, mounted on paper. Paper mount: 18 3/4×24 5/8 inches (47.6×62. 6 cm); paper support: 12 1/4× 18 3/4 inches (31.3×47.7 cm). Solomon R. Guggenheim Museum, New York. Estate of Karl Nierendorf, by purchase. 48.1172.142. © 2009 Artists Rights Society (ARS), New York/VG Bild-Kunst, Bonn.

Gallery March 5 to April 10, 1950).[3] In *Intention* (*Vorhaben*, 1938) (figure 8), the figure is "behind" or obstructed by a line that feels like a wall or barrier, presumably watching as well as experiencing feelingly the drifting of the materials on either side (interior and exterior spaces). "Insula Dulcamara" (1938), "Demonry" (1939), and "Early Sorrow" (1938), in the same exhibit, also have a figure who "hides" within the lines and material that make up both his body and the environment. In the 1948 Buchholz exhibit, *Young Moe* (1938), *Sextet of Genii* (1937), and *Child and Aunt*[4] (1937) all hold the figure or figures in a state that also opens toward and dissolves into the lines or fabric of the environment. Sometimes, as in *A Park and the Tresspasser* (1939), also at the 1948 Buchholz exhibit, the figure is tiny, set at the margin of a large landscape, with openings and barriers. Klee provided Bishop with one way of imagining the lyric speaker held in a state that also opens toward and dissolves into the lines or "fabric" of the environment.

Figure 8. Paul Klee, *Vorhaben* (*Intention*). 1938, 126. Colored paste on paper on burlap; original frame 75.5×112.3 cm. Zentrum Paul Klee, Bern. © 2009 Artists Rights Society (ARS), New York/VG Bild-Kunst, Bonn.

The entire mid-section of the volume *A Cold Spring* experiments with the holding of subjectivity in the materials of the environment. "Insomnia" and "The Prodigal," as we shall see, are more extreme examples; but "View of the Capitol from the Library of Congress" hides the figure apart from and embedded within the field. Composed in fall 1950 after Bishop had seen the Klee retrospective at the Phillips Gallery, "View of the Capitol" implies a speaker standing in an upper story of the library. The speaker feels off to the side, behind a barrier, and not quite in the scene, yet we can also say that the whole scene holds the subjectivity of the speaker, who is suspended somewhere in it. The poem is built on variant kinds of absorption of line, texture, or material. Bishop thematizes the role of line emerging from and becoming absorbed into the landscape: "unceasingly the little flags / feed their limp stripes into the air" (*CP* 69). The qualities of light ("heavy" and "coarse") alter as the light crosses another surface ("the Dome"). In some places, light cannot be absorbed or incorporated: "one small lunette turns it aside / and blankly stares off to the side" (*CP* 69). The opacity of a surface, the sense of obtuseness or closing to another material or mode, emerges as the theme of the poem, which includes the semiblindness or opacity of a "wall-eyed horse." The closed surfaces present the opposite portrait from the openness thematized in "Song for the Rainy Season." Incorporation of different objects or materials can barely occur. Although uneven rhymes permit otherness in some stanzas to "intervene" between two rhymes, by the end rhymes come so closely together that no other sounds or meanings can "intervene" (especially in the closing "boom-boom"). The music of the Air Force Band cannot quite "come through" the "giant trees" but is held by each "big leaf" that "sags" (*CP* 69). The variant interfaces among materials here, their (obstructed) crossing into or interpermeating one another, clearly carries Schwitters's compositional method into the urban and political world, beyond the nature scenes of "Cape Breton" and "At the Fishhouses." Yet the strange effaced presence of a located lyric speaker in "View of the Capitol" approaches the unusual holding of subjectivity within the lines and materials of Klee's *Intention*. The lyric speaker's consciousness is detached and held aloof and able to see all, yet it is held beyond a kind of membrane or wall inside the scene. The speaker, the central consciousness of the poem, is composed of opacities and deflections parallel to the window across from which she stands—nothing "gets in" to illuminate her interior, yet her report of the landscape partially composes that interior. The depth of subjectivity emerges from the complex play of open and opaque surfaces that can or cannot incorporate other parts of the environment. The speaker becomes one of the variant surfaces inventoried in the poem. Lyric again becomes the site that allows materials to meet, cross, and transform or become opaque, deflect, close, and obstruct, and subjectivity itself appears or is held as an interface among these elements.

Verse as a Fabric That Tilts and Turns, Subjectivity
Falling into Extent

In "Insomnia" and "Prodigal," Bishop seems to go even farther in altering or widening the arena for Schwitters's interpermeating materials and fabrics that modulate from surface to depth so that the materials appear to hold subjectivity inside or open to a surrounding environment. Bishop composed "Insomnia" and "Prodigal" as a contrasting pair, each holding subjectivity in a particular material: silvered mirror and mud. "Insomnia" produces a complex interaction between verse imagined as a fabric and the stretching out of other materials. One of the major subtopics of "Insomnia" seems to be "extent"—the way states of mind can stretch and the relationship between that kind of stretching and the way distance and time stretch. Large sheets of material fold out or away—like the fabric that falls in the opening stanza of "The Unbeliever" when "the sails fall away from below him / like the sheets of his bed" (*CP* 22). In "Insomnia," with the moon hanging in or on it, the blank expanse of a silvered mirror suddenly stretches out expansively, beyond the frame of the bureau mirror, and looked at another way, pivots and falls outward, becoming the night sky:

> The moon in the bureau mirror
> looks out a million miles
> (and perhaps with pride, at herself,
> but she never, never smiles)
> far and away beyond sleep, or
> perhaps she's a daytime sleeper. (*CP* 70)

The reflective surface of the mirror, holding darkness, seems to open expansively, turning into the space of the night sky between the speaker's bedroom and the moon, a space that stretches "far and away beyond sleep" "a million miles." Left alone in her place in the sky ("by the Universe deserted"), the moon then falls into or on a stretched-out surface ("a body of water"). With a simple *or* ("she'd find a body of water, /or a mirror, on which to dwell"), Bishop transforms the material of water into a blank sheet of mirror. Later, the "shadows" (reflections in a mirror) seem to turn into body, or, thought about from the other way round, real bodies fall into the insubstantial reflections ("shadows") in the mirror, a realm that itself falls and turns into the material of sea:

> Into that world inverted
> where left is always right,
> where the shadows are really the body,
> where we stay awake all night,
> where the heavens are shallow as the sea
> is now deep, and you love me. (*CP* 70)

The women fall into one another, into the space of bodily embraces that feel materially like shadows, where bodies feel insubstantial or not quite solid. The lovers' bodies lie in a space between two extensive planes—one shallow, one deep—of heaven and sea. The closed reflective surface of mirror and sea has opened downward, and the lyric speaker has fallen through that surface and now is held by a deeper, much more capacious space.

In these turnings, where one material folds out from another or "reverses" to become another, the poem enacts other falls from surface into depth. The opening lines flipped from contemplation of the surface (the mirror) to an experience of the depth of loneliness. The second stanza—in which the focus is first on the surface of water on which the moon's face will be reflected—suddenly shifts to the depth beneath the surface of the well water. The third stanza opens with a focus on the mirror's surface, but turns and falls from there into the depth of sea and of love. The body of water at first has no depth (it is at first only the mirror in the bureau), but it suddenly falls away from itself and becomes deep. The heavens and the sea appear to be facing one another as two surfaces; then, as we turn around the line break, each seems to fall into "depth." The poem passes through the oddly angled juxtapositions of different kinds of depth that fall into or out of one another: loneliness, sleeplessness, time, love, the sea, the sky, two lovers' mingling bodies.

The "turns" also comprise reversals of subject position. Just as the moon looked *at* in the mirror is also imagined as looking *out from* the mirror, so too the speaker looking at the moon ("The moon in the bureau mirror") is suddenly reporting on the scene as if she is located inside the moon's interior ("looks out a million miles"). The moon, who distances herself from the world, is subjected to a reversal so that she is deserted by that world, as if the world falls away from in front of her. The speaker, as if for a moment located in a stable place and able to drop an object down a well, "turns" in the middle of the third stanza so that it is she herself who has fallen into the well and found there an inverted world. The lonely speaker "turns" to speak from the position of a "we" (CP 70).

In "Insomnia" the subjectivity of the speaker becomes sequentially coextensive with the materials depicted in the poem. In each reversal of subject position, the subject becomes open to or part of a new field. The movement of the verse appears less as an undulating or immersing net and more as a series of fabrics that tilt or turn. The prosodic fabric of "Insomnia" takes on the qualities of mirrored or watery reflective surfaces. The quicksilver "turns" in prosody are like the rippling of light on the reflective surface of the mirror. Iambic quickly falls away to anapestic or reverses to trochaic, feminine and masculine line endings alternate, and the fabric of the verse never settles into a pattern but shimmers in its changeable rhythms, lightly turning this way and that. Bishop's light touch makes the poem feel like the lightest of fabrics, and that lightness is most apparent when set in direct contrast to the heaviness of "The Prodigal" (*CP* 70, 71).

We should note first that parallel subject matter makes the two poems a set;[5] both poems undertake portraits of loneliness. The imagery in "Insomnia" turns up reversed in "The Prodigal." The mirrored surface of "Insomnia" appears in "Prodigal" as "glass-smooth dung." The moonlight that the speaker in "Insomnia" sees in the mirror appears as the glazed light of the sunrise on "barnyard mud." The moon that moves "far and away" in the distance in "Insomnia" becomes the much more frightening "the sun, going away" in "Prodigal." But, beyond these deliberate contrasts in the imagery of light, Bishop seems to have taken care to contrast a poem that keeps "turning" in "Insomnia" with a poem that cannot "turn over" in "The Prodigal." The logic of the double sonnet of "The Prodigal," with its displaced voltas in delayed or chaotic places, can't quite manage to "turn." It produces no symmetrical and clear-edged sequence of turns but, rather, a muffled, heavy movement like turning over a heavy woolen blanket. The poem begins with the impossibility of judgment or choice: "The brown enormous odor he lived by / was too close, with its breathing and thick hair, / for him to judge" (*CP* 71). Moving through the revolting description, which should lead to a "turn" homeward, does not lead there. The brightening of the imagery turns the prodigal, instead, back toward his life with the sow ("but sometimes mornings after drinking bouts / . . . the sunrise glazed the barnyard mud with red; / the burning puddles seemed to reassure"). The couplet that should record an act of will to return home turns back on itself so that the prodigal decides only that he might be able to "endure / his exile yet another year or more." Even this conclusion, this turning to stay, fails to decide how long. The "turn" that opens the second stanza, that re-turns the prodigal toward home by at least bringing a warning, somehow remains a staying (locked in the barn at night). "Ark" (hope and rescue) and "dark" collapse into one; light and lightning are one (*CP* 71). "The Prodigal" is an insomnia poem in which the motion of the "sleeper" seems to be a heavy turning over, from side to side, from "but" to "but," which occur like thuds and do not advance to any release from the question or problem of the night.

Especially set in the original edition's facing-page opposition, the poems show that Bishop designed starkly different kinds of "fabrics" for the "surface" of verse in the two poems.

> The moon in the bureau mirror
> looks out a million miles ("Insomnia," *CP* 70)

has a lightness and mobility in the verse line that accentuates the slug-gishness of the opening of "The Prodigal":

> The brown enormous odor he lived by
> was too close, with its breathing and thick hair. (*CP* 71)

The force of the many spondees in "The Prodigal" ("too close," "thick hair," "glass-smooth dung") contrast markedly with the rising and falling rhythms of "Insomnia," in which iambic turns over to become even lighter anapestic ("and perhaps with pride at herself," "where the shadows are really the body"; *CP* 70–71). Whenever "The Prodigal" lifts toward hopefulness by moving into iambic, it quickly falls backward into something thick and immoveable. By the second stanza of "The Prodigal," the uncontrollable trembling of the wastrel, caught by the trembling shudder of the dactylic ("carrying," "staggering," "shuddering"), even after it rises briefly in the emotional "touching him," merely flattens out exhausted and plodding:

> Touching him. But it took him a long time
> finally to make his mind up to go home. (*CP* 71)

In contrast to "Insomnia," "The Prodigal" cannot manage to lift or glitter.

On the other hand, "The Prodigal" retains the strange turning from subjectivity to material that Bishop created in "Insomnia." The human figure of the prodigal keeps emerging from and turning back into material. The poem opens with a moment in which the "enormous odor [the prodigal] lived by" stretches out in extent and feels like the tangible material of the pigs' "breathing and thick hair," which is so "close" that his own being cannot pull away far enough from it either to judge it or see it. Bishop creates a mind in which internal "turning" occurs almost simultaneous with or coextensive with the turning of the landscape. The "bats' uncertain staggering flight" becomes "his shuddering insights, beyond his control, / touching him." The "edge" between the landscape and the prodigal appears to flip over so that interior and landscape turn into one another. It is not a romantic merging with landscape but, rather, the creation of a boundary line that has two sides; one that, like a reversible fabric, can turn over. The phenomenon occurs also in the flip from inside to outside in Bishop's characterization of the "overhanging clouds of hay" in the barn that make the interior of the barn feel like an outside. Then, the lightning storm that would usually occur outside reverses and occurs inside: "The farmer whom he worked for came at dark / to shut the cows and horses in the barn / beneath their overhanging clouds of hay, / with pitchforks, faint forked lightnings, catching light" (*CP* 71). In "Insomnia" and "Prodigal," the verse materials stage a mobile encounter where interior and exterior materials turn or sink into one another, surfaces drop into depths, and different kinds of extent fold outward or inward.

Klee's Wandering Line: Subjectivity Held in Line

In "Insomnia" and "The Prodigal," the lyric subject, held in the variable and tilting or turning fabrics of verse, becomes open to the various fields in which it is held. Just as the silvered expanse of mirror tilts slightly and becomes a different expanse—the night sky or the surface of water—so too the expanse of the lyric speaker's emotional loneliness tips and becomes the visual expanse of night or a well. It is not that the boundary between the speaker's emotions and the landscape disappears into merging or complete resemblance; their different "registers" remain. The speaker of "Insomnia," tipping from location to location, is successively held within different expanses and shifting materials. The subjectivity of the man in "The Prodigal" has effaced boundaries; he is too close to mud, dung, sows, and bats. Both speakers feel too close, closed in, by these materials. Yet there are still "edges" between subjectivity and these materials. Loneliness can sense its own extensiveness by falling into the material of a mirror as dark and infinite as night sky or the surface of the sea, or loneliness can sense its own bottomless depth by "falling into" the dark well. But it is the tilting from one to the other that also becomes the site of subjectivity and expresses the particular feel of its mobility: the pace at which it transforms, its lightness or heaviness, the density or intensity of its feeling states, and how their duration is experienced.

Beyond his visual works, such as *Lying as Snow* or *Intention*, Klee's writings—translated at mid-century—offer another way to imagine the entanglement of subjectivity falling into or opening toward the surrounding materials. The most well-known excerpt from Klee's writing about line, which came to be designated as "taking a walk with a line," appears in Margaret Miller's edition of the MoMA publication about Klee. Bishop was clearly very familiar with the phrase "taking a walk with a line." In a letter to Lowell, she jokingly refers to a child in her house walking upstairs with a crayon brushing the wall by remarking, "as Klee said—Monica 'took a walk with a line'" (Bishop 2008, 451). In the excerpt of Klee's writing reproduced by Miller, "taking a walk with a line" involves a journey that surveys the variety of lines that express both interior and exterior space:

> Let us develop, let us make on the basis of a topographic plan, a little journey into the land of greater insight. The dead point must be overcome with the first act of movement (line). After a short time, stop to get your breath (broken line, articulated by repeated stops). A look back to see how far we have already come (counter-movement). In your mind consider the road from here to there (bundle of lines). A stream wishes to hinder us; we use a boat (wave movement). Further on there would have been a bridge (series of curves).
>
> On the other side we find someone of like mind who also wishes to go where greater insight is to be found. At first a joyful agreement (convergence), but gradually all kinds of differences arise (independent direction of two lines). A certain excitement on both sides (expression, dynamics and spirit of the line). We cross an unploughed field (lines crossing a plane), then thick woods. He goes astray, searches and once even goes through the classic movements of the meander.

I, too, am not entirely cool; over new river-land lies fog (space element). Soon it becomes clearer. Basket-makers return home with their wagons (the wheel). With them a child with gay curls (cork-screw movement). Later it becomes sultry and dark (space element). Lightning on the horizon (zigzag line). Above us there still are stars (field of points). Soon we reach our night's lodgings. Before falling asleep many things come back to the mind, for such a little journey leaves strong impressions. (Klee 1945, 10–11)

The line is attached to the subjectivity of a person with desires and anxieties, who will experience pleasure and obstacles. In the passage, there is a strange way in which the line that expresses the subjectivity and travels of a person also serves to characterize the landscape through which the person is moving. The "feeling" of the person taking the journey does not stay "inside" any body with contours where subjectivity is located as a kind of condensed point. Instead, the description of the person temporarily becomes coextensive with the changing landscape as the person moves through "sultry and dark" space, sees "lightning on the horizon" and senses or sees "above us there still are stars (field of points)." A person feeling divergence from a companion travels along/encounters lines that diverge or take on a dynamic excited quality. The lines that express interior emotion also occur as physical landscape. The end of the passage strengthens the impression that the lines that the traveler encounters abide both inside and outside of the mind: "before falling asleep many things come back to the mind, for such a little journey leaves strong impressions" (Klee 1945, 11]).

In "Argument," we can most clearly see Bishop thematizing line as expressive of both interior and exterior space. In this poem, unlike "View of the Capitol from the Library of Congress," the lyric speaker is not so much "held" in relation to materials of the environment but "living" the quality of the line, emotionally. Many of Klee's drawings use the line that creates a figure to also express the emotion of the figure; so, for example, in "Fight" (1930), which Bishop would have seen at the 1940 Buchholz exhibit, the jangly, harsh "fight" of lines represents figures fighting. Many of Klee's works in the exhibitions that Bishop saw contain images that use line in this expressive way. For example, "Child Consecrated to Suffering" (1935), which was reproduced in Margaret Miller's MoMA publication on Klee; "She Howls, We Play" (1928); and "The Mocker Mocked" (1930) all use scrambly lines criss-crossing inside the figure and going outside the bounds of the figure to indicate anguish, excitement, or other emotions.

In "Argument" and in "Four Poems," Bishop seems to experiment with a verse line that falls away, becomes weak, or falters as a way to express the faltering or tenuousness of the lyric speaker. Published in spring 1947 and probably written in summer 1946 when Bishop was separating from Marjorie Stevens, "Argument" was composed shortly after Klee's excerpts appeared in print. In this lyric, Bishop uses a looser and more ragged verse line than she does in any previous poem. Long lines that waver or drop away become expressive of the lyric speaker's vacillation:

> Days that cannot bring you near
> or will not,
> Distance trying to appear
> something more than obstinate,
> argue argue argue with me
> endlessly
> neither proving you less wanted nor less dear. (*CP* 81)

The short line carries the speaker's dropping away from a line of thought or conviction. The separation from the lover appears impossible and then drops away from that conviction ("or will not," dropping away from the solidity of that first declaration). An insistent, repetitive driving motion ("argue argue argue with me") drops away into a softer line that simply dies away ("endlessly"), expressive both of fatigue and of the potential that the speaker will relent and return to her lover.

In addition to a logic that keeps flipping over (for example, from "cannot" to "will not" or from wanting to leave to wanting to return), the subjectivity of the speaker flips across a membrane of interior and exterior space.

> Distance: Remember all that land
> beneath the plane;

that coastline
of dim beaches deep in sand
stretching indistinguishably
all the way,
all the way to where my reasons end? (*CP* 81)

The stretching of the land proves that no return is possible; the lyric speaker sees the line as leading "all the way, / all the way to where my reasons [for leaving] end." It is as if the speaker falls into fusion with the "line" of the coast and its "line" of argument, and then, suddenly, pulls away, veers off, and separates. The stanza turns at the end so that the lyric speaker emerges out of the "coastline" that is "stretching" (*CP* 81). The visual image is a long long line, stretching to an unseen end. The line then becomes expressive of the line of mental reasoning in which the speaker is engaged (as well as an indicator of the geographical and emotional distance between the lovers). As in Klee's writing about line, the characteristics of the line vacillate or tilt over an edge, expressing interior and exterior landscapes.

After the jangly, clashing "argument" in stanza three, in which the perspective of each woman, almost metallic in feel, becomes an "instrument" for "canceling each other's experience," in the final stanza of the poem, Bishop brings back the tenuous and gentle verse line, expressive of a resigned but still hopeful tenderness toward the lover.

The intimidating sound
of these voices
we must separately find
can and shall be vanquished:
Days and Distance disarrayed again
and gone
both for good and from the gentle battleground. (*CP* 81)

The faltering of a line, its loosening within a more taut stretch, opens the possibility for a change of heart. Inside the "box" of the rhymes, the lines are uneven and seem disarranged, frayed. To lock the experience into the straight line of coastline, stretching to the south, would close the relationship into "distance." To lock the experience into the series of jangling rectangle shapes in the "hideous calendar" of

"Compliments of Never & Forever, Inc." would close the relationship into sharp conflict. To waver, to disarrange the lines, to put "Days and Distance" into "disarray" would allow for the possibility of returning to the ex-lover (*CP* 81). The wavering mind, thematized as softening or disintegrating line, can accommodate the other, open to her.

Around this period, Bishop's notebook included several drafts of a poem that thematized dots, cavities, closed shapes, and several kinds of lines. She was clearly using categories from visual art as she tried to articulate the ending of her relationship with Marjorie Stevens. She wrote about "definition perfectly bound" and noted "all 'pool?'" in the margin, as if using a private shorthand for the way that she had thought about the pool in "Pleasure Seas" carrying the clarity of a closed, defined shape. Against such a closed shape or line to define the end of the relationship, she renders the softness and delight of a "spray of red-gold integers" (created by dust from a smoke stack at twilight) that falls on the perhaps still-sleeping lover ("your wrists & temples, where demons play"). Bishop renders the relationship as in-between the states of spray, cavity, and line, with such phrasing as, "cavity or lines . . . (also for a heart)" and "definitions go on & on / see you also their conclusions"—as if the relationship seems unable to arrive at its still inevitable edge, boundary, or line that will make a conclusion for the relationship and define it. The rhyme "falters / alters" associates disarrangement or softening of line with the difficulty of either reaching an end or maintaining the love; "the definition perfectly bound" is undone by "falters / alters" (VSC 75.3a, 66–67).

Surfaces, Lines, Membranes, and Intimacy

In "The Museum," another unpublished fragment, Bishop imagines the closed surface as the failure of intimacy. The poem focuses on two lovers who could have but did not quite manage to "arrange" their connection in quite the right way. Their failure to reach one another is "caught" by the display of materials that cannot change or touch. Bishop presents the museum as a Schwitters-like space, where worn papers and other materials are held in place.

> Dear—please let's go back
> To that little provincial museum,

& through its little rooms again,
. . . .
& This time let us translate
the labels more carefully
on brownish paper, as if scorched
printed in a quaint /black /type.   19th cent.

Some of them had slipped
to the bottom of the cases & lay
face down, or stood on one corner.

Some of the rooms were   dim
dry smell or a damp smell

A column of sunlight fell
clear & thin & alive
almost like a stream of water—
alive as a stream of water
as if it lived there
        commenting fastidiously on lighting. (Bishop 2006, 72)

The papers, scorched on the edges, slipped down or standing on a
corner, and stuck in the museum cases behind glass, untouchable,
with some face down, unreadable, become motifs of the not to be
touched or changed. Bishop sets material against material: scorched
paper against glass; a river of sunlight against a room that is "dim";
sunlight that is streaming and "alive" against the less vivid, dead,
electric light of the museum (Bishop 2006, 72). She arranges the "fabrics" of her collage. The barely seen speaker and her lover move
through this space, their distance from one another expressed by the
lack of modulation, the mutual inaccessibility of the various materials. The lovers' past, like the array of materials in the museum, is understood to be inaccessible to touch, behind glass, although it is in
need of having its disarray rearranged.[6] Although there is no way to
know why Bishop chose to complete and publish some drafts rather
than others, we can note that, in this case, the environment begins to
take on a metaphorical or allegorical relationship to emotions rather
than holding subjectivity in a more interactive relationship with the
environment. Here, the figures are passing through an environment

that resembles them, whereas, in the poems that Bishop chose to publish, the interior and exterior environments, and the verse lines and verse materials, become more entangled, opening toward or falling into one another.

The sequence "Four Poems" surely stands as Bishop's most extreme experiment in the entanglement of verse materials, interior subjectivity, and exterior landscape. The rendering of human interiority and intimacy becomes a meditation on the interfaces among lines, surfaces, materials, and skins. Before turning to a close reading of this sequence of poems, it is instructive to look at one of Bishop's own paintings, the watercolor of the Aladdin lamp, a painting Bishop gave to Lota for her birthday in 1952. The painting suggests Bishop's imagination of sexuality as the movement across intricately dense layers from physical sensation deep in the body, up through layers of the physical body, to unfold across the layer of one's own skin and the layer of another's skin, opening into and across layers of visual and emotional sensation and pleasure. The Aladdin lamp that Bishop depicts is a kerosene lamp, presumably the one that she and Lota lived with in Samambaia. A kerosene lamp needs to be cleaned every few days in order to burn correctly, so Bishop would have been familiar with the lamp's parts. The white, incandescent "bulb" of the lamp is a mantle, a flimsy piece of textile held up by the wires at its side. When lit, some of the cloth mantle's substance burns away and the rest is inflammable and incandescent. The fluid kerosene is drawn up into the flimsy cloth and vaporizes at the skin of the mantle. So the lamp is a mechanism for altering substances or materials, allowing them to permeate one another and then transform into another material— cloth becomes flame and light. The use of this kind of lamp to represent her love for Lota shows that she associated love with one material crossing over a boundary and turning into another material. Her handwritten message "Many Happy Returns" is a pun on the "turning" of the lamp knob to intensify both the flame and sexual desire. The "turning" keeps turning one material (the mantle made of fabric) into another material (flame and light). Or it allows the modulation of physical sensation deep within the body to turn into love. The painting stresses a range of materials (Bishop 1996, 61). The wood grain texture has a see-through aspect, in some places fading to reveal the brown paper beneath so that flat brown paper is juxtaposed to paper "grained" as wood. As in a Schwitters collage, there is a sequence of ascending solidity or "filled-in-ness"—the brown wrapping-paper-like background, the painted trompe-l'oeuil wood surface more "filled-in," and then, most surprising, an actual piece of cork that is patterned like the ink depicting the wood surface. With this small "burnt" sticklike shape touching the glass shade (invisible in the painting except for the two lines that indicate its sides), Bishop makes her tribute to love and touch also a tribute to the art of assemblage, where wood can "meet" glass. By attaching a strip of real cork to the "glass" surface of the lamp, Bishop draws attention to the "touch" of material against material as code for the act of love. The strange detail of the solid cork touching the glass demonstrates that Bishop associated assemblage or collage—different materials touching one another—with human intimacy.

In the sequence, "Four Poems," Bishop renders bodies and minds closely entangled, crossing and touching at intricately delineated multiple borders. The folding out of one surface into another occurs mostly inside and across the lovers' bodies and minds, although interior becomes actively entangled in landscape in both "Rain towards Morning" and "While Someone Telephones." In these poems, the skin of the body and the "skin" of verse open. In the first poem, the interior of the lyric speaker occurs as lines and multiple membranes opening and closing, with a line that only temporarily and tenuously bounds forms that appear and disappear. In the second poem, the interior of two lovers and landscape seem radically open to one another, as if the boundaries of skin and house cease to exist. In the third, boundaries between minds and environments cross, open, and close, and in the fourth, we see the fraying or wearing away of the verse fabric and a focus on the skin that separates and bounds. These four poems by Bishop have been written about in only the briefest terms and seem both difficult to read and unlike anything else that she wrote. One way of understanding them is to see their themes of opening out of surfaces and lines that rhythmically waver or drop away and make the surface of verse wobble, tear, or fray as the theme of *A Cold Spring* as a volume. Another way of gaining access to "Four Poems" is to read the poems closely, paying attention to the interplay of the poems as a sequence in the way that they rework questions about membranes opening out, the sudden and temporary production or awareness of depth and its dropping away, and the mobile and tenuous holding of subjectivity in lines and fabrics.

All four poems have a remarkable intimacy. We are watching the "I" emerge from and sink back into a field or a background that is part of and keeps seeping into the self. The background (within the mind but outside or underneath the "I"; or outside the body—either the lover's body, the sky, or the landscape) becomes active, opens, and pulses into or penetrates or becomes closed, resistant, and opaque to the foreground. The "canvas" of the poem becomes the body of the "I." We feel a seeping in from elsewhere, a turning toward, quickenings, and fadings. A form or thought or feeling becomes distinct, then indistinct, then insistent, and then fades away and is lost. Bishop produces the physicality of the feeling mind, experienced as if from within, as it is touched, aroused. At about this period, Bishop wrote in her notebook a phrase that opens up a poetic project: "Into the wild realms of Touch / still almost unlettered on the Maps" (VSC 72.B.5, 23), and "Four Poems" appears to be the execution of that plan. "The Realms of Touch" are surprisingly explored not just on the skin of two lovers' bodies but in the full "touch" of interior and exterior experience. We experience the mind as it feels interior "touch"—the dropping away of intention or attention, as the "I" loses "shape" and disperses or diffuses. A "brightening" opens from inside a field as if an all-over emulsion appears and produces a sense of release. A line crosses the space of the self and attenuates it. Blankness is encountered not as one overwhelming nihilistic experience but intermittently as part of a moment-to-moment lived reality. The speaker becomes the object of movements that are sensed as remote, then intimate, coming from within and from without, movements that cross the membrane of an "I." The "I" is less a bounded form than a field with multiple interior boundaries or membranes, up through which sensations or emotions emerge or erupt. The field of the "I" experiences states or events hosted by backgrounds that can emerge into forms. The line between two people becomes a thick mobile frontier, unstable, shifting, unlocatable, and full of the textural and tactile experience of ripplings and punctures. The fabric of verse becomes the site within which the "touch" inside and across body, mind, lover, and landscape can be felt.

"Conversation" renders a quietness of voice that fades away, out of the "plane" of the visible poem, almost to nothingness, and then resurfaces. To read the poem is to experience a speaking consciousness that itself intermittently almost fades away. This quietness first arises in the radical disjunction between the reported experience of "tumult" and the extreme gentleness of the tone of voice that is reporting on that tumult:

> The tumult in the heart
> keeps asking questions.
> And then it stops and undertakes to answer
> in the same tone of voice.
> No one could tell the difference. (*CP* 76)

The tone of speaking about this "tumult" could hardly be more tranquil. We are being asked to imagine "tumult" in the heart as an insistent voice that "keeps asking questions." The voice that "undertakes to answer" speaks "in the same tone of voice"; that is, it must be equivalent to the insistence, vociferousness, and passion that arises naturally from "tumult." Yet the lyric speaker's voice we actually hear is almost without emotion, passionless and resigned. The voice is so quiet, with so little driving forward motion, that it nearly stops almost as soon as it begins. The opening iambic ("The tumult in the heart") begins to drag backward by line 2 ("keeps asking questions") and, after a tiny resumption of energy ("And then"), comes to a complete stop midline ("it stops"). The voice manages to move along for another two lines before another dying out (" . . . and undertakes to answer / in the same tone of voice"). Rhythmically and syntactically, the poem feels as if it could end right there, but it manages to go on for one more exhausted line with a weak feminine ending that seems to fade off into the blank space that follows ("No one could tell the difference"). There appears a long wait, through the blank space between stanzas, before the voice reemerges with remarkable uninsistence in the word *uninnocent* followed by a pause, another blank. In *uninnocent*, breathy, with so many vowels and the soft "n's" strung through the word, the voice is barely there and has barely begun before it disappears in the following caesura (*CP* 76).

This radical discontinuity between the gentleness of the reporting voice and the "tumult" of the other voices creates some curious effects.

The speaker who is reporting the conversation appears distant and detached from an interior drama to which she has privileged and intimate access. Thus, there are not just two voices in this "interior" but actually three, given the implied third consciousness or voice of the speaker, who must also be inside or close by the heart. The strange locution of *"no one* could tell the difference," when the speaker must mean that the speaker herself cannot tell the difference, gives off the sense that the speaker has no special status in her own heart but is as unlikely as anyone on the outside to be able to distinguish between these two voices on the basis of tone. Thus, multiple voices inside the self are too close (essentially indistinguishable from one another because the answerer and the tumultuous questioner cannot be distinguished from one another), while, simultaneously, the stanza implicitly asserts that there are multiple voices in the self so removed from one another that one can watch the others as if she were a stranger to them (the passionless reporting voice that observes the "tumult"). The effect is one of a tangle of voices, so intertwined or fused, that they cannot be distinguished; farther off, another voice, not part of the tangle, watches it from a position that cannot be located as entirely inside or outside, given that the intimate access cannot be distinguished from an outsider's lack of access. An interior boundary is hard to distinguish from an exterior one. Certainly, this distant "insider" has as little power as any self on the outside to affect this tangle of questioner/answerer. The extreme tranquility of the reporting voice conveys an utter resignation about the inevitable recurrence of this conversation. The reporter can do nothing but watch, although she is ostensibly inside the self. The strands of self bound together are simultaneously intimate and remote from one another, bound into one form and open in the other direction, at their "backs," to separate fields with no visible borders.

The first stanza produces an almost complete absence of an "I" because the "I" has the status of "no one" and because it appeared to be remote from the other contents of the self, as if witnessing its own inner thoughts and feelings, as if not in the same "place" as itself. There are many objects and forces in the interior, and the "I" is only one of them. In the second stanza, the self appears to be invaded, but softly, as if something else is seeping in or, rather, up through:

> Uninnocent, these conversations start,
> and then engage the senses,

only half-meaning to.
and then there is no choice,
and then there is no sense. (*CP* 76)

The story of this stanza tells of an engulfing of the "I" that previously was somewhat distant from the drama taking place in another part of the interior. The engulfing occurs with volition in an in-between state. The voices only "half-[mean]" to do what they do. They lean toward or allow rather than intend to initiate a forbidden action or open a sequence. The in-betweenness—the middle state between willed and involuntary action—is produced by the double negative of *uninnocent* (which implies some volition) and by the missing agent of the action ("these conversations" just "start" rather than anyone beginning them). There is a seeping through from layer to layer of the self, as voice, which began without actual choice but with some degree of intentionality, "engage[s] the senses" and then falls completely away from will ("And then there is no choice") and falls away from the ability to think ("And then there is no sense") (*CP* 76).

The theme of lines or spaces merging and then diverging, an indistinguishability, continues in this stanza, not only in the ambivalence about that which is voluntary or involuntary, innocent or guilty, but also in the very nature of the self that cannot separate—and actually becomes the site of crossing for—the strands of vague prelinguistic desire, linguistic interior conversation, physical and erotic sensation, will, and intellect. These areas bleed into one another or across one another's boundaries. In its brevity, the third stanza ("until a name / and all its connotation are the same") conveys a falling out of "choice" (*CP* 76). The voice is simply taken over by a phenomenon and ends. Nothing more to be said. Event complete. The saga of an interior conversation, with its tangle of voices and emotions, has come to a close. We realize that the reporting self will no longer be able to distinguish anything to report in the welter of connotations that has now been sucked in, whirlwind-like, into a name that will be so "full" that it can no longer function as part of linguistically articulated thought. Rather than falling away into a blankness, the poem ends with the voice swallowed up into a fullness. It is too saturated for any "figures" to be distinguished.

The voice of the speaker, which earlier had nearly faded out and only so lightly—so passionlessly—started up again, merely drops away.

The quickening of the rhythm in "And then there is no choice, / and then there is no sense" betrays the quiet, passionless resignation of the reporting voice and enacts its "trauma" by allowing us to feel the "conversation" sweep the remote "I" into the feelings of the tumult so that we feel the rush of all the "connotations" of the lover's name; all the emotions, questions, resistances, and desires flow into the "name" (*CP* 76). The boundary between the remote "I" that was also inside the self, but to which it had incomplete access, now experiences the rush of emotion about which previously it had only been reporting. We feel the figure that had been distinct fall into the ground of the self and become part of its substance.

"Conversation" enacts the emergence of desire and voice from inside the mind. They are experienced seeping up from silence or blankness, quickening and then dying away, falling into and out of volition and recognition. Desire, sensation, language, and volition bleed across one another's boundaries. Voices and desires expand or degrade, swell up and diminish in volume or intensity, are remote from one another and then fall into one another, becoming indistinguishable.

The second poem in the sequence, "Rain towards Morning," imagines the same kind of events but across different kinds of boundaries. No longer located inside one mind/body, this poem holds two lovers and a landscape. Just as the voices and desires of "Conversation" appeared to seep up from regions beneath the level of discrimination or awareness, so too in "Rain towards Morning" something is released as if opening up from inside a field. The field is both the air that surrounds the lovers (or is outside their bedroom) and their own bodies. The poem's own "body" reiterates the feeling of release because it moves like a sonnet. Although it is too truncated to complete the traditional fourteen lines, the poem moves through a sonnet-like sequence, a kind of opening up, then a volta, and then a "solution" or closing down.

In the first sequence of images, the bars of a cage that would normally mark the boundary between an inside and an outside are all "outside" in the air.

> The great light cage has broken up in the air,
> freeing, I think, about a million birds
> whose wild ascending shadows will not be back,
> and all the wires come falling down. (*CP* 77)

The "light cage" is without materiality, without substance, and has no location but is everywhere. It appears and disappears by a kind of airy emulsion. Even the "birds" that have been released may be birds without materiality, may be only shadows that ascend *like* birds. "Answering" this ascension, in an opposite motion ("wires come falling down"), a new cage emerges. The rain cage has more substance than light, an even denser materiality than rain would normally possess. One cage has "broken up in the air," dispersed from no central point into an everywhere, and another cage has emerged from the air, producing "wires" that fill the space. Whereas "Conversation" enacted the insistence of voices and desires emerging from a background blank of silence, "Rain towards Morning" enacts the disappearance, dispersal, and emergence of light, shadows, and rain from a background blank of air. Atmosphere itself, without boundary, just seems to open ("the rain is brightening now"; *CP* 77). Likewise, from the bodies/minds of the two lovers on the bed, a release and a brightening emerges. The movements and desires have no locatable origin but softly erupt all over the (seemingly deep) surface. The outdoors has boundaries everywhere (light that has multiple bars like a cage and rain composed of multiple wires). The indoors or interiors of bodies also have multiple interior boundaries or membranes, up through which sensations or emotions emerge or erupt.

The multiple locations of boundaries, both internal and external, make it impossible to mark any one line as the boundary between inside and outside. This mobility of boundary lines is marked linguistically by the ambiguity of pronouns and their referents in "Rain towards Morning," an ambiguity absolutely anomalous in Bishop's poetry. I can think of only one other example of such ambiguity, in "In the Waiting Room," in which Bishop allows *from inside* to refer both to inside the dentist's office (from where Aunt Consuelo may be screaming) and inside the speaker's body (from which a scream may have arisen (*CP* 160). As in "In the Waiting Room," the lack of clear referents in "Rain towards Morning" is purposive. The "face," like the communal "their" of "their prison" belongs to *both or either* of the lovers.

> The face is pale
> that tried the puzzle of their prison
> and solved it with an unexpected kiss,
> whose freckled unsuspected hands alit. (*CP* 77)

The lines deliver a set of surprises. The first surprise: the lovers are in a prison, and the prison is a shared space. The second surprise: they are both inside the prison, yet one lover can free the other *as if* from outside. As in "Conversation," separate beings who are in some sense remote from one another appear located inside one interior. The third surprise: a prison can be unlocked from the inside. The unlocking or release emerges from nowhere, out of the air. The kiss is "unexpected" both by the one who receives it and by the one who gives it. Again, the ambiguity of referent is purposive. Does the kiss release the other person's hands to move, eliciting the answering gestures that constitute the lovers' approach to one another? Or do hands, alighting on one person's body, alight (elicit or provoke) the gesture of a kiss? The extreme ambiguity of *unsuspected*, married in internal slant rhyme to *unexpected*, allows the owner of the hands to be as surprised by the action of those hands as she was by the kiss.

Like "Conversation," this poem explores a blurred area between volition and "happening to." The owners of bodies are surprised by their own movements, as well as by their partners' movements. Emotions are released upward or outward from inside the body as well as from outside, elicited by the "face" of a lover or a landscape. A whole body can experience a "brightening" that emerges from within or is touched off by a gesture from without. Partly because no house or walls are mentioned, the boundary between landscape and lovers has dropped away, and it feels as if the lovers are located outdoors. But more than being located outdoors, the bodies and minds of the lovers feel like the material of the landscape and atmosphere. The paleness of the face, the way that the "prison" of the shared face moves into love, feels like the "face" of the atmosphere in "the rain / is brightening now" (*CP* 77). In the opening of the poem, light is arriving (or leaving, that too is ambiguous) and initiating movement but in a soft all-over effect; so too, the kiss and the hands open into movement from stillness. Light emerges, movement emerges, and love or desire emerges—eruption up through a surface that suddenly acquires depth or becomes aware of itself as deep.

These bodies, minds, atmospheres have boundaries that open to other internal or external forms, open "all over," open from within, and have internal events that interact with an outside across an intermittent or missing membrane. The figures do not bound an object in a stable way; the contour that bounds the shape melts away or turns to interact with or bound another. Both poems conduct an anatomy of kinds of boundaries, multiple and not privileging the "line" at skin or wall of the house or around the "I." In "Conversation," distinguishing and being indistinguishable, even inside the self, becomes the first theme, as the voices inside the self (which are not as distinct as voices because they are turbulent and mangled) veer close and then away, like two lines diverging and converging. In "Rain towards Morning," the lovers, the atmosphere, and the reader experience the falling away of something, or the unfolding or opening of something, that feels like a release. Coming down or closing down is followed by opening out, a brightening that is also an opening up from inside a field. It is as if space itself can open out to something, fold open at all its interior edges, and as if a body or mind can do the same. Skin itself becomes just one of many membranes that can be crossed through, both by internal and external movements or changes.

In the third poem of the sequence, "While Someone Telephones," the central moment, the volta, enacts another opening out from within a field. Like "Rain towards Morning," the field is partly the atmosphere itself, the landscape. But, strangely, time also becomes a kind of atmosphere and a field that can open out. The complex nature of the field is produced in the title and opening two lines, in which Bishop ambiguously attaches "barbaric condescension" both to the "minutes" themselves and to a person who is using the telephone in a hallway while the speaker waits.

> III / While Someone Telephones
> Wasted, wasted minutes that couldn't be worse,
> minutes of a barbaric condescension. (*CP* 78)

The emotion "barbaric condescension" has spread out across multiple kinds of objects—time and a person. The minutes themselves seem to contain the "barbaric condescension" because Bishop says "minutes of a barbaric condescension." Because minutes are not usually given the ability to be condescending, the quality begins to roam in search of an owner. It can appear to derive from the stranger who is using the telephone while the speaker waits either to receive or to make a call. The quite conventional politeness of someone who is using a telephone while someone else is waiting feels to the desperate speaker as a kind of "barbaric condescension" (*CP* 78). Last, the quality can "roam" even further and attach itself to the person whom the speaker expects to eventually reach on the telephone. Given the placement of the poem in a sequence of four poems about a difficult relationship, we can surmise that the speaker anticipates a conversation with a person whose polite condescension can only feel barbaric to the speaker, who loves beyond that level of politeness.

The emotion "barbaric condescension" therefore has a kind of all-over feel to it. It comes at the speaker from the landscape, from the minutes through which she is living, from the vague shape of a stranger down the hall, and from the disembodied lover who is anticipated to appear on the other end of the line. Playing with sonnet form, the poem's volta involves the emergence of a feeling of release or a solution to this all-over feeling of "barbaric condescension." In the middle of the poem, the speaker, who never rises close enough to the surface of the mind to speak the word "I" and who hangs in a blank space that is also blank time, feels a release.

The wasteland of the opening lines ("Wasted, wasted minutes that couldn't be worse") first descends into a bitterer space than waste, filled by the malice of an environment out the bathroom window, where "fir-trees" can be seen with "their dark needles, accretions to no purpose." The enlarged eyes of the speaker, implied by the strongly accentuated verb *stare* at the start of the line ("Stare out the bathroom window at the fir-trees"), seem too dangerously close to the needles, accentuating the threat of the landscape. This dark and menacing landscape becomes the place "where two fireflies / are only lost." The *only* heightens the sense of emptiness and waste, implying either that the only beings that this landscape can hold are "two fireflies" or that the fireflies can only ever be in the condition "lost." In this empty and menacing landscape, the speaker can "hear nothing" and, with the same strange in-betweenness of description as imperative that we found in "stare," she seems to *command* herself to "hear nothing." The only sound the landscape can hold is a highly tense one, in fact "tension" itself ("Hear nothing but a train that goes by, must go by, like tension; / *nothing*. And wait:"). The field of the waiting speaker is crossed by a highly pitched, highly wrought "tension" that does pass away, leaving in its wake, again, the "nothing" of the opening of the poem. The "wasted, wasted minutes" have been interrupted only by the emergence of something worse. Although the minutes "couldn't be worse," they immediately became worse by the malice of the fir trees' needles, the sensation of other creatures who are "only lost," and a train whistle "like tension." The truncated line *"nothing*. And wait:" with its two full stops and extremely emphatic *nothing* at the start of the line, produces only emptiness. The strange elision of the subject pronoun "I," leaving only the emphatic verbs *stare* and *hear*, produces the subject as an empty but tense field without any firm boundaries. The self is composed of an unbounded open "stare" and "hear," which are filled by the up-close looming of the fir trees and the attenuated waiting for the sound of the train whistle (*CP* 78).

Out of this blank space, which is also blank time, emerges the "host" of that nothingness, as if stepping out from behind landscape, time, and emotion—the fields that had held the speaker up until this point.

> Hear nothing but a train that goes by, must go by, like
> tension;
> *nothing*. And wait:
> maybe even now these minutes' host
> emerges, some relaxed uncondescending stranger,
> the heart's release. (*CP* 78)

One plane moves away to reveal its "host." It is as if the stranger was occluded before but now steps out into the foreground and reveals that he has, all along, been the "ground" of these other figures, the "place" from which that atmosphere had its origin, and because he is nothing like what he had seemed, the landscape (both outer and inner) is transformed. Just as in "Rain towards Morning," an atmosphere "brightens." The despair that had formerly suffused the speaker's response to catching sight of the fireflies "only lost" in the trees becomes merely a ground or condition that holds, potentially, in "maybe" position, the lover's warmth and his "green gay eyes": "And while the fireflies / are failing to illuminate these nightmare trees / might they not be his green gay eyes" (*CP* 78).

The unfolding of a plane or figure emerges from a ground that was itself the figure to some other ground. Figures, atmospheres, landscapes, and emotions fold out into one another, becoming "host[s]" for one another's emergence or transformation. The "surround" of the outdoor landscape, the feeling of waiting and nothingness, the sound of the train whistle "held" the speaker as a background loosely holds within itself a figure. But now the ground itself is strangely shown to have been held all along by another ground, and that one is not diffused like a landscape or like nothingness but concentrated in the shape of a person, a "host." Whether the simple ending of his own telephone call, passing the opportunity to the desperate speaker, has "turned" him in her eyes from barbaric to generous host or whether, in the interim, the speaker has actually reached her lover and found *him* to be warm rather than condescending, the poem does not make clear. Because, just as the stranger who uses the telephone can shift almost instantaneously from barbarian to host, the anticipated conversation partner can move from the position of stranger (someone who could potentially treat the speaker with barbaric condescension) to the position of host of welcome, warmth, and gaiety that would mark him as lover: "might they not be his green gay eyes" (*CP* 78). This shift occurs on the aural level in the movement from *lost* to *host* and on the visual level by the shift from eyes that "stare" at emptiness to eyes that convey human warmth and love.[7]

As we might expect, the fourth poem in the sequence, "O Breath," draws on, varies, and extends the development of the themes and techniques in the preceding three poems. Again, we find Bishop using a technique that is completely anomalous in her oeuvre—typographical indicators of blank spaces that occur within the line. Like "Conversation," the first poem in the sequence, which shows a voice that emerges out of and fades back into the blank "canvas" of silence that precedes the eruption of poetic voice, in "O Breath" the poetic voice fades out of and back into existence from silence. At each break in the line, the voice appears capable of simply never going on or, at least, lapses into a momentary silence where an implied nonthinking nonlinguistic substratum of self subsists.

> Beneath that loved and celebrated breast,
> silent, bored really blindly veined,
> grieves, maybe lives and lets
> live, passes bets (*CP* 79)

The rhythmic, almost rhetorical opening ("Beneath that loved and celebrated breast") becomes, after "silent" only a kind of mumble ("bored really blindly veined"). There is a sense of something rising to excitement and then dissolving, rippling away. The thought of the poem has a zigzag feel, the speaker capable of changing her mind almost completely within the space of one word ("grieves, maybe lives and lets / live"). From the little energetic push and certainty of opening the line with "grieves," the idea becomes marked as little better than a wishful conjecture ("maybe") and then to a supposition that the lover is so indifferent as to hold the attitude toward the other of a mere "live and lets live." The "line" of thought begins to move in one direction and then undercuts or reverses, veering 90 degrees or even 180 degrees. Intensity becomes conjecture and ends in something much diminished—to be "let live" by a lover is not to be loved. The strange phrase "passes bets" diminishes the negotiations of the love affair, from the point of view of the other, to a kind of card game in which one can "pass" and then "bet" on another, future companion (CP 79). The sweep of a rhetorical line dissipates here, cannot "get going," peters out, and has to restart itself from zero.

Corresponding to the crucial human and lovers' question, "What moves you?" the poem considers a speaker/lover's attempt to divine the tiniest of movements in the other, signs of that other's desire or interior life. Movement of the heart at its most intimate is placed next to/against physical movement in its most intimate, minutest manifestation—the breath and the quivering of hairs on the skin. It is as if Bishop wishes to explore the actual membrane between emotional and physical life (emotional and physical movement). Beginning with "something moving," "beneath," we feel the quickening hope of the speaker's ability to sense the movement of the other, to catch a glimpse of the interior of the other, his desire, his heart. However, the hope is undercut immediately, in that zigzag shape of thought, by the close of the line, "something moving but invisibly"; the movement is sensed but not actually seen. The rhythm of the speaker's voice and thoughts expand and contract like breath, as if the mind and body are moving together. The dynamics increases ("and with what clamor") and diminishes ("why restrained"). The barrier between the lovers grows dense and diminishes, opens and closes down. The boundary line between the two lovers is itself moving, expanding and contracting, becoming solid and then lighter and more diffused: "Something moving [I can sense you, your interior] but invisibly [no, it's closed to me] / and with what clamor [I can hear your interior] why restrained [no, it's not loud enough and I don't understand its movement] / I cannot fathom [I cannot go deeply enough into you] even a ripple." The only rippling movement that the speaker can sense is actually her own, her own voice and breath, her words creating a rippling effect ("even a ripple"). The materiality of the speaker's own emotions and voice, inflating from whisper to insistence and dropping away again (to "even a ripple" and then silence), becomes the skin or membrane of her boundary interaction with the skin/breath of the lover's body and his interior (*CP* 79). The "canvas" of the poem is slashed or interrupted by the sometimes painfully delayed pauses between breaths. The surface of the poem's own words becomes a kind of body that breathes and stops breathing, a surface that is also strangely the membrane or ever-shifting boundary "line" between the two people lying so close to one another.

Refused entry to the interior of the other, the speaker retreats to contemplate the membrane between them—the skin and the items on the skin that appear to reveal movement and so might "mean" a revelation of the interior. Yet the "thin flying," the tiniest of signs, actually reveals only something that has already become exterior to the lover, his exhaling breath. The closest that she can come is skin, or the movement on the skin, the exterior part (the hairs) that, while part of the lover's body, are moved by something at least emerging from the interior, his breath. In spite of its humorous reworking of Catullus's jealousy over the little bird that can touch the girl's hand while Catullus cannot (after all, Bishop here is jealous of nine black hairs around two nipples), the poem's tone here is more grieving than risible. The depth of regret is expressed by the *intolerably*, which cannot comfortably be retained only as modifier of the hairs' flying and attaches itself to the speaker herself, who finds the remoteness from the other intolerable (*CP* 79).

During the course of the poem, the question has shifted. "What moves you?" (a question that has lying behind it, "Do you love me?") becomes "Is it possible ever for me to know what moves you?" and later, "Is it possible for me ever to enter inside you?" "Equivocal" is Bishop's answer to all three questions: undecided, of uncertain disposition. The togetherness of lovers, their ability to "become one," is under the most intense and closest scrutiny. In the zigzag motion that we have come to expect in the poem, a little burst of hope, the assumption of intimacy in "what we have in common," is undercut immediately by a reminder that the speaker cannot know, has no access, and is left merely with the ambivalence of conjecture ("bound to be there"). Closeness becomes only "own[ing] equivalents for" an unnamed, unknown, presumed "whatever," a "something." The "something" then becomes the ground, or "host," with which the speaker could "bargain," "make a separate peace beneath," even position herself "within," but that place "within," inside the other, will not be a "with" (*CP* 79). Even inside the boundary of the other, the speaker will not be close enough.

Thus, the circle of the four-poem sequence closes with a structure similar to the first poem's "Conversation"—one entity inside another, intimate within it but also remote from it. In "Conversation," multiple voices inside the interior of one body/mind become tangled, indistinguishable, while another "interior" voice stands as a remote bystander and witness. Intimacy and remoteness exist inside one person. In "O Breath," intimacy and remoteness occur across the thinnest possible membrane between two people. For a moment, imagined or projected but felt, the two people are "within" one membrane, but they remain remote from one another, not "with" one another. The location (between or within) and quality (thickness, fuzziness, or translucency) of the boundary line itself keeps modulating. Skin, hair, heart, breath, thought, and emotion each can act as both boundary line, barrier, interior membrane, or enclosing shape that can turn to include more or exclude much.

FIVE

"COMPOSING MOTIONS"

Alexander Calder, "Gypsophilia," "A Cold Spring,"
"The Moose," and "North Haven"

> Our bodies are still cardinal but the separation of this cardinality
> from the presumed larger order of the world is one of the
> fundamental things characterizing us as modern.
>
> —David Summers, *Real Spaces*

Bishop had trouble selling "Four Poems," and she associated the poems with despair (letter from Bishop to Loren MacIver, August 12, 1949, VSC). In the early 1950s, both before and after she moved to Brazil, she deployed Alexander Calder's aesthetic as an antidote to the radical disintegration and mobility enacted in her four-poem sequence. She seems to have used Calder's hanging mobiles as a means of imagining a kind of coherence that could stabilize or organize mobility without betraying it. Bishop's use of a geometrical three-dimensional space to counteract the disorientation from materials falling into one another can be glimpsed in "Sunday, 4 A.M." In this poem, Bishop again imagines human subjectivity, like the surface of verse, as a mobile interface opening toward other materials and environments, other registers of experience. She arranges "dream dream confronting," where the dreamscape of Brueghal's painting *The Crucifixion* coincides, momentarily with the speaker's dream of that painting. The "meeting" of dream and painting glance off one another, coinciding and diverging: "cross- and wheel-studded" accoutrements of the crucifixion glance off the twentieth-century iconography of "tick-tack-toe"; the "Mary"s of the Christian story are held in some strange aslant relation to the ordinary "Mary"s who have occurred in the speaker's life, the rusty nails of the crucifixion appear as rusty nails in the speaker's own kitchen, and the "wail" of human grief at the crucifixion turns into a memory from the speaker's childhood. The hinge of the poem ("Turn on the light. Turn over"), when the speaker wakes, makes the facing surfaces of painting and dream, in their coinciding and diverging, encounter or "confront" another surface—the everyday reality of the speaker's bedroom. The "black-and-gold gesso" of the cat's "smutch" makes the arena of the altarpiece painting and painter's gesso coincide momentarily with the "altered cloth" of the bedsheet. The violence of the crucifixion occurs as/ diverges from the cat's murder of a moth; the flooded lowlands in the dream occur transformed or translated into the "brook feel[ing] for the stair." The wavering and mobility of these momentary aslant similarities across dream, painting, and bedroom come to some momentary standstill only when the turn toward the outside of the bedroom is fixed in place by a "bird [who] arranges / two notes at right angles" (CP 129–30). The spatial geometry or border provided by these sounds, like the temporal border of the beginning of the day, encloses the experience in a frame that stabilizes or pauses the movements across these multiple interfaces, so putting an end to the sequence of the troubled night. These planes of experience—dream, painting, the far distance of a childhood memory, and physically lying in bed inside a house—hold still for a moment and cease falling into one another's extents.

In a 1959 letter to Ilse Barker, Bishop claimed that she could visualize "almost every" Calder that she had seen exhibited in Pittsfield, Massachusetts, almost thirty years before: "his very first mobiles, that had cranks, or little electric motors. We spoke of this show the last time he was here [in Brazil]—and it was funny how many of the pieces I could still remember, so it must have made a big impression (September 30, 1959, PUL).[1] She also stressed the vividness of her long-term memory of that exhibition when writing to Anne Stevenson in 1964 (March 6, 1964, WUL).[2] Whether or not Margaret Miller accompanied Bishop to that exhibition in 1933, some of Bishop's knowledge of Calder probably came from Miller, who worked for James Johnson Sweeney, the most important early advocate for Calder's work in the United States. In 1943, Sweeney arranged for the sculptor to hold a one-man show at the MoMA, and Miller worked with Sweeney on the catalogue of the exhibition, the first comprehensive analysis of Calder's work. Given Bishop's interest in Calder and her friendship with Miller, we can assume that Bishop was quite familiar both with Sweeney's descriptions and with the mid-century critical reception of Calder. Later, Bishop had access to the writings of Henrique Mindlin and Mário Pedrosa, the most influential Brazilian critics of Calder. Even their commentary that preceded Bishop's arrival in Brazil would probably have been available to Bishop because Lota had played a prominent role in Calder's reception in Brazil (Saraiva 84).[3] Drawing on her experience of Calder's work and these mid-century critical responses to Calder, Bishop creatively transformed the work of Alexander Calder, using his hanging mobiles to conceptualize lyric structure and orient the lyric speaker. We can see particularly strong evidence of the poet's incorporating features of Calder's aesthetic in "Arrival at Santos," "Armadillo," "Gypsophilia," and "A Cold Spring." Moreover, some of Bishop's strongest late poems—"The Moose" and "North Haven"—gain their beauty and power from Bishop's having combined in them the aesthetics of Schwitters's "interpermeating materials" and Calder's "composing motions." By drawing on these aesthetics, Bishop reimagined the structures by which lyric poetry can incorporate event into continuity, unfurl or open toward emotion, orchestrate movements from minimal to abundant, and set the willed and the unwilled in relationship to one another. In these poems, she creates containers in which the lyric speaker is poised within a larger space of unknown dimensions from which unwilled events drift into the space of the self but where elements can also be held apart or arranged. Stability can incline toward freedom, pleasure, anxiety, or grief without overwhelming or collapsing the space of the lyric speaker.

Calder's Aesthetic and His Mid-Century Reception

The pieces that Bishop remembered so vividly from Pittsfield were Calder's early small mobile sculptures, "some of the constructions were driven by small electric motors, others were moved by tiny hand cranks" (Sweeney 1943, 30). In the catalogue for that show, Calder announced his program: "Why not plastic forms in motion? Not a simple translatory or rotary motion but several motions of different types, speeds and amplitudes composing to make a resultant whole. Just as one can compose colors, or forms, so one can compose motions" (Calder). Explicating his work in 1932, Calder had emphasized that he was composing by setting the disparate kinds of motions in changing relation to one another: "Each element can move, shift, or sway back and forth in a changing relation to each of the other elements in this universe. Thus they reveal not only isolated moments, but a physical law of variation among the events of life" (quoted in Giménez and Rower 47). Calder's remark makes clear that, although the mobiles drew on the motion of planets and constellations, they had a wider relevance, illustrative of the intersecting trajectories and shifting relations between objects, motions, and events of lived realities. Mário Pedrosa and Pietro Maria Bardi, Brazilian critics, emphasized the insertion of the mobiles in architectural and natural environments, the sculptures' becoming part of lived realities (Saraiva 33, 74).

In her watercolor of the room in Samambaia that holds one of Lota's Calder mobiles, Bishop slips the mobile into the environment in such a way that she reinforces Calder's view that his mobiles captured the cross-rhythms and disparate shapes of parts of the environment (Bishop 1996, 65).[4] Bishop draws attention to the play of shapes in the room that "answer" the mobile's shapes. The closed rectangular stove, with its filled-in volume of heavy black, is poised against the lightness and openness of the mobile. With its closed shapes arranged in a "spray," the Calder mobile occupies a middle realm between a series of pictures on the back wall of the room, each enclosed by a prominently outlined rectangular frame, and a spangle of dotted flowers, an open spray, in a vase in front of the wall. Bishop situates the little stove-door opener next to the Calder mobile so that it hangs at the same height as the center of gravity of the mobile. This little tool is composed of line, curve, and circle, with a blank middle resembling the open-holed sphere of the Calder shape closest to it. Positioned so that it is at the same height as the middle of the Calder, the mechanism of the stove pipe, which can move and open, draws attention to the qualities that the stove and the mobile share across their immense differences. The arrangement of shapes in the painting conveys Bishop's sense that any environment can be experienced as one of Calder's hanging mobiles.

The reception of Calder at mid-century helps to characterize the nature of that aesthetic and lived experience. Midway between closed geometric shape and open organic biomorphic form, the Calder mobile, according to mid-century art criticism, acted as a conciliator in the split between the geometric and the biomorphic that prominently structured the art scene at mid-century. To see Calder as associated with but deviating from the school of geometric abstraction was a commonplace in the 1940s, especially after Robert Motherwell's recapping of the famous report of Calder's visit to Piet Mondrian's studio, which appeared in the winter 1944 *Partisan Review*: "I was very much moved by Mondrian's studio, large beautiful, and irregular as it was, with the walls painted white, and divided by black lines and rectangles of bright color . . . like his paintings . . . and I thought at the time how fine it would be if everything MOVED" (Motherwell 1944, 97). Like Paul Klee, Calder was seen as inventing an alternative aesthetic to Mondrian's, partly because he combined biomorphic and geometric shapes and partly because of his use of the "wandering line" that broke loose from Mondrian's straight-lined geometric forms. The sketchiness of Calder's line in his early wire sculptures, like Klee's wandering line, became associated with the human qualities of tentativeness and hesitation.[5] These qualities continued to be linked to Calder, even in the later mobiles, because of the hesitation and "waiting" as one element hovered before taking on speed and direction when impelled by a neighboring element. In a 1947 catalogue for Buchholz, later reproduced in multiple locales, Jean-Paul Sartre wrote: "The 'mobile' . . . weaves uncertainly, hesitates, and at times appears to begin its movement anew, as if it had caught itself in a mistake" (quoted in Giménez and Rower 70).[6] Calder's work seemed to his critics to gather the qualities of improvisation and human frailty, partly in opposition to the coldness and certainty implied in the straight-edged geometric abstractions of the followers of Mondrian. In that hesitation and improvisation, critics perceived a sense of freedom from constraint in opposing the straight-lined tradition.

Calder, however, set tentativeness, hesitation, and improvisation inside an organized three-dimensional deep space, where an observer experienced more than just fluidity and flux. Compared to Bishop's first attempt in "Pleasure Seas" to think through the issues of the amoeba versus the square as tidal currents versus a still rectangular pool, Calder's mobiles allowed an organized experience of disparate relations among still and moving objects that ascended and descended, moved out and in, and curved around in different directions. Calder placed the observer among "floating motifs." The "motifs," Calder's orbiting shapes, literally floated above the observer's head, like Paul Klee's "fish swimming in all directions" (Hayter 130). Yet the floating elements were organized by their relations to one another. Sweeney asserts that "the organization of contrasting movements and changing relations of form[s] in space" was "the first feature of [Calder's] new approach" in creating the hanging mobiles (1943, 30). Gabrielle Buffet-Picabia emphasizes Calder's "extraordinary command of the interaction between weight and motion" and describes the way that the sculptor arranged elements' responsiveness to other elements (quoted in Giménez and Rower 68).[7] In his own writing, Calder emphasizes that he composed by arranging disparities: "Disparity in form, color, size, weight, motion, is what makes a composition" (quoted in Giménez and Rower 59). Some commentators include sound as one of the elements ("sounds of a thin metallic nature emerging from the scarcely touching forms"; Janis 28). Amid these disparities, Calder manages to create a place for the observer, a position inside the mobile structure so that the viewer imagines him- or herself set inside this space of changing relations. The observer has a place in the "field" without the observer's having given rise to the motions. There is a sense of the observer suspended among objects with different weights and trajectories, part of a system in which these elements impact one another. The system allows the observer to sense the disparities between the elements so that the randomness and "accidents" feel peaceful, gentle, and orderly without becoming fixed or rigid.

Partly because of that gentleness, freshness, and surprise, in the 1940s Calder began to be associated with pleasure and buoyancy at a time when the country struggled with the experience of the war. Almost as though he himself were an element in one of his mobiles, Calder was seen as a counterweight to that grief (Marter 202). Sweeney and others spoke of Calder's humor, playfulness, and vitality (again, this feature became prominent, particularly in contrast to Mondrian's emphasis on formal relations as geometric). Sartre declares that, "A 'mobile', one might say, is a little private celebration" (quoted in Giménez and Rower 69). In 1950, Marcel Duchamp pays tribute to this pleasure and characterizes it more precisely: "Through their way of counteracting gravity by gentle movements, they seem to 'carry their own particular pleasures. . . .'" (quoted in Giménez and

Rower 77). The sensation of pleasure arose partly because of the weightlessness and mobility of these floating elements but also in response to the freshness and surprise of not being able to predict the events that occurred. The most prominent Brazilian commentator, Henrique Mindlin, also characterizes Calder's mobiles as "contain[ing] a human, unexpected and joyful element that is Calder's own" (Mindlin, "Alexander," 55). This system, harboring spontaneity, playfulness, pleasure, humor, buoyancy, and a sense of private celebration, counteracted and replaced the more frightening characteristics of the "system" of a world that had moved to a scale too large to accommodate individual desire or defiance. Hesitation, then, had a humanist quality and gathered the sensation of freedom (one was not locked inside a rigid system; there was space for "wandering" and for surprise) as well as a sensation of gentleness and privacy. Suspension in space became expressive of a suspension in time, with its rich human variation of directions and speeds and openness to a (pleasantly) unpredictable future.

Bishop's Composing Motions

With the help of manuscripts in the Vassar Collection and the recently published volume edited by Alice Quinn, we can see Bishop's invention of a lyric structure and experimentation with a compositional method that resembles Calder's "composing motions." The poem "Gypsophilia," set in Samambaia after Bishop moved to Brazil in 1951, carries the title of two Calder mobiles from 1949 and 1950.[8] Calder's *Gypsophilia II* is extremely delicate. The mobile offers large spaces between small white circles and then a kind of spray of smaller circles, clusters of which move somewhat independently or in pairs. There is a sense of gentleness, balance, ascension and descent. Because of the asymmetrical arrangement, the center is off-balance. Some of the upward-tending wires look slanted or veering.

By titling her poem with the title of one of Calder's works, Bishop indicates that she is trying out a version of his mobile in her own medium. The poem draft "Gypsophilia" suspends the speaker (as "we") on top of a mountainside, in a field of shapes, sounds, and events above and below her that float toward and away in trajectories of varying speeds and directions. A dog's "*oblique* barks" float upward and sideways, as if "chop-chopping at the mountains with a hatchet" and then "flake off in yellow sparks." Far below, the "last clangs" of "somebody beat[ing] the hanging iron bar" at the orchid nursery, float away, as if off to sea. Floating upward, a "lighter" variant on that clanging, "A child's voice rises, hard and thin." Below the speaker, Manuelzinho's family is crossing at a "half-trot"; the parents each carry branches that make a variety of series of horizontals, moving in a swath. A "spray" appears: "each child with an enormous sheaf of Gypsophilia, baby's breath" (Bishop 2006, 128–29). In another draft of the poem not published by Quinn, Bishop arranges above the speaker a weightless "spray" of white stars balanced high above the gypsophilia carried by the children: "one can just make out / the tiny blossoms [of stars] glimmering white. . . . Now it is so dark / the tiny blossoms glimmering white / in systems of their own" (VSC 66.5). The poem ends with descending and ascending motions: Venus setting and a question rising.

Amid these "motions of different types, speeds, and amplitudes," the speaker herself is suspended but not motionless. She floats in a weightless three-dimensional field. The repeated but incrementally softer sounds from a bell-buoy's clang on water give off the sensation of the presumably sedentary speaker traveling, floating further away while standing still. Each object of attention resituates the consciousness of the speaker so that the "center" where the speaker is located "tips" in relation to another object or "moves off." The use of the word *sub-stratum* ("we're in / some cold sub-stratum of dew") repositions the speaker so that she appears to be at the bottom of a space while still above, high on the mountain. In another draft, she is suspended and borne: "in those minutely-blossoming sprays all about us, [we are] [c]aught up, somehow, and carried, carried." In this version, Bishop invents an image of condensation for the "we"—she imagines the "we" (the couple on the mountain or the Earth itself) as a small, dark, condensed black seed ("a dead black seed / caught somewhere / caught, somehow, and carried, carried / in those glimmering sprays about us.") Another variant ends: "we live aslant / an invisible round seed / caught up somehow, and carried, carried / fascicles / about us / borne in the fascicle." "Fascicle," the exfoliated, bursting shape of a flowers' stamens, characterizes our space; invisible at the center of a circle of a white spray of stars, we are suspended, borne along, "carried" (VSC 66.5). In this unpublished poem, Bishop seems to be experimenting with setting the lyric speaker as one of the elements in a Calder hanging mobile. The speaker is held and carried as a moving element among gently ascending, descending, and circling shape motifs that, condensing and unfurling, poising their disparate weights and motions, carry the timbre of gentleness, accident, and pleasure.

Being "borne" or carried, subjected to motions and set in a world of motions, does not always occur in the key of pleasure and balance. Calder's mobiles also involve a more robust "bump" as one element meets another in mid-trajectory. In Bishop's "Arrival at Santos," the speaker inhabits a Calder-like system, in which disparate elements appear seemingly out of nowhere and knock or move into other elements, sometimes with the humor that commentators mentioned frequently in their characterizations of Calder's work. The speaker and Miss Breen, climbing down the ladder backward, cross into the orbit of another more determined motion—the boat hook, which has suddenly swung into view as if from another part of the "mobile" and which then produces its effect (lifting Miss Breen from shipside to land). As in a Calder hanging mobile, objects appear on the horizon, their sources not seen; while the speaker and her friend are eating breakfast, from the margins of experience, from the periphery, floats in another element: "Finish your breakfast. The tender is coming, / a strange and ancient craft, flying a strange and brilliant rag" (CP 89). Like Calder, Bishop links suspense in time (the always being poised in one's own mental motion for the next event that will enter the "scene") with suspense in space (traveling on a trajectory that will "hit" or "be hit"):

> Oh, tourist,
> is this how this country is going to answer you
>
> and your immodest demands for a different world,
> and a better life, and complete comprehension
> of both at last, and immediately,
> after eighteen days of suspension? (CP 89)

In this pun, Bishop links the physical sensation of suspension (traveling toward a destination on a boat) to the existential one of human waiting and expectation, motioning toward, in desire. The lyric speaker moves on her own trajectory—of travel and of desire—toward other elements that have their own independent motions.

Whereas Calder's mobiles cannot easily incorporate human thought as an element of the mobile itself, in Bishop's linguistic medium, the speaker's thoughts enter as part of the set of objects acting on one another. Her thoughts "slip off" or away, set off in a little chain of one thing "knocking" another, from ports to other necessities like postage stamps or soap. Bishop calls our attention to the way that the elements participate in the "hesitation" or "uncertainty" that Sartre says characterizes the motion in Calder's work. The objects themselves and the lyric speaker's thoughts about them do not have enough self-assertiveness to make an impression. They are so unassertive that they cannot hold in place but move off ("slip," "waste"):

the unassertive colors of soap, or postage stamps—
wasting away like the former, slipping the way the latter

do when we mail the letters we wrote on the boat (*CP* 90)

The sequence resembles the movements in Calder's hanging mobiles—large motions (the trajectory of the ship moving South, the crane, the tender) set off a frisson of smaller shakes and shivers (the little quotidian items that cannot stay in place) and the speaker's "cascading" from one thought to another, resembling, in a lighter, smaller-scale register, the speaker's slipping from one locale to another. Postage stamps, soap, and glue ricochet off one another without actually "taking" or sticking. The little rustling movement of this cascade then ceases abruptly when a new trajectory "bumps" into it in mid-line: "We leave Santos at once; / we are driving to the interior" (*CP* 90). It is as if Bishop is "composing" by setting motions in relation to other motions, setting disparate levels of certainty and hesitation in the speaker's mind in a field of objects that move with varying degrees of certainty. A new kind of motion enters the "picture" at the end, one with more initiative, less gentle and more in a straight line.

As we see in chapter 2, Bishop's poem, "On the 'Prince of Fundy,'" draws on some excerpts from Klee published by Margaret Miller in which thought and feeling ascend in the midst of, and in relation to, a collection of other kinds of motions. In that poem, too, the last line emerges from the matrix of circling and ascending shapes to move off, forcefully, in a straight line. It seems as though Bishop was experimenting with closure for the lyric—how to produce a sense of an ending from a drifting or wandering set of images and occurrences by bringing in a more forceful movement at the end. Calder provided Bishop with a more fluid means of translating Klee's ideas about multiple trajectories and "fish swimming in all directions" into lyric structure. Calder's work allows for lyric images and verse lines, with their disparate weights and trajectories, to be arranged as events emerging in responsiveness to other events, arising from and moving into one another. Whereas Klee's excerpts and his paintings with floating motifs tend to produce an evenly distributed set of experiences through which the observer floats, Calder's mobiles clarify the role of relative weights of elements and dynamics of pace and timing, a slow drift followed by a stronger jolt, or vice versa.

In "The Armadillo," Bishop is clearly "composing motions," including even the "breeze that disturbs [the mobile and] configures it differently at each moment" (Mindlin, "Calder," 123). Bishop may have been responding to a small brochure from the 1948 exhibit in which Pietro Maria Bardi announces: "In a few days, Alexander Calder will be planting his superlative equations of color, shape and balance in our halls; in some countries where the curiously-shaped colored paper balloons of St. John's day represent 'abstractionist release and aspiration' for the majority of the population, the mobiles will be warmly, or even enthusiastically received" (Bardi 148). Delicately composing the vagaries of movement in verse lines that lift, drift, and hover, Bishop arranges for the "frail, illegal fire balloons" to appear and rise, "flush and fill with light / that comes and goes," and "with a wind, / . . . flare and falter, wobble and toss." The "Venus going down" arranged against the balloons that, when the wind disappears, "steer [straight up] between / the kite sticks of the Southern Cross" orchestrates human-made shapes balancing against or moving among the cosmic ones. One action releases a corresponding but disparate motion, varying by speed, direction, and weight: a flame runs down; a pair of owls fly up; when the armadillo "left the scene," "a baby rabbit jumped out, / *short*-eared, to our surprise." Bishop arranges the shapes and motions with the lyric speaker oriented in the midst of these disparate trajectories: fire balloons "receding, dwindling, solemnly / and steadily forsaking *us*" (emphasis added). The motion is felt as a moving away from a (tipped) center. The orientation produces a sense of potential (unrealized) threat to the speaker from the sudden and "dangerous" "downdraft from a peak." The rising up of objects from other motions ("owls who nest there flying up / and up, their whirling black-and-white" visible "until they shrieked up out of sight") creates a structure that prepares for the surprise emergence of an even fiercer movement at the end of the poem, "weak mailed fist / clenched ignorant against the sky" (*CP* 103–4). As is true of most of the other objects in the poem, we do not know previously about the existence of this creature who "speaks" in motions at the end. Again, the close of the lyric brings in from an unseen periphery an unpredicted, more solid, and straight-lined and forceful movement.

Clearly, Bishop had begun to experiment with translating Calder's aesthetic into her own poetry even before she came to Brazil. With the title poem "A Cold Spring," written in 1950, Bishop opened her second volume of poems in the "space" of one of the later Calder mobiles. Although there are moments in this poem when a small motor or spring generates movement, the atmosphere of the poem more often contains the gentler trajectories and sense of suspension characteristic of Calder's mature hanging mobiles from the 1940s. After hesitation and delay, elements rise freely and spontaneously out of other sets of relations, and the whole "constellation" is associated with pleasure and offers Sartre's sense of a "private celebration." The pieces in the poem incline from inertness to wavering and then to a freshness and surprise, prominently allied with pleasure. The lyric speaker is situated within this constellation not just as observer but as one among the unequally weighted shifting elements.

"A Cold Spring" orients the lyric speaker as a heavier and more stable element within the curving, ascending, and descending, and shifting relations of shapes and motions of the landscape. There is an amplitude and ease in the massing of large shapes ("your big and aimless hills"). Ease is associated with extent, with a curving line, with volume, but also with the leisurely pace of movement. The expanse and aimlessness of those shapes seem connected to the length of time that is leisurely passing in a state of "waiting" (the hesitating of trees, flowers, and leaves and the length of time that the mother takes eating the after-birth). At times, Bishop composes by setting one motion against another of unequal weight or activity. The first stanza's long, aimless, seemingly passive drift erupts at the close in a little explosion of activity and initiative: "the calf got up promptly and seemed inclined to feel gay." Two disparate objects are poised: "the after-birth, / a wretched flag," remains lying on the hillside, whereas the calf rises up and carries the "gay" movement that is ordinarily associated with a flag (CP 55).

Each element wavers between receiving motion and initiating it. These are elements that, as Sartre says, are "halfway between . . . servility . . . and independence" (quoted in Giménez and Rower 70). The mother cow does not so much give birth to the calf as have the birth happen to her. "The little leaves" hover between active and passive. Passively, they are waiting and must be impelled from inside— actively, they are engaged in "carefully indicating their characteristics"; however, even in this latter activity, their "characteristics" are not chosen by themselves but are determined for them. Elements shift or swing from passivity to activity: "a calf was born" to "the calf got up promptly / and seemed inclined to feel gay" (CP 55). Green limbs on a hillside receive rather than cause the emergence of lilacs, whitening in their tops.

Bishop's closing of that first stanza with the verb "inclined" captures the sense of a landscape inclining toward spring. This event in time has its correlative in the sense of physical "tipping" or incline (the calf born "on the side of one" of the big hills). As the atmosphere warms up ("The next day / was much warmer"), the sense of one element leaning on another or tipping into one another becomes energized; there is more infiltration and diffusion: "greenish-white dogwood infiltrated the wood" (CP 55). The shape of a form seems so open that it becomes a blur, "like movement." As in a Calder mobile, the shapes are seen in their double identity between objecthood and movement. The "inclining" or drifting of elements from one arena into another includes the activity of the human mind as one element among others in the whole of the composition. Bishop inclines human metaphor-making so that it crosses over into the register of the natural. She humorously marks the drifting over as "like" a physical touch; the dogwood petals' ragged edges are "burned apparently, by a cigarette butt," as if the human activity of thought, its special kind of motion, could lean over and into nature (CP 55). These linguistic qualities (the crossing from description into metaphor, the mind and its words crossing into nature) are set inside a natural world that has similar qualities of trajectories crossing, passivity/activity, receiving, inclining, leaning toward certainty, and speeding up.

As in a Calder mobile, the movement of elements begins hesitatingly and speeds up after one object or "line" has leaned into the other. Now "deer practised leaping over your fences," and "the infant oak-leaves swing through the sober oak." Calder's characteristics of liveliness, youthfulness, and gaiety (swinging through) appear. In this section of the poem, Bishop brings in the language of the mechanism of action for the little Calder mobiles with their springs, each piece acting on the other and sending it into complementary but different motion. "Song-sparrows were wound up for the summer"; their "spring" causes the cardinal to sing, and in motion relayed to other elements, the cardinal wakes the landscape (*CP* 55). The pun on winding up a spring not only recalls the early Calder mobiles but humorously plays on the most traditional of poetic topoi, the complementary relations between the seasonal moment of the awakening landscape in spring and the feeling of movement, initiative, that, passively received from the interior by the mind and heart, prompts desire and action. Living creatures having been woken up and touched— set into motion by other motions—themselves set in motion human love. This love that rises up from the human soul is set in relation to other gentle movements, such as the "spray" that first appears optically (in the "cap" of the hills) and begins to move, drift, and fall or fireflies that begin to rise from "thick grass" (*CP* 55–56). New objects arrive unexpectedly from a previously unseen periphery. A new moon arises in the midst of, around the corner from, or in relation to other objects. The emergence of a new object is not something that the "frame" in which the speaker stands had centered on until the object appears and creates a new center. So, as each new object appears, the place of the observer is reset. Subjectivity is pulled toward, but also stands as counterweight to, each new shape or object that emerges.

As each event occurs, the positioning of the speaker alters. The moon rising makes space expand in relation to the speaker; the bullfrogs deepen space, their heavy and low sounds setting a boundary at another distance, as do the fireflies when they appear.

Now, from the thick grass, the fireflies
begin to rise:

up, then down, then up again:
lit on the ascending flight,
drifting simultaneously to the same height,
—exactly like the bubbles in champagne.
—Later on they rise much higher.
And your shadowy pastures will be able to offer
these particular glowing tributes
every evening now throughout the summer. (*CP* 56)

Without losing their own position, the stationery observers here are pulled out into that experience of depth where elements float. The celebratory mood arises gently as one element responding to the drifting of others. The passivity itself, the allowing oneself to be opened and moved, has also its counterweight of stability or location. The lyric speaker is "held" in a mobile container with disparate textures and movements, located among them, "re-arranged" as they coalesce and part, open, close, and shift. The fireflies that "later on . . . rise much higher," tipping upward, after some delay alter the relative positions of the (comparatively) heavy, stable speaker and the now "higher," lightly floating objects. The poem "A Cold Spring" feels like a giant "warm" Calder.[9]

Combining the Aesthetics of Schwitters and Calder

Bishop took advantage of possibilities in her own linguistic medium and revised Calder's aesthetic while adapting it for the lyric. She expanded the materials that could be used, beyond even those deployed by a sculptor known for democratizing the range of sculptural materials. In "A Cold Spring," she slips a tiny Schwitters collage into the mobile of the poem:

Beneath the light, against your white front door,
the smallest moths, like Chinese fans,
flatten themselves, silver and silver-gilt
over pale yellow, orange, or gray. (*CP* 56)

The collage orchestrates tiny modulations of color ("silver" to "silver-gilt" to "pale yellow") and tiny modulations of depth (the moths "flatten themselves" into a relief sculpture). Part of the sense of release in the finale of the poem derives from the emergence from the restrictions of collage—a medium never fully able to arrange its own escape from flatness and stillness—into the mobile. The moths arranged on the white door hover between flatness and depth; they make the slightest departure into relief sculpture and, with their potential for flight, hint at full emergence into three dimensions. The transition, only potential for the moths, becomes enacted in fact and abundantly by the fireflies that "begin to rise." Almost as if she is reaching back to George Herbert's "Easter Wings," Bishop makes the physicality of her own words on the printed page open and close, constrict and then expand into a fuller verse line. In a more expansive crescendo than "The next day / was much warmer," Bishop offers:

> Now, from the thick grass, the fireflies
> begin to rise:
> up, then down, then up again:

The verse line "warms up," inclining from the minimal "now" to the more expansive phrase "from the thick grass" and repeating that unfurling movement as "begin" expands ever slightly to the more elongated vowel of "to rise." It creates, as if *ex nihilo*, from the blank flatness of the page a mobile and welcoming world, where motion quickens, space opens, and liveliness flourishes.

This pivot from the minimal to the abundant, in a motion that is not self-willed, resembles Bishop's notebook descriptions of Jane Dewey's meadow, the setting for the poem: "They [the fireflies] begin close to the ground, go down & then, as they go up, light. Over & over—as if the light was what pushed them up, like jet propulsion. That's in the first part of the evening. Later they are all over the place & even up in the tops of the maple trees. The view from the porch was hazy, deep lavender, & *sparkling—goldnesses*" (VSC 77.4, 18, emphasis in original). The passage comes as a surprise in the pages of the 1950s notebook where Bishop often barely got going before her writing stalled and petered out. The depression verging on despair that Bishop reported in her letters during this period can be sensed in that paucity of language in the notebooks. So, when Bishop rapturously described her evenings at Jane Dewey's farm, joy arrived as palpable relief. The notebook passages combined a Schwitters-like cherishing of materials and textures with Calder's orchestration of movements that emerge and shift in relation to one another. "Drifts" of flowers are "shot through" with fireflies. Joyousness arises from the midst of abundance and variousness. Dotted textures are held loosely by wavy outlines of "meadow slopes," and there is a swelling up of forms punctuated by the levitation of the moon above the irregularity of the fields:

> Monday evening just as it was getting dark I went up to the enormous overgrown meadow behind the barns. It is almost completely filled with daisies—the ones that grow in sprays . . . about 2 ft. high black-eyed Susans, other daisies, Queen Anne's Lace, & here & there tall [?] & some pink weed—All these grow in drifts, first this one then that one—huge Q[ueen] A[nne's] L[ace], sticking up above the rest here & there like little moons—. All these drifts of gold & greenish white in the twilight, shot through all over by fire-flies—I've never seen anything more beautiful. The meadow slopes down rather steeply to big trees— then those wonderful fields & fields beyond—Just then the new moon appeared just over them. (VSC 77.4, 19)

As in the memoir fragments quoted in the introduction and in the poem draft "Gypsophilia" earlier in this chapter, multiple edges emerge between materials so that space appears to close and open, resituating the observer:

> The fireflies begin all over the grass at once just as it is getting dark—&, as I said, go up, lit, at first only about a foot when the lights are extinguished. Finally . . . it looks like & Jane agreed with me—Since they all stop glowing at the same height it gives the illusion of a *surface*—& the effect is exactly like the bubbles . . . in a glass of champagne. (VSC 77.4, 19; emphasis in original)

> A big Q[ueen] A[nne's] Lace looked at from underneath looks just like when you're in swimming & go under & look up at foam floating on the surface of the water overhead. (VSC 77.4, 19)

To have a new "surface" open up, resituates, or reorients the observer inside a new "container," where instability opens toward possibility without becoming chaotic or mere flux. Tipping or inclining seems to invite such a sensation, and in another passage that turns rapturous, the observer's own "tipped" station contributes to the sense of subjectivity held within an orchestration of other movements: "Driving home to Jane's was wonderful—up & down & round & round through cornfields & over little streams, animals moving mysteriously on the hillsides" (VSC 77.4, 25).

The structure allows for the unfurling of emotion from within the multiple "edges" of the observer's interior spaces. In a draft poem from the mid-1960s, titled "the first color," Bishop again places the lyric speaker among a set of shifting motions, "tipped" and suspended in the midst of the inclining, tilting landscape of the town of Ouro Preto:

> the town unsh[a]dows   unshadows
> church by church falling
> from th[ei]r sheer coco[o]ns
> and ope[n]ing, shini[n]g, half-opening glisten
>
> half-open moths
> stuck sleeping to the hillg[r]een hill
>
> the streets go down
> the three or four red veins
> the purity pure pink
>
> the first color see[n] is blue baby blue
> Pity pity pity the
> quaresma blossoms grieve and allig[a]tor pears
>   glazed green and rotten—purple—
>
>   cabbag[e] moths invade the gauze
>
>   St Iph[i]genia
> in fresh blue and white
> her sweet black face with lowered eyes
> and silver
>
> holds her toy church tight and bright f[la]mes peep
> the bright flames peep, and leap
> from the closed windows, in the dawn— (VSC 68.3)

Here in the baroque movements of rising and falling, furling and un-furling, texture after texture is presented as opening out into one an-other. The town "unshadows" as if a robe or cloth has been pulled open or away. While the speaker is looking down onto the town from above, the churches appear to be both falling further down ("church by church falling") and simultaneously "opening" up to reveal their "glistening." Whereas "the streets go down," the lifting of the shad-ows and the glistening makes the town seem to float upward. Emo-tions emerge or rise up from the landscape as merely another kind of unfurling, like color or texture—the blossoms give rise to grief ("que-resma blossoms grieve") and unfurl a soft immense gentleness ("pity pity pity"). The emotion seems to drift over and take up residence in the visual icon of the saint, the "sweet black face with lowered eyes" of the St. Iphigenia, whose hugeness emerges from contrast with an-other object (she "holds her toy church tight") and serves to magnify her tenderness. Surfaces open toward one another with different kinds of "touch" at the end of the poem as the reflection of the dawn light from the church windows now shifts from the mere "glistening" of the opening stanza and the gentler action of "opening" to the ener-getic mobility (they "peep, and leap") of "bright flames" (VSC 68.3). In this fragment, we have no "speaker" emerge as "subject," yet the implied observer of this dawn is set amid these shifting materials and objects, elements that have their own trajectories and whose surfaces can accommodate the leaning of one on another or the unfurling of one into the other.

Bishop's own linguistic medium, of course, had mechanisms for producing movement that extend far beyond the possibilities for most visual artists, even for Calder. Yet it does seem as though "unfurling" became one means for Bishop to organize movement across layers. This action of unfurling in Calder's hanging mobiles was emphasized by Mário Pedrosa in one of the major pieces of Brazilian criticism on Calder (Pedrosa 132). In "The Moose," the poem that Bishop contin-ued to work on for twenty-six years (between 1946 and 1972) and that of course had multiple influences beyond the visual arts, Bishop integrates Klee's wandering line; Schwitters's materials modulating toward and away from one another; and Calder's dynamic structur-ing of three-dimensional space, his composing by motions with dis-parate objects of varying weights held in relation to and responding to one another, and his action of "unfurling" toward a pleasantly un-predictable future.

The slightly divergent materials of sea and bay, river and bay, in their actions of entering into one another, repelling, swaying for-ward, retreating, and mingling, open the poem in the space of materi-als and motions in all their varieties of trajectory, weight, and cross-ing. As if expanding the 1929 poem that Bishop had recopied in her notebook so many times in the 1940s ("A lovely surface have I seen"), "The Moose" gives us each surface "regrained" by surfaces that cross, diffuse, or alter (Bishop 2006, 11). The sun, itself crossed by the atmo-sphere and so "silted red," alters the surface of the sea to become red in its own medium, whereas the sand flats redden and become sun-like in their "burning." But in the mirroring, the materials alter; color modulates when red tilts to "lavender," and material modulates when red sea becomes red mud. This is Schwitters's aesthetic, the interpermeating materials varying in tiny degrees of likeness and dif-ference modulating one another as they touch. The red roads' "grav-elly" texture varies the "silted" sun. Just as "mist" tilts over into "spirit" and "ghosts" in "Cape Breton," the clapboard of the farmhouses, a small degree away from clapboard churches, tilts into resemblance to "bleached, ridged" "clamshells." Bishop incorporates into the land-scape first the white of human-made houses and churches, naturalized by their resemblance to the white of the clamshells, and then the in-creasingly unnatural, mechanical, and garish "pink" and "blue" wind-shield glass, metal, and enamel. And, like "Cape Breton," the poem has as its subject the crossing and dispersion of materials. Light thick-ens into and alters fog. Fog, in its own "thin" drifting material ("shift-ing, salty, thin") holds or accommodates the increasingly solid and dense "cold, round crystals," which then cross over on to even more stable objects ("white hens' feathers"). Like the "sprinkle of grass" held next to and against the "stains, like dried blood" on the rusted capstan in "At the Fishhouses," the materials modulate toward and away from one another, holding some aspects in resemblance (white fog or white hens' feathers) and differing in other aspects (lightness and drift vs. stability). The poem takes as its subject the diffusion and thickening of materials as they meet, accommodate one another, alter, and unevenly permeate (e.g., "moonlight and mist" "caught" in "hairy, scratchy, splintery" woods). These modulations across different kinds of materials include the modulations of vegetable to flower ("glazed cabbages" and "cabbage roses") and the modulations in language (the shift from "cabbage" as noun to "cabbage" as adjective). Slant rhymes modulate or turn words toward and then tilt them away from one another; the close embrace of "dog" and "fog" or "thin" and "in" slides away to "crystals"/"settle," "crystals"/"feathers," "roses"/"apostles." We can almost feel the "scratchy" materiality of the "limbs" of the consonants in "apostles" hold in its embrace the softer sounds of "roses." The visuals of line against plane—"wet white string" modulates into and across "whitewashed fences"—become the winding of verse line across the surface of the world, undulating, crossing, diffusing, holding, draping, looping, and becoming taut or condensed (*CP* 169).

Although the poem can be understood as a Schwitters-like arrangement of interpermeating materials modulating across tiny intervals of resemblance and difference, "The Moose" also has the qualities of a Calder-like hanging mobile. The observer is set among materials that swing into view, unfurl, drift across, and bump. The infiltration and diffusion of materials occur through Bishop's "composing motions": tides moving toward and away; the bus moving "down hollows, up rises"; and the fog "closing in." After "bumblebees creep / inside the foxgloves," Bishop's description rises to an understated Prospero-like act of ritual invocation. She pronounces that "evening commences" (*commences* is defined as "to enter upon: begin; to initiate formally by performing the first act of" in Webster's). Actions now speed up, and from the substratum of the continuity of tiny events of interpermeating materials emerge more distinct events. These events rise up from the unknown, out of the darkness of a space that has no outer boundary or graspable dimensions.

> A pale flickering. Gone.
> The Tantramar marshes
> and the smell of salt hay.
> An iron bridge trembles
> and a loose plank rattles
> but doesn't give way.
>
> On the left, a red light
> swims through the dark:

a ship's port lantern.
Two rubber boots show,
illuminated, solemn.
A dog gives one bark. (*CP* 170–71)

Each object has its own stability or independent motion, almost its own freedom and dignity. Yet each is sensed in relation to the observer moving in her own steadier but winding "line." In a "constellation" moving around the reticent observer, Bishop arranges the drifting of objects of disparate forms, colors, weights, and motions. In spite of the anxiety and tension of a space that oscillates between "vague alarm and familiar comfort" (Millier 469), the fact that the observer does not call up these events, the fact that they arrive of their own "free will," produces a strange kind of tranquility. As in Bishop's other Calder-like lyrics, human language is one of the elements that drifts, with its own trajectory, across the speaker's space and can infiltrate: The passengers lie back. / Snores. Some long sighs. / A dream divigation / begins in the night, / a gentle, auditory, / slow hallucination. . . ." The moose has its own independent existence and its own distinctive motion: "a moose has come out of / the impenetrable wood / and stands there, looms rather . . . approaches . . . sniffs" (*CP* 171–72). It wanders across the trajectory of the moving bus. The "bump" as the trajectories cross, carrying some of the humor of the same phenomenon in "Arrival at Santos," also has the seriousness of larger questions of realms crossing. Like Calder, Bishop creates a means of holding the disparate realms in a dynamic relation. The weight of the speaker and passengers, sinking down into their seats, and the conversation and thoughts rising up are held in a suspension of relations of disparate "objects" that move along particularized trajectories that include "drift" but also remain distinct, are held apart, in relation, orderly and contained, but free. In a moving world, and moving herself, the observer nevertheless has a place.

In "North Haven," the dead body of Robert Lowell becomes the motionless counterweight to the drifting "constellation" of the moving world in all its freshness, lightness, gentle improvisation, and surprise. As in "A Cold Spring," the gradual "start up" of emotion occurs enfolded within three other kinds of emergence: from the inert to moving, from flat plane to three-dimensions, and from line to wave. This beautiful and deeply affecting little elegy draws on associations extensively worked through in much of Bishop's previous oeuvre. Here, Bishop brings back the imagery of Alfred H. Barr's "the silhouette of the square confront[ing] the shape of the amoeba" that she first used in "Pleasure Seas," with its bounded rectangular pool set against the drifting of currents and tides (Barr 1935, 19). As in a still collage where materials cannot modulate toward one another, cannot cross, and do not resemble, the opening of "North Haven" arranges disparate elements in stationary display: one large object, the schooner, in the distance; the spangle of smaller objects suspended nearby ("new cones on the spruce"); the flat opaque surface that extends ("the pale bay wears a milky skin"); and a fuzzy line ("no clouds, except for one long, carded horse's-tail"). As if constructing the opposite of "Pleasure Seas," "At the Fishhouses," and "Cape Breton," Bishop, in this first stanza, allows nothing to move. No element drifts or infiltrates, touches, opens to another. Lines (the rigging and the one long cloud) and planes (the sky and the surface of the bay) are held purely apart. The skin of the surface of the world lies as surface that cannot open. Bishop orchestrates the poem by allowing this still landscape to open out into increasing depth, movement, and emotion.

Human thought, human desire, and freedom enter the picture as the elements begin their tiny shifts in relation to one another. The freedom first occurs in the key of illusory movement, the desire for the still to be able to move—"the islands haven't shifted since last summer / even if I like to pretend they have." Grief is permitted only the gentlest presence, the slight emergence of wish uttered in the acknowledgement of conditions of impossibility. So, too, the gentlest note of pleasure enters with this wish, pleasure in the drift and dreaminess associated with that imagined and illusory shifting, the sense of freedom within a structure: "they're free within the blue frontiers of bay." Like the islands themselves, the line that expresses a slight desire is allowed to float loosely within boundaries on either side.

The islands haven't shifted since last summer,
Even if I like to pretend they have
—drifting, in a dreamy sort of way,
a little north, a little south or sidewise,
and that they're free within the blue frontiers of bay. (*CP* 188)

The first line's feminine ending is closed by the iambic finish of the second line; the feminine ending of the fourth line is closed by the even longer "wall" of the stricter iambic of the final line of the stanza. Between these two blocks, the middle line ("drifting, in a dreamy sort of way") floats untethered within limits. Likewise, and resembling "A Cold Spring's "The next day / was much warmer," the listing structure of the next stanza, with its play on elegy's typical catalogue of flowers strewn on a bier, permits a tiny sense of momentary release and freedom each time the catalogue of proper nouns opens out to more mobile expansive rhythmic phrasing: "Hawkweed *still burning*, Daisies pied /. . . . the Fragrant Bedstraw's *incandescent stars*" (emphasis added). Pure description of the world opens toward emotion when the poet allows an emotion to be explicitly stated: flowers "returned, to paint the meadows *with delight*" (*CP* 188; emphasis added). Emotion enters the landscape, simultaneously, with the landscape and the verse line entering into freer movement. Emotional depth increases together with spatial depth. Flowers stuck close to the surface of the landscape thicken the plane into sculptural relief and then into three dimensions as birds float up or down, move off and return, with more freedom. Song emerges. Lyric "opens."

The opening toward delight is also an opening toward sorrow. "This month, *our* favorite one" acts as a reminder that a shared delight will no longer be shared. The dilation toward emotion, the permission to feel, only means that pleasure is twinned with grief. So, the entrance of "song," coming with the insistence on the theme of return, comes back along with its twin, no return ("The Goldfinches are back, or others like them"). Finally, "five-noted song" (perhaps a reminder of Lowell's own beauty-stricken, grief-stricken "magnolia blossoms' murderous five-days white"; Lowell 2006, 131) inclines toward the crescendo of "pleading and pleading" and the appearance of "tears to the eyes." Again, Bishop characteristically tilts the surface of verse so that it alters gently from natural description to emotion and then closes its surface again, like water that opens a facet to glimmer with light and then subsides. "Nature repeats herself, or almost does" closes the surface of verse to that erupted emotion and settles back into statement. Modulation becomes tiny again. The two phrases of the line almost repeat, almost stand still ("Nature repeats herself, or almost does"), and then modulation becomes even smaller ("*repeat, repeat, repeat; revise, revise, revise*") (*CP* 188). Then white space. The paper page. Silence. No song. Pure plane. Pure closed surface. Then, as the next stanza opens, the shift into another material, into the language of story, and into memory of Lowell at the shore in his early years.

In "Argument," "The Museum," and "Four Poems," Bishop associates the opening or rearranging/disarranging of closed lines and closed surfaces with human openness and warmth, and these associations reappear in "North Haven." The strong recurrent associations in Bishop's oeuvre of movement, crossing, infiltration, inclination, opening, and swaying allied with human warmth and touch, with human intimacy and life, make the stillness that opens "North Haven" gain its extra measure of quiet grief. The unmoving Lowell becomes "anchored" like the island of North Haven itself, an unmoving rock in its sea of blue. The motionlessness of Lowell makes the "you've left" into a kind of lie; Lowell—incapable of change, movement, or drift—would be more truly captured in the unspoken but evoked phrase "you're left." The two phrases—one almost said, one explicitly said—balance in equal measure Bishop's sense of abandonment with Lowell's having been abandoned. In the slight modulation of "derange, or re-arrange," Bishop permits again the slight pleasure involved in fluidity, unavailable to the dead man who is "anchored" against "afloat." The solidity of the phrases that pronounce life gone ("you've left / for good"; "you can't"; "the words won't change again"; and "you cannot change") stand as rocks of language. Other phrases linger and waver floating among those stable rocklike elements of language ("But the Sparrows can their song" and "sad friend"). In her lyric as mobile, Bishop creates the gentleness and sadness of North Haven, where among the disparate elements the unchanging Lowell can no longer move, no longer change. Building a space in which to hold the experience of the death of her lifelong colleague and friend, the friendship that anchored her all her life, Bishop arrays the world's movements in a constellation around the dead body of Lowell. He appears in the constellation as an unmoveable rock or anchor and also in a gesture of floating off ("you've left / for good") as the lyric speaker herself becomes the weighted one, left behind (CP 189). His motionlessness, arranged both underneath and against the lovely precious drifting up and down and across of other elements (islands, water, flower petals, sparrows, and song) gives him a place in which he can also be "borne or carried" and in which Bishop's grief can also be carried and borne. The elements held "apart"—because they are arranged and suspended against one another in the poem—become a container or structure in which Lowell, Bishop, the elements of nature, and the elements of verse can be "together."

MIRRORS AND FIELDS

Three Ways of Appearing

Both the unpublished draft "Something I've Meant to Write about for 30 Years" and the late "Sonnet" offer up *ars poetica* images representing the poem as the surface of a mirror. Making an art object as "homely" as the nailed-together wood of "The Monument," the artist in "Something I've Meant" had "fixed / with nails, half hammered in, then bent, / a piece of broken mirror to each picket top" of a fence (Bishop 2006, 139). This unexpected creative act catches the speaker's attention and produces a wonder and delight that has lasted thirty years. Bishop establishes the status of art as superfluous human inventiveness: "why not *decorate* morning?" (Bishop 2006, 138). Balanced against the slight sense of ridiculousness is a triumphant tribute to a human vitality that goes beyond the necessary and moves toward sheer delight. With stunning minimalism, "Sonnet" distills the action of art as mirror: a holding, flicker, and flash, a surface that "catches" then releases sensations of glancing off, freedom, gaity and delight. In both poems, the positioning of the lyric speaker in relation to these mirrors has an uncanny, almost "missing person" effect. In both, Bishop holds steady for our gaze the strange phenomenon of an empty mirror that glances or flashes, where the face that would look into the mirror does not appear.

The title of "Something I've Meant to Write about for 30 Years" announces the staying power of the image in the poem and its special hold over Bishop's imagination. As Bishop thematizes the image, we can glimpse her in the process of working out what it was about the scene that made it stick so long in her memory. During the course of the poem, a revelation is precipitated by the slightly vertiginous experience of the train coming to a jerky stop, reversing and correcting itself: "We jerked back and forward there" and "I saw it slide back then forward like a slide several times" (Bishop 2006, 137). The motion sets up an intensified experience of the relational dynamics between the movement of the train and the relative stillness of the yard. Understood as composed of disparate motions, the poem holds in relation the jerky movement of the train, the still scene of the yard, and the "irregular jagg'd disconnected mad" stagger of the many tiny mirrors (138). The speaker is positioned in some resemblance to the "jagg'd" movement of mirrors and to the stillness of the yard. She is understood to be flickering between or arriving at those two "states." Flickering herself, the speaker passes by the moving work of art and, almost as voyeur, is permitted to see art reflecting the world without an artist or an observer present. Of course, the lyric speaker is the observer of the scene, but there is a strange sense in which she is off to one side, merely peripheral to a private and agentless mirroring that catches and produces light: "only the mirrors seeing the morning coming" (138). The art object "sees" morning even without the presence of a human being. The speaker has been granted privileged access to the artwork in its pristine state, open to and interacting with the world, going about its work of reflecting but missing its human maker and observer. Bishop marks that mirroring as accomplished "sadly, over and over again," and the sadness, here, seems to arise because of the absence of any subjectivity ("only the mirrors seeing the morning coming"). The interface between world and art, as lively encounter, contains no subject to participate in it aside from the temporary observer in the train, the speaker of the poem, who is about to depart. Other images of the natural world in Bishop's work have the same feel of an object alone and abandoned with an almost unpeopled world as witness. In "Pleasure Seas," water "lightly, lightly, whitening in the air / An acre of cold white spray is there / Dancing happily by itself" (CP 196). And a note from one of the early notebooks described "thunderstorms on & off all day": "pink flashes in the sunset-pink thunderhead—strange & lovely effect— . . . huge flower-like cloud flashing away to itself, in perfect silence?" (VSC 77.3, 21). The world has relations with itself that seem unconcerned, self-pleasuring, and witnessless. In "Something I've Meant" and "Sonnet," Bishop fashions images for art that partake of that sense of privacy and delight in an action that needs no observer.

In many ways, "Sonnet" condenses and sharpens this poem draft, repeating many of its themes. Perhaps because it was sent off to the *New Yorker* but not published until after Bishop's death (Millier 545), and perhaps because it has no defined place for the speaker to stand, "Sonnet" comes to us as if spoken by the flown or dead, almost as Bishop's self-elegy. The sheer emptiness of a mirror that holds no human face gives the poem its sadness, particularly because it appears as Bishop's final words, their originator having vanished into thin air. The subjectivity of the writer does not appear in the frame, at least not as visible figure. Yet the speaker does and does not appear in the body of the poem. She hovers on the beveled edge between presence and absence. Because she cannot be held by the words of the poem (has disappeared from them, has no presence as a character in the poem) and has also died, she exists as the unappearing observer of the scene that she reports. Yet she is there, somehow held in the spirit of the "rainbow-bird" that glints. The figure of the "rainbow-bird" finally released and the unmistakeable joy in the speaker's own emotion expressed in "flying wherever / it feels like, gay!" collect the speaker and the glint of light into a shared existence.

The subject of the poem is partly the mechanism by which such a figure is precipitated—the production of a flash at the place of interval, interface, pivot, facet, or bevel. The action of the poem takes place at the beveled edge of the mirror, where flat plane leans up to become three-dimensional. That action is modulation—by means of likeness, a fragment of rainbow-colored light that seems to fly becomes a figure so real that it does fly, having modulated into a bird. The turn occurs compactly in a hyphen that allows a crossing over, as if it is only a tiny interval between the real (a piece of light) and art (the fictional bird), between material (light) and living creature (bird). As in "North Haven," the poem holds still, forever, the opening toward three dimensions, toward liveliness, movement, and emotion. Reading "Sonnet" over and over, we can rise repeatedly from pure description to joy, pure description to grief. And it is almost as if Bishop has also held in perpetual flicker the modulation between life and death for the speaker. Bishop, as now-dead spirit, keeps being reborn at the beveled edge of the mirror, pronouncing herself still speaking, "gay!" The speaker of the poem, like the glint of light, both exists in pure unadulterated joy and disappears forever, irretrievable, having transitioned from "empty mirror" to empty space. In giving "life" to a bit of light that escapes from the beveled edge of the mirror, Bishop allows it to escape from the reader's view, unbound forever, living forever, and unavailable to earth and to others in perpetual flight. Yet the disembodied, un-framed life is also "caught" forever, inside the rectangle of the poem.

The poem enacts the analogy that Bishop imagined in a lifetime of work—the surface of verse as a mirrored plane that can open out to three dimensions; hold elements in moving "constellations"; and tilt from stillness to movement, reticence to emotion, natural description to human metaphor. "Sonnet" focuses on surface at the moment that it tilts. Where the surface of the mirror, as plane, reaches its edge and bends upward, at the bevel, the glint of light, merely a tiny fragment of "rainbow," because of its liveliness "tilts" through likeness and be-comes "bird." The poem enacts up close and in slow motion, isolated for our attention, the suture between the purely descriptive action of naming the natural world and metaphor arising from the human mind that notes resemblances. A plane (the mirrored surface) tilts up to release, into three dimensions, an object, a bird. The flat plane of verse on a white page seems to release a figure into the world. That figure hovers forever among a glint of light, a bird, and Bishop's spirit.

In some sense, the difference between painting and lyric is that in a painting the painter does not have to be "in" the scene as its subject. But in impressionism, the mode of painting that Bishop most envied, the artist, although not appearing as figure in the painting, becomes the body of the painting by recording nature as it fell on to or fell into the responding mind of the artist. Could a poem do the same? Meyer Schapiro, in an essay on Eugene Fromentin that thrilled Bishop, sug-gests that writing could (Bishop 1994, 181). The essay explained the reasons that impressionists in Fromentin's time had become interested in the older masters such as Rembrandt and Vermeer. So, Schapiro de-scribes the link between the two schools of art that Bishop often men-tioned as close to her heart: Vermeer and impressionism. According to Schapiro, Fromentin's book on sixteenth- and seventeenth-century Dutch painters excelled in the "keen, tireless observation of the fabric of the painting as a sensory matter" (1949, 25). That attentiveness revealed the "painting as a personal object" in which "everything in the work of art—the attitude to the subject, the execution, palette, and forms—belongs . . . to the individual and is an expressive end as well as a means" (26). According to Shapiro, "the interest of Fromentin lies in his power to make us see that the highest human values are involved in a patch of color the bend of a line" (28). Like these older painters, who, while focused on direct observation of things, could be "personal," Fromentin's "imaginative writing represent[ed] the exterior world through a reacting sensibility" (Schapiro 1949, 29). Yet Bishop wrote Anne Stevenson that the *post*impressionist Edouard Vuillard is the painter with whom she most identifies (April 8, 1964, WUL). And when Stevenson failed to take the hint, Bishop reminded her again (letter to Anne Stevenson, November 14, 1964. WUL). We have very few clues in letters, notebooks, or poems about Bishop's identification with Vuillard. The only real thread to follow occurs when Bishop tells Jarrell that she has been working on an elegy about Maud, her aunt, in the mode of Vuillard (Bishop 1994, 312). I suggest that although Bishop may have longed to be the poet-equivalent of an impressionist painter or a Vermeer, wishing the poem to record nature as it fell on to the mind of the artist who never had to appear as figure on the canvas, she instead did appear in her work more in the mode of Vuillard's women, who emerge from and melt back into the wallpaper. Rather than "an art in which the subjective and external were fused" (Schapiro 1949, 29), Bishop created an art that enacted the observer emerging and falling back into the "scene" that is separated from her by seams or edges that become palpable and fade, shift, clarify, and become prominent and then effaced.

Given Bishop's remark to Randall Jarrell that her poems on Maud were composed in the mode of Vuillard, the draft of Bishop's elegy for Maud may provide some sense of her translation of Vuillard's visual aesthetic into her own medium. In "For M.B.S., buried in Nova Scotia," tilting plane, bunched-up material, curving line, and the unseen field of the gently moving bay are gathered to lie next to/against one another, holding close the dead aunt:

> Yes, you are dead now and live
> Only there, in a little, slightly tip-tilted graveyard
> Where all of your childhood's Christmas trees are forgathered

With the present they meant to give,
And your childhood's river quietly curls at your side
And breathes deep with each tide. (Bishop 2006, 98)

The human figure is held inside materials that sequence modulation among human life (not present but invoked); the inanimate, still, tilted earth; and the "life" of trees and moving water. The translation from the visual aesthetic to linguistic composition allows movement to be folded into the pictorial scene. Stillness is held against movement, the unseen still body held against the curling river that "breathes" with the slow diurnal rhythm of the tide.

The "holding" of human figures within the materials of a scene occurs in a more fully developed draft about her aunt in "One afternoon my aunt and I . . . ," in which Bishop is clearly thinking about visual art as she writes. The poem deploys the language of drawing, opening with "scribblings" and "chalk." The opening emphasizes the "layering of pattern and arabesque" characteristic of Vuillard (Easton 34).

One afternoon my aunt and I
went picking blueberries. The sky

the line of marsh
like scribblings with green chalk
the berries were chalk-like, too
someone, perhaps Pythagoras,
had idly dotted over the pasture
with thick blue chalk, billions of dots. (Bishop 2006, 99)

Bishop sets her human figures in a background, a field, composed of "billions of dots." The layering of patterns (blueberries dotting the hills; the berries, stems, and leaves layered over one another in the pail), fields without pattern ("the sky"), and the loose and fluid line ("the line of marsh / like scribblings with green chalk") provides the substratum out from which the aunt emerges as the most distinct figure: "she wore a pair of overalls / her husband's, and an old straw hat" (Bishop 2006, 99). The wicker of her hat—a modulation in material and shape from the wicker basket and "the horses' velvet wickering"— make her emerge from and fold back into the field of other patterns and materials, much as Vuillard's figures recede into and out of the wallpaper. Bishop mentioned this feature of Vuillard in a notebook poem: "unobtrusive / Have given up not quite the ghost—the ghost is there—/ (like Vuillard's sister in the wall-paper) NO—/ weak, stunned, dazed, pale, pining" (VSC 66.10). In a painting by Vuillard that Bishop could have seen at the Smith College Art Museum, "Interior (L'Atelier) 1893, "the young woman . . . literally blends into the *ground* of the painting since her spotted dress is composed of a network of black dots scattered over the blank, unpainted surface of the cardboard. . . . Marie's head blends with the wallpaper as much as her torso does (Easton 50; emphasis in original). As in the painting, Bishop's poem allows figures to emerge from and fold back into background, pattern, other materials of landscape, language, and also time.

The "wicked family anecdote," although another kind of material, a fragment of the linguistic, is added to the summer landscape: "our afternoon's addition / summer's sum" ([99–100]). The poem begins to funnel into a thematic climax, becoming an encomium to this kind of layering or addition.

Haycock on haycock in the wagon
berry on berry in the pail
Pythagoras
One more
berry, one more baby, no more fuss. (Bishop 2006, 100)

With "one more / berry, one more baby, no more fuss," Bishop drops herself into both landscape and family as unobtrusively as "berry" modulates to "baby," settling among the "background" of similar rhythmic phrasings. The story of an orphan added to the family, slipped into the landscape, into the portrait, into the summer in that place at that time becomes, although a singular event, part of a "dotted" pattern, in which event can slip into continuity like a slightly different syllable into a string of varying syllables. Bishop, and her story, almost do not "appear" in the painting. She almost disappears into the landscape, the way that she has been slipped into the ongoing life of her mother's family.

To be held in the patterned fabrics is to be "held close," as "A Short, Slow Life" puts it: "We lived in a pocket of Time. It was close, it was warm. Along the dark seam of the river / the houses, the barns, the two churches,/ hid like white crumbs / in a fluff of gray willows and elms" (Bishop 2006, 103). In "One afternoon my aunt and I . . . ," material set next to material ("tin-mug," "lard pail," and "basket"; "berries," "thin blood-red stems," and "thick little leaves"; Bishop 2006, 100) provides the containing collage into which the speaker can be inserted or hid. It is a Schwitters-like space—Bishop's word *glaucous* emphasizes the surface of the berries, where color modulates into color (blue to gray) and layers peel off (*glaucous* is defined as "a fuzz or coating that rubs off the fruit" in Webster's). The "idly dotted," Pythagorean pasture, a series in space, eventually becomes the "plop-plop" of the berries falling into the pails "almost inaudibly / softly," a slow steady series in sound and in time (Bishop 2006, 99–100). Poised next to/against the series, "a cricket held a high hot note / all afternoon." In this image, as if composing sounds rather than motions, Bishop sets an intermittent dropping sound next to one of much longer and more insistent duration (100). To set an event inside a duration becomes something like composing motions, but Bishop also sets both sounds and motions inside materials, making a space in which the "I" of the child (intermittently enduring in the intermittent memory of the adult speaker) can be held together with the now-gone figure of the deceased aunt. Bishop arranges patterns of continuity that held intermittent event, materials that hold human figures, and figures that emerge from and are held by fields.

As these unpublished drafts demonstrate, it becomes a habitual mode of composition for Bishop to arrange the materials of lyric as fabrics or materials of the world that are held next to/against one another. The materials often interpermeate or modulate toward one another; in "Something I've Meant," the air "started to crystallize," taking the shape of wisteria "dripping half-crystallized" down a porch and "the unpainted houses were almost the color of the air" (Bishop 2006, 138). The interpermeating materials modulate across bevels or shifting edges, where a mirror "catching the light, reflecting, white" modulates toward and away from the actual white light of dawn, and where, as dawn progresses, "white" modulates toward "bluish." Within this landscape of disparate materials and shifting edges, Bishop arrays sounds, actions, and events in disparate trajectories, speeds, and durations. Human figures are enfolded in these moving constellations, in this sea of materials, which become like the patterned wallpapers and dresses in Vuillard's interiors, opening and closing from two dimensions into three. As the materials embed a human figure or allow it to emerge, so the surface of verse tilts toward emotion and then recloses, the language of natural description tilts toward metaphor then recedes. Lines of verse open to a freer movement and then reclose to a more hard-edged container.

> And the compass needle
> Wobbling and wavering,
> Undecided. (*CP* 192)

Bishop composes her poetry out of these edges among kinds of materials, kinds of lines, and kinds of languages. She composes out of their variant interfaces and the place of the human within them.

In "The End of March," materials seem unable to "hold" the human. The landscape is "withdrawn as far as possible, / indrawn: the tide far out, the ocean shrunk." The landscape is closed ("inaudible rollers / in upright steely mist") and colors do not modulate toward one another even if they seem alike: "the sky was darker than the water /—*it* was the color of mutton-fat jade" (*CP* 179). Among the collage of materials, the edges of materials become lines or waver between edge and free-standing line.

> Then we came on
> lengths and lengths, endless, of wet white string,
> looping up to the tide-line, down to the water,
> over and over. (*CP* 179)

Bishop arranges three kinds of "moving" lines: the curving irregular edge of the tide-line in the sand, always moving and shifting in its location; the white edge of waves, a curving irregular line that rises and falls, holds together, and dissipates; and a three-dimensional real string that loops and comes close to and resembles the "flatter" tide line drawn in relief on sand. These moving lines wobble between the linear and the edge of a plane and between the still and the moving. One of the lines, the string, then tilts toward figure when it ends in "a thick white snarl, man-size, awash, / rising on every wave" (179). With our understanding that the suggestion of a dead body is resonant with Bishop's mourning over Lota, we can feel the verse opening up, almost, to emotion and metaphor and then closing back, receding, into natural description:

> Finally, they [the loops of string] did end:
> A thick white snarl, man-size, awash,
> Rising on every wave, a sodden ghost,
> Falling back, sodden, giving up the ghost . . .
> A kite string?—But no kite. (*CP* 179)

The human figure embedded in the material, emerging, falling back. Verse that provides a substratum and then allows to emerge a new object, a new event, a metaphor, an emotion—and then recedes and recloses. A proselike line that rises toward meter and then subsides.[1] This is the "moving marble" of Bishop's surface of verse as fabric, mirror, sea surface, and field. Here we find multiple and shifting interior and exterior edges that, like bevels, tilt toward and away, landscapes or "we's" from which lines, figures, or "I's" emerge and fall back.

NOTES

Introduction

1. See also letter to Kit and Ilse Barker, July 28, 1968, PUL.

2. Lorrie Goldensohn (1992, esp. chap. 6) has also written in depth about the many aspects of Bishop's poems that derive from her interest in ways of seeing.

3. Bishop names Klee and Schwitters in letters to Anne Stevenson, March 18 and March 20, 1963, and January 8, 1964, WUL. Suárez-Toste (2001) has explored the affinity between Bishop and Joseph Cornell. See also Keller (1987, 114–15).

4. See Summers (332–37) for a more extensive discussion of surface.

5. That Margaret Miller was studying at New York University with Max J. Friedländer, a specialist in seventeenth-century Dutch painting, and that Bishop spent a long time with Miller in Paris after Miller's accident make it almost certain that the women would have found either Claudel's two articles about Dutch art in the popular literary magazine, *La Revue de Paris* (February 1 and 15, 1935), or the Gallimard book-publication of the articles.

6. Christiane Hertel establishes a long orientalist tradition of describing the Netherlands as "mysterious."

7. My work focuses on some of the features that Goldensohn first describes as essential concerns in Bishop's poetry: "Bishop as poet dealt with the problem of illusionism created by the act of reading common to both poetry and painting. The page is a way station, a port. Reading, one wants to fall through the print on the paper, to penetrate its light scrim, behind whose features through some peculiar method of evocation are suddenly located an interior body state, which is literally neither here nor there, but in some spaceless energy of mind, created by mind, off page. Bishop's fascination with objects,

with the visual look and feel of existence, again and again calls up this questionable relation between internal and external, between depth and surface authenticity" (1992, 119).

8. See Molesworth (243–44, 289) regarding Moore's "leveling of the hierarchy of surface and depth" (244).

9. Cristanne Miller does not consider Moore's voice to be either self-effacing or impersonal and shows how crucial it was for Moore to fight against the masquerading of authority as objectivity, a struggle that her poetry wages by exhibiting a strikingly personal bias in reporting of facts. Miller argues that the speaker in Moore's poems is personal—the poems include a "thinking, remembering, feeling, resolving, self-correcting individual 'I'" and "the poem's form announces a speaker's presence at the outset" of the poems (Miller 1995, 70, 73).

10. See also Leavell (116) on the relationship between collage and Moore's use of quotation to avoid subjectivity.

11. Alternatively, at times, painting's "bodiliness, its immanence, its spatial presence, attracted Stevens as a cure for rhetoric" (Costello 1985, 66).

12. I do not want to overstate the distinctions between Bishop and Stevens. As Altieri argues, Bishop "shares Stevens' sense that what matters about the imagination is not its quasi-mythmaking abilities but its capacity to bring the psyche into direct vital engagement with its world" (1995, 229). But the consensus among scholars in the *Wallace Stevens Journal* special issue on Bishop and Stevens is that "however compelling Bishop found Stevens' conception of the imagination, she could not share it" (Gelpi, 159), that Bishop "stood at a much more deeply ironic moment than Stevens" (Page 1995, 170), and, compared to Stevens, included "persistent reminders of mediating artifice" between natural and rhetorical modes (Page 1995, 171).

13. Bishop goes on to suggest a solution: "poetry should have more of the unconscious spots left in" (VSC 75.3A, 89). But, although she did maintain that "mystery" was a crucial ingredient for poetry, she did not pursue the direction of the unconscious made available by surrealism and, instead, invented alternative conceptions of depth.

14. Margaret Miller seems to have shared this distaste for Mondrian, finding him restrictive, unrelentingly "flat" and oppressive (see undated letter, probably from 1942, from Margaret Miller to Elizabeth Bishop, VSC). Weldon Kees, who Bishop met in Washington, D.C., in 1949, and who had replaced Greenberg as the art critic of *The Nation*, complains about Mondrian's "general sense of refrigeration" (Kees 451).

15. Goldensohn notes that Bishop "rarely breaks open the space of her poem in cubist imitation, or in modern juxtaposition, as Moore or Eliot, or Williams or Pound all do" (1992, 198). Schwitters provides the model for Bishop's alternative aesthetic. See Rudi Fuchs for a more wide-ranging discussion of the differences

between Schwitters and other figures that have been considered more central to modernism.

16. Thomas Gardner has also written sensitively about Bishop's navigating within a skeptical space and the sense of her lyric speaker as experiencing "alertness actively opening up within a limited space" (47).

17. The phrasing of the last term belongs not to Klee directly but to S. W. Hayter's 1946 description, p. 130.

18. It has been "increasingly recognized since the mid 1980s that postmodernism actually inherited a range . . . of techniques, and attitudes from all areas of modernism" (Sheppard 358). Jacqueline Vaught Brogan (2001) has emphasized the way that postmodernists such as Bishop continued aesthetic strategies developed well before World War II.

19. Travisano (1999, 10–17) places Bishop's reticence in the larger context of cultural and aesthetic pressures on mid-century poets.

20. On Bishop's ecphrastic poetry, see Costello (1991, 214–33).

21. Regarding Loren MacIver, Bishop's 1938–1939 notebooks reveal that her reflections on landscape and the arts were partly stimulated by MacIver's paintings. In addition, MacIver shared some of the aesthetic interests of Miller and Bishop; critics of MacIver's work saw Klee as an important influence for her work (although MacIver denied the claim). A *Magazine of Art* piece about MacIver in 1948, by Renée Arb, described a painting as "emphasiz[ing] surface and depth simultaneously" (Arb 14), and MacIver was interested in veils of translucent materials layered over or through other materials and did speak about the environment becoming part of the "observer"—all features that interested Bishop. Bishop did go to see MacIver's exhibits (October 1949, VSC 29.11), and during the difficult period just before taking up the position of consultant in poetry to the Library of Congress, Bishop begged MacIver to send "the little picture of the lights so I can take it to Washington with me" (August 2, 1949, VSC 29.10), as though the painting would provide some kind of life raft for her. However, I have found little evidence that MacIver served as a significant mediator for Bishop's understanding of visual art. Although MacIver had considerable success as a painter, showing at the Matisse Gallery and selling work both to MoMA and the Phillips Collection, she was not particularly articulate about her work, and Miller's ability to translate visual experience into language may have been one reason that Bishop relied more on Miller. Miller had the art historian's ability to bring visual art closer to the linguistic realm; and this linguistic facility must have appealed to Bishop (it is useful to remember that Miller was the one who came up with the phrase "black-tongued piratical vigor" [Bishop 2008, 74] to describe Robert Lowell's poetry). Likewise, although Bishop must have had many conversations with Louise Crane about visual art (given that they traveled in Europe together and given that the Crane family had a substantial art collection), I have found no

evidence that Crane served as a significant influence on Bishop's understanding of visual art.

22. The letters from Bishop to Margaret Miller do not survive.

23. I am especially indebted to Adrian Sudhalter, associate researcher in painting and sculpture at MoMA, for sharing with me her characterization of Margaret Miller's correspondence with and about Schwitters and for alerting me to additional correspondence by Miller in the MoMA Archives.

24. Letter from Margaret Miller to Kurt Schwitters, July 17, 1947, Curatorial Exhibition Files, Exh. #1400. The Museum of Modern Art Archives, New York.

25. Bishop first developed a passion for Calder when she saw an exhibit in Pittsfield in 1933. She does not mention visiting the exhibit with Miller.

26. Not only did Miller take a course from Schapiro at New York University in 1935, but she clearly felt both inspired by and grateful to him. In the preface to her master's thesis, she writes, "This thesis was begun under Professor Meyer Schapiro who suggested the manuscript as a subject for study, and to whom I am indebted not only for much helpful criticism in the course of the preparation of this paper but also for my general conception of Romanesque art, an obligation that exceeds footnote acknowledgement" (Miller 1941, 2). Bishop and Marianne Moore shared an enthusiasm for Schapiro (letter from Marianne Moore to Bishop, February 28, 1937, VSC). See also the Barker correspondence, March 23, 1956, PUL. In the late 1930s and 1940s, Schapiro had a cult status among writers and artists, who came to hear his lectures at the New School and who read and circulated his unpublished manuscripts.

27. We might guess that "On a Bridge at Night," with its affecting portrait of the union and solitude between a woman and child so like the photograph of Bishop and her mother (Millier fig. 5), would have been one of the Daumiers, but this painting had been exhibited in the period when Bishop frequently visited the Phillips Gallery while serving as consultant in poetry to the Library of Congress, and it is therefore puzzling that she would react so strongly to the painting only in the 1970s.

28. Bishop's *The Complete Poems 1927–1979* (1983) is cited as *CP* throughout this book.

29. See Lee Zimmerman for a discussion of Bishop's movement between containment and freedom, in which freedom feels like dread.

30. In this respect, I consider this memoir passage the imaginary scene that counteracts the scene of night, fire, crib, wallpaper, cage, and lines that Lorrie Goldensohn (1992, 50–51) describes.

31. Bishop therefore can be seen to contribute to the line of poetics that Elisa New proposes and so richly describes in *The Line's Eye: Poetic Experience, American Sight,* and her descriptive terms of "thick reciprocity" (21) and "adjacencies and interfaces" (150) become important for my understanding of Bishop's aesthetics.

32. See the foundational comparisons between Moore and Bishop (Keller 1987, 108–14; Costello 1984).

33. The phrase is from Bishop's notes on Erwin Panofsky's course on baroque art, which Bishop audited (VSC 71.1, 20).

CHAPTER 1. VERSE AS DEEP SURFACE

1. Celeste Goodridge (11–14) provides a broader study of Moore's self-concealment and self-presentation as well as her protection of other writers in her reviews.

2. On the importance of this early essay for Bishop's later poetics, see James Longenbach (23–33); see also, Barbara Page (1993, 202).

3. Even though in 1964 Bishop told Anne Stevenson that "Another man who influenced me—not with his books but with his character—was John Dewey, whom I knew well and was very fond of" (letter to Anne Stevenson, March 20, 1963, WUL), Bishop clearly did read Dewey in 1938, experimented with his ideas in "Pleasure Seas," and continued to read Dewey and experiment with poems that drew on his language and ideas (VSC 65.7).

4. See Travisano (1999, 10–17) for commentary on aesthetic theory and mid-century poets, including Bishop.

5. For a more extensive exploration of the philosophical resemblances between Bishop and Dewey, see Frances Dickey.

6. The reviews of Seurat's own experiments beyond impressionism, exhibited at several shows in New York in 1937–1939, situated him as arising from the flux of impressionism yet leaning toward both depth and form. Margaret Breuning describes Seurat's work as opening to allow an unusual depth to emerge: "Its blonde suavity of color form[s] a vibrating mirage through which the landscape is seen to emerge, with an extraordinary sense of depth" (44). James Johnson Sweeney declares that Seurat, like Cezanne, "imposed a sense of compositional organization on Impressionism" (1938, 10).

7. A passage in "The Riverman" also puts in close proximity images of a gas lamp and river surface as threshold: "I went down to the river / and the moon was burning bright / as the gasoline-lamp mantle / with the flame turned up too high, / just before it begins to scorch" (CP, 105). The image is associated strongly with the idea of moving through a threshold between realms; the next lines show the speaker moving through a doorway in the water.

8. *Resists* is written above the uncancelled word *escape* (VSC 75.3b, 197).

9. See Bonnie Costello (1991, 180–84) for a reading of Bishop's "Quai d'Orleans" that also thematizes the dynamic interfaces and resemblances of water, verse line, mind, and nature.

10. Lorrie Goldensohn (1992, 194–95) discusses a similar passage in which Bishop's mind is suspended among the differing speeds of clouds, wake, and horizon.

11. For other commentary on mind and water in Bishop's poems, see Costello (1991, 180–82); Goldensohn (1992, 35). Jeredith Merrin (1993) tentatively suggests that Bishop is repressing the "depth" of personal experience in the poem; I am attempting to describe the full range of the thematics of surface and depth in the poem.

12. The phrase "keying up chromatic intensity" is from the discussion of impressionist and postimpressionist color in Robert Hughes, 129–35).

Chapter 2. Infiltration and Suspension

1. In a letter from Bishop to Marianne Moore (January 5, 1937, VSC), regarding the MoMA exhibition "Fantastic Art, Dada, and Surrealism," she wrote, "Have you been to the surrealist show and didn't you like the Paul Klees?"

2. Stanley W. Hayter describes one of Klee's compositional structures as, "spatial organization through three dimensional energies (fish swimming in all directions)" (Hayter, 130).

3. The painting was also reproduced in André Masson's "Eulogy of Paul Klee," first published by Fontaine (Paris, 1946) and then in English by Curt Valentin (in 1950). Masson compares Klee's use of space with the limited depth of cubism: "The slight antenna of a scarab will suffice to measure the desert, and the trail of a gust of pollen will humiliate the Milky Way."

4. In the opening section of the 1945 catalogue, Miller also chose to reproduce Klee's "Refuge" (1930), which features a figure with all the qualities that Bishop mentions ("Modesty, care, *space*, a sort of helplessness but determination at the same time"). The figure "swims" straight toward the viewer, as if fleeing forward; two arms, one with a foot attached, push off or away to propel the figure forward. The expression is "determined," but the circumstances and the solitude of the figure, his clear expectation that he must save himself without assistance, within an environment that is inhospitable to the human, makes the painting a haunting one.

5. Many years later, Bishop's tribute to Wesley Wehr links small size (and implied modesty) to Klee (implicitly contrasting his intimist work to the large-scale monumentality and myth-making of the abstract expressionists). Millier quotes from Bishop's unpublished notes for Wehr's gallery show: "It is a great relief to see a small work of art these days." Millier continues, "she [Bishop] goes on, comparing Wehr's work to Chinese scroll paintings, Klee, Bissier, and the instrumental pieces of Webern" (Millier 390).

6. Miller wrote enthusiastically to Christian Zervos about the first edition of *Cahiers d'Art* (1945–1946) to appear after the war, which began with a fifty-page tribute to Klee (letter from Margaret Miller to Christian Zervos, July 22, 1947,

Registrar Exhibition Files, Exh. #385. MoMa, New York. Many of the paintings reproduced in that issue involved the sense of deep space, the viewer wandering among motifs, or people submerged in a landscape.

7. Paintings with eyes in the landscape at the 1940 Buchholz exhibition included *Fishes in the Deep* (*Fische in der Tiefe*, 1921) and *Nocturne for Horn* (*Nocturno für Horn*, 1921).

CHAPTER 3. MODULATION

1. For Panofsky, see the letter from Margaret Miller to Bishop, April 14, 1943, VSC. For Gasquet, see Miller's letter to Bishop, December 28, 1942, VSC. For Kahnweiler, which Miller was reading in a manuscript lent to her by Curt Valentin, see Miller's letters to Kahnweiler, September 30, 1946 (REG Exh. #385, MoMA Archives, NY); January 26, 1956, PUL.

2. The materials reemerged years later (mingled with Bishop's impressions from visiting the Galapagos and reading Darwin) in Bishop's "Crusoe in England," where Crusoe reports "nightmares of other islands / stretching away from mine, infinities / of islands, islands spawning islands, / . . . knowing that I had to live / on each and every one, eventually, / for ages, registering their flora, / their fauna, their geography" (*CP* 165). Crusoe's combination of pride and despair in his small "island industries" is reminiscent of the descriptions in *Arts of the South Seas* that covered the "home-made" artifacts of these cultures. The poem ends with one of the most important ideas shared by the Oceanic peoples—the existence of a power that could attach to objects and that "could be destroyed in various ways" (Linton and Wingert 12), like "the living soul [that had] dribbled away" (*CP* 166) from Crusoe's knife and the emptying out of power and significance from the other objects in the last stanza of that poem.

3. Stanley Hayter's work on engraving is another possible influence on Bishop's interest in the movement of engraving between two and three dimensions. The *MoMA Bulletin* description of the 1944 show titled "Hayter and His Studio 17" (June 27–September 17) states, "With Hayter and his associates burin engraving has recovered its dignity as a medium of original expression. For them the copper plate is not merely a plane-surface in which to draw, like paper, a lithographic stone or a canvas. Thanks to the different depths and types of strokes possible to the burin, line engraving exists in a middle realm between relief-sculpture and drawing—perhaps closer to goldsmith's work than to either" (Sweeney 1944, 4).

4. Thomas Travisano captures the modulation in his description: "Icons of sorrow and loss detach themselves from the static field of the almanac and enter the dynamic field of the child's drawing, taking on a dreamlike life of their own" (1999, 224).

5. The show was scheduled to go up in 1946 but had to be postponed, perhaps due to the difficulty of collecting pieces from Europe immediately after the war.

6. She did give a presentation on collage at the College Art Association in late 1946, but no transcript or abstract of the talk has been preserved (letter from Margaret Miller to H. W. Janson, February 9, 1947, REG, Exh. #385. MoMA Archives, NY).

7. "I've just read a marvelous life of Juan Gris, the best book I've read in a long time, I think" (Bishop 1994, 161).

8. In this letter, Bishop misdescribes the collage show to the Barkers, remembering it as devoted to Schwitters: "[S]he [Miller] put on the Museum of Mod. Art show of him [Schwitters]." Bishop also told Anne Stevenson, her biographer, "I am also extremely fond of Schwitters" (letter to Stevenson, March 20, 1963, WUL).

9. Orchard reports nineteen, but four of the nineteen originally chosen were not actually hung in the show (REG Exh. #385. MoMA Archives, NY). I am grateful to Adrian Sudhalter, assistant research curator, Bauhaus Exhibition, Department of Painting & Sculpture, MoMA, for alerting me to this fact.

10. This collage is *Merzzeichnung 305 Lobositz* (*Merzdrawing 305 Lobositz*) (1921).

11. Bishop's letter to May Swenson indicates that even as late as 1953, Bishop thought that Schwitters was less likely to be known than the other artists that she names (Klee, Calder, and Ben Shahn) (September 19, 1953, WUL).

12. The Schwitters collage given to Miller can be seen in the catalogue raisonné #3374.

13. A letter from Bishop to Marianne Moore establishes that Bishop did visit Miller at the MoMA, in this case in December 1945 (Bishop 1994, 129).

14. The exception is Carola Giedion-Welcker's article in *Magazine of Art* (1948). In addition, there was brief catalogue copy of an exhibit at the Pinacotheca Gallery (1948).

15. Both Dietrich and Elderfield consider Klee to be one of the most important influences on Schwitters: "Yet it was one artist above all who seems to be Schwitters's unacknowledged source of inspiration and model for his own career: Paul Klee" (Dietrich 100).

16. Even if Miller's emphasis on the earlier Schwitters's collages may have been dictated by her desire to "place [Schwitters] in an historical context among the artists with whom he was sympathetic or in opposition" (letter from Margaret Miller to Katherine Dreier, May 18, 1948 [REG Exh. #385, MoMA Archives, NY], Miller reveals her preference for the 1920s collages in a letter to Bishop: "The $150 choices were of his late period, which are usually not as good as the ones he did in the '20s" (undated [1953], VSC).

17. Descriptions of Schwitters's collages are necessarily inexact because of the complex conservation issues. For an example of such issues, see the "Conservation Notes" in Anne Umland and Adrian Sudhalter with Scott Gerson (285).

18. I thank Patricia Phagan, curator of prints and drawings, the Frances Lehman Loeb Art Center, Vassar College, for generously allowing me to view

the work and for helping me to categorize the materials used in it. Errors in the naming of those materials are, of course, my own.

19. "No I have never been to Hanover, and have only met you through your work, your article in Ararat and your 1927 exhibition catalog," (letter from Margaret Miller to Kurt Schwitters, October 14, 1946, REG Exh. #385, MoMA Archives, NY). Given Miller's special interest in Schwitters and her plan to publish a description of his work separately from the catalogue for the collage exhibit (letter from Margaret Miller to Kurt Schwitters, February 3, 1947, CUR Exh. #1400, MoMA Archives, NY), and given that she tells Schwitters that she knows this article, it seems likely that she would have read the article in German before it was published in translation by Wittenborn in 1951. By May 18, 1948, Miller records that the MoMA library owned "a considerable number of copies of the Schwitters magazine, Merz" (letter to K. Dreier, MoMA Reg. Exh. #385).

20. This collage was not part of the 1948 MoMA exhibit, but it is included here as a particularly clear example of modulation from fabric to net.

21. The quotation is part of a larger passage in which Barr explains that "cubist interest in textures increases during 1912–14 in such complex arrangements as the [*Still Life with Chair Caning*] and the Card Player composition . . . in which a variety of actual and simulated surfaces is combined in one composition" (Barr 1946, 79).

22. Bishop continued to be interested in Panofsky. In a April 14, 1943, letter, Miller asks, "If you have finished with the Panofsky book, would you send it back to us, if it's not too much trouble. I used it to work on a poor paper I wrote for Friedländer, which he has taken an unshakable fancy to" (letter from Margaret Miller to Elizabeth Bishop, April 14, 1943, VSC).

23. It is likely that Bishop used Panofsky's theories while working on "Roosters," given that the poem enacts the explicit alteration of the meaning of a visual motif for "rooster," changing its iconography in the final section of the poem.

24. This crossing of similarities across divergent materials can also be seen in the Seurat (*Evening at Honfleur*) that Bishop singles out for praise in a letter to Anne Stevenson. The dots of color—beautiful deep lavenders, blues, and grays—cross from sea, to rocks, to sky, and even pass over on to the frame of the painting, into the "real" (January 8, 1964, WUL).

25. For the list of Baudelaire poems, see VSC 75.3b, 175–76.

CHAPTER 4. IMMERSIBLE NETS, LINES, FABRICS,
AND ENTANGLEMENTS

1. The drawing was available to Bishop in Grohmann (1934). Grohmann's 1934 book on Klee's drawings was suppressed in Germany; few copies circulated, and it "would only reach a wide public in 1944 when it was reprinted in English by Curt Valentin" (Lanchner 99).

2. Goldensohn traces the motif of line more fully in *Elizabeth Bishop: The Biography of a Poetry* (1992, 37–52, 85–86).

3. The title of the exhibit was "Paintings, Drawings, and Prints by Paul Klee from the Klee Foundation, Berne, Switzerland, with Additions from the American Collections," March 24, 1949–May 24, 1950 (Soby).

4. *Child and Aunt* is listed as *Aunt and Child* in the 1948 Buchholz exhibition catalogue.

5. "Insomnia" and "The Prodigal" are set on facing pages in both *North & South and A Cold Spring* and *The Collected Poems*.

6. Uncharacteristically, in the mid-1940s Bishop copied many times into her notebook a poem that she had first written in 1929: "A lovely finish I have seen . . ." (Bishop 2006, 11). The rare recopying of such an early poem hints of Bishop's continued fascination with the subjects of beauty, depth, materiality, texture, and human intimacy and the way that a closed surface or mere surface produces human distance.

7. May Swenson, puzzled about "Four Poems," told Bishop that she thought they were "non-objective" (letter from May Swenson to Elizabeth Bishop, August 24, 1955, WUL). That is, she categorized them as in the aesthetic of the nonobjective painters, some of whom were experimenting radically with figure and ground. Especially in the work of Willem de Kooning, background and foreground keep "hosting" one another. Bishop did compose these poems at about the time that de Kooning emerged into wide acclaim with his black and white paintings at the Egan Gallery exhibit (which occurred just at the moment that Bishop returned to New York from Key West) in May 1948. In de Kooning's new work, the surface of the painting became a field of emerging and disappearing forms; lines create a shape that folds in or away to become background for another shape. Other galleries were also exhibiting work that experimented with the tangible feel of space. In a gallery brochure for the "Intrasubjectives" exhibit (September 14–October 3, 1949), Harold Rosenberg writes: "The nothing the painter begins with is known as space. Space is simple: it is merely the canvas before it has been painted. Space is very complex: it is nothing wrapped around every object in the world, soothing or strangling it. It is the growing darkness in a coil of trees or the trunk of an elephant held at eye level. It is the mental habit of a man with a ruler or a ball of string—or of one who expects to see something delightful crop up out of nowhere. Everyone knows it is the way things keep getting larger and smaller. . . . such recognition is not really very difficult. The spectator has the nothing in himself, too" (Rosenberg). Bishop's notebooks from this period became thinner, and it is more difficult to trace her engagement with the visual arts; therefore, here I merely point out the possibility that Bishop's radical experiment in poetry at least partly arose from her response to current work of the abstract expressionists. Bishop does mention liking de Kooning, Franz Kline, and Jackson Pollock (letter to the Barkers, July 24, 1959; PUL).

Chapter 5. "Composing Motions"

1. Bishop mistakenly gives the date of the exhibition as 1931 to Stevenson and 1932 to Barker.

2. From 1934 on, Bishop continued to have access to Calder's work, which was exhibited in New York City at the Pierre Matisse Gallery (the gallery that represented Loren MacIver) and later at the Buchholz Gallery, which represented Calder in the 1940s.

3. Lota also owned three of Calder's mobiles (letter from Bishop to Kit and Ilse Barker, March 12, 1960, PUL). In 1959, Bishop came to know Alexander Calder personally, when he visited the house at Samambaia.

4. The mobile represented in the painting is a composite of several mobiles and does not accurately represent any actual Calder work (2008 conversation with Alexander S. C. Rower, Calder Foundation, New York).

5. Mid-century criticism linked Klee to Calder, and they were exhibited together in two exhibits in 1944. For Klee's influence on Calder, see Turner (229).

6. Beginning as catalogue copy for a 1946 show at the Louis Carré Gallery in Paris, the brief commentary on Calder by Sartre was widely translated and reproduced.

7. Picabia's article was originally published in the same issue of *Cahiers d'Art* (1945–1946) that extensively covered the work of Paul Klee, about which Margaret Miller expressed enthusiasm (REG Exh. #385. MoMA Archives, NY), so it is likely that Bishop saw this article.

8. Drafts of the poem can be found in Bishop (2006, 128–29) and VSC (66.5). Note that the titles of Calder's works are sometimes used for several pieces. Bishop's poem seems closest to either 49.MO.019 (A07525), which was labeled *Gypsophilia* at a Buchholz exhibit in 1949, or 50.MO.003 (A00529), which was sold by Buchholz in 1950 and so was probably on display in the gallery. A reproduction of the latter mobile also appears in the reissue of James Johnson Sweeney's catalogue *Alexander Calder* in 1951.

9. In "The Mountain," originally part of *A Cold Spring* but not included in the *Collected Poems*, Bishop experiments with the appearance and ascension of objects drifting upward and downward across an inanimate subject, each event unwilled by that subject (*CP* 197–98).

Coda. Mirrors and Fields

1. I suspect that Bishop was playing on Klee's "taking a walk with a line" in announcing "the end of [the] march." Some of Klee's most vulnerable human figures, drawn with such a loosely looping line that they are only tenuously able to maintain their shape and seem about to collapse into just line, or just

string—such as *Shame, Burden, A Sick Man Making Plans,* and *Symptom, to Be Recognized in Time*—were continuously available to Bishop in the large Klee volume by Will Grohmann that she bought in 1954; others, such as, *Flight from Self (First Stage),* were on view in the 1949–1950 Klee exhibition that Bishop saw three times (and were available in the catalogue for the Guggenheim's 1967 retrospective of Klee).

BIBLIOGRAPHY

Archives

MoMA Museum of Modern Art Archives, Registrar's Exhibition Files #385 and Curatorial Exhibition Files #1400, New York.
PUL Princeton University Library, Manuscripts Division, Department of Rare Books and Special Collections, Kit and Ilse Barker Collection of Elizabeth Bishop, C0270.
VSC Vassar College Library, Special Collections, Elizabeth Bishop Papers, Poughkeepsie, New York.
WUL Washington University Libraries, Department of Special Collections, Manuscript Division, St. Louis, Mo.

General

Altieri, Charles. "Ann Lauterbach's 'Still' and Why Stevens Still Matters." *Wallace Stevens Journal* 19, no. 2 (fall 1995): 219–33.
——. *Painterly Abstraction in Modernist American Poetry* Cambridge, UK: Cambridge University Press, 1989.
——. *The Particulars of Rapture: An Aesthetics of the Affects.* Ithaca: Cornell University Press, 2003.
Anderson, Perry. *The Origins of Postmodernity.* London: Verso, 1998.
Arb, Renée. "Loren MacIver." *Magazine of Art* 41 (January 1948): 13–15.
Axelrod, Steven Gould. *Robert Lowell, Life and Art.* Princeton: Princeton University Press, 1978.

Bardi, Pietro Maria. "Calder and the Mobiles at the Coming Exhibition." In *Calder in Brazil, The Tale of a Friendship,* ed. Roberta Saraiva, trans. Juliet Attwater, 147–49. São Paulo: Cosac Naify, 2006.

Barr, Alfred H. Jr. *Cubism and Abstract Art.* New York: Museum of Modern Art, 1935.

——. *Picasso: Fifty Years of His Art.* New York: Museum of Modern Art, 1946.

Bishop, Elizabeth. "As We Like It." *Quarterly Review of Literature* 4 (1948): 127–35.

——. *The Complete Poems 1927–1979.* New York: Farrar, Straus, and Giroux, 1983. [cited as *CP*]

——. "Dimensions for a Novel." *Vassar Journal of Undergraduate Studies* 8 (1934): 95–103.

——. *Edgar Allan Poe & the Juke-Box: Uncollected Poems, Drafts, and Fragments.* Ed. Alice Quinn. New York: Farrar, Straus & Giroux, 2006.

——. *Exchanging Hats: Elizabeth Bishop's Paintings.* Ed. William Benton. New York: Farrar, Straus and Giroux, 1996.

——. "Gerard Manley Hopkins." *Vassar Review* 23 (February 1934): 5–7.

——. *One Art: Letters.* Ed. Robert Giroux. New York: Farrar, Straus, and Giroux, 1994.

——. *Words in Air: The Complete Correspondence between Elizabeth Bishop and Robert Lowell.* Ed. Thomas Travisano with Saskia Hamilton. New York: Farrar, Straus and Giroux, 2008.

Bousquet, Joe. "Paul Klee." *Cahiers d'Art* 20–21 (1945–1946): 50–51.

Breuning, Margaret. "Exhibitions in New York." *Parnassus* 9, no. 4 (April 1937): 39–44.

Brogan, Jacqueline Vaught. "Postmodernist Crossings: Aesthetic Strategies, Historical Moment, or a State of Mind." *Contemporary Literature* 42, no. 1 (spring 2001): 155–59.

Brown, Ashley. "An Interview with Elizabeth Bishop." In *Conversations with Elizabeth Bishop,* ed. George Monteiro, 18–29. Jackson: University Press of Mississippi, 1996.

Calder, Alexander. "Modern Painting and Sculpture." Exhibition Catalogue, Berkshire Museum, Pittsfield, Massachusetts, August 12–25, 1933.

Claudel, Paul. *The Eye Listens.* Trans. Elsie Pell. New York: Philosophical Library, 1950.

Costello, Bonnie. "Effects of an Analogy: Wallace Stevens and Painting." In *Wallace Stevens: The Poetics of Modernism,* ed. Albert Gelpi, 65–85. Cambridge, UK: Cambridge University Press, 1985.

——. *Elizabeth Bishop: Questions of Mastery.* Cambridge, Mass.: Harvard University Press, 1991.

——. "Marianne Moore and Elizabeth Bishop: Friendship and Influence." *Twentieth-Century Literature* 30 (1984): 130–49.

——. *Marianne Moore, Imaginary Possessions.* Cambridge, Mass.: Harvard University Press, 1981.

——. *Planets on Tables, Poetry, Still Life, and the Turning World.* Ithaca: Cornell University Press, 2008.

Dickey, Frances. "Bishop, Dewey, Darwin: What Other People Know." *Contemporary Literature* 44, no. 2 (summer 2003): 301–31.

Dietrich, Dorothea. *The Collages of Kurt Schwitters: Tradition and Innovation.* Cambridge, UK: Cambridge University Press, 1993.

Dewey, John. "Art as Experience." In *The Later Works, 1925–1953, Vol. 10: 1934,* ed. Jo Anne Boydston et al. Carbondale: Southern Illinois University Press, 1986.

Duthuit, Georges. "Á Paul Klee." *Cahiers d'Art* 20–21 (1945–1946): 20–21.

Easton, Elizabeth Wynne. *The Intimate Interiors of Edouard Vuillard.* Washington, D.C.: Smithsonian Institution Press, 1989.

Elderfield, John. *Kurt Schwitters.* London: Thames & Hudson, 1985.

Ellis, Jonathan. *Art and Memory in the Work of Elizabeth Bishop.* Burlington, Vt: Ashgate, 2006

Fountain, Gary, and Peter Brazeau. *Remembering Elizabeth Bishop: An Oral Biography.* Amherst: University of Massachusetts Press, 1994.

Fuchs, Rudolf. *Conflicts with Modernism: Or the Absence of Kurt Schwitters.* Bern-Berlin: Gachnang & Springer, 1991.

Gardner, Thomas. *Regions of Unlikeness: Explaining Contemporary Poetry.* Lincoln and London: University of Nebraska Press, 1999.

Gelpi, Albert. "Wallace Stevens and Elizabeth Bishop at Key West." *Wallace Stevens Journal* 19, no. 2 (fall 1995): 155–65.

Giedeon-Welcker, Carola. "Schwitters: Or the Allusions of the Imagination." Trans. C. Ritter. *Magazine of Art* 41 (October 1948): 218–21.

Giménez, Carmen, and Alexander S. C. Rower, eds. *Calder: Gravity and Grace.* London: Phaidon Press, 2004.

Glaesemer, Jürgen. *Paul Klee: The Colored Works in the Kunstmuseum Bern, Paintings, Colored Sheets, Pictures on Glass, and Sculptures.* Trans. Renate Franciscono. Bern: Kornfeld and Cie, 1979.

Goldensohn, Lorrie. *Elizabeth Bishop: A Biography of a Poetry.* New York: Columbia University Press, 1992.

——. "The Homeless Eye." In *Divisions of the Heart: Elizabeth Bishop and the Art of Memory and Place,* ed. Gwendolyn Davies and Peter Sanger, 103–11. Wolfville, Canada: Gaspereau, 2001.

——. "Written Pictures, Painted Poems." In *"In Worcester, Massachusetts": Essays on Elizabeth Bishop, from the 1997 Elizabeth Bishop Conference at WPI,* ed. Laura Jehn Menides and Angela Dorenkamp, 167–76. New York: Peter Lang, 1999.

Goodridge, Celeste. *Hints and Disguises: Marianne Moore and Her Contemporaries.* Iowa City: University of Iowa Press, 1989.

Greenberg, Clement. "Art." *Nation* 167 (November 27, 1948): 612–14.

Grohmann, Will. *Paul Klee: Handzeichnungen, 1921–1930.* Potsdam and Berlin: Müller & I. Kiepenheuer, 1934.

——. "Un Monde Nouveau." *Cahiers d'Art* 20–21 (1945–1946): 63–64.

Harrison, Victoria. *Elizabeth Bishop's Poetics of Intimacy.* Cambridge Studies in American Literature and Culture. Cambridge, UK: Cambridge University Press, 1993.

Hayter, Stanley W. "Paul Klee: Apostle of Empathy." *Magazine of Art* 39 (April 1946): 126–30.

Hertel, Christiane. *Vermeer: Reception and Interpretation.* Cambridge, UK: Cambridge University Press, 1996.

Hoffman, Katherine, ed. *Collage: Critical Views.* Ann Arbor: Michigan University Press, 1989.

Hughes, Robert. *The Shock of the New.* New York: Alfred A Knopf, 1981.

Janis, Harriet. "Mobiles." *Arts & Architecture* 65, no. 2 (February 1948): 26–28, 56–59.

Johnson, Alexandra. "Geography of the Imagination." In *Conversations with Elizabeth Bishop,* ed. George Monteiro, 98–104. Jackson: University Press of Mississippi, 1996.

Kagan, Andrew. "Paul Klee's Influence on American Painting: New York School, Part I." *Arts Magazine* 49, no. 10 (June 1975): 54–59.

Kahnweiler, Daniel-Henry. *Juan Gris, His Life and Work.* New York: Valentin, 1947.

Kalstone, David. *Becoming a Poet: Elizabeth Bishop with Marianne Moore and Robert Lowell.* New York: Farrar, Straus, and Giroux, 1989.

Kees, Weldon. [Art column]. *Nation* 169 (November 5, 1949): 451.

Keller, Lynn. *Re-making It New: Contemporary American Poetry and the Modernist Tradition.* Cambridge, UK: Cambridge University Press, 1987.

——. "Words Worth a Thousand Postcards: The Bishop/Moore Correspondence." *American Literature* 55 (1983): 405–29.

Klee, Paul. *Exhibition Catalogue.* Buchholz Gallery, New York, October 9 to November 2, 1940.

——. "On Creation." [1941]. In *Paul Klee,* ed. Margaret Miller, 10–15. New York: Museum of Modern Art, 1945.

Lanchner, Carolyn. "Klee in America." In *Paul Klee, His Life and Work,* ed. Carolyn Lanchner, 104–8. New York: Museum of Modern Art, 1987.

Leavell, Linda. *Marianne Moore and the Visual Arts: Prismatic Color.* Baton Rouge: Louisiana State University Press, 1995.

Linton, Ralph, and Paul S. Wingert with René D'Harnoncourt. *Arts of the South Seas.* New York: Museum of Modern Art, 1946. Reprinted New York: Arno Press, 1972.

Longenbach, James. *Modern Poetry after Modernism*. New York: Oxford University Press, 1997.

Lowell, Robert. *Selected Poems*. Expanded ed. New York: Farrar, Straus & Giroux, 2006.

Lucie-Smith, Edward. "No Jokes in Portuguese." In *Conversations with Elizabeth Bishop*, ed. George Monteiro, 12–13. Jackson: University Press of Mississippi, 1996.

MacLeod, Glen. *Wallace Stevens and Modern Art: From the Armory Show to Abstract Expressionism*. New Haven: Yale University Press, 1993.

Marter, Joan M. *Alexander Calder*. Cambridge, UK: Cambridge University Press, 1991.

Masson, André. *Eulogy of Paul Klee*. Trans. Walter Pach. New York: Valentin, 1950.

McCabe, Susan. *Elizabeth Bishop: Her Poetics of Loss*. University Park: Pennsylvania State University Press, 1994.

Merrin, Jeredith. "Elizabeth Bishop: Gaiety, Gayness, and Change." In *Elizabeth Bishop: The Geography of Gender,* ed. Marilyn May Lombardi, 153–72. Charlottesville: University Press of Virginia, 1993.

Miller, Cristanne. *Marianne Moore: Questions of Authority*. Cambridge, Mass.: Harvard University Press, 1995.

Miller, Margaret. "Loan Exhibition of Post War Art Held at Vassar." *Art News* 32 (May 19, 1934): 8–9.

———. "The Eleventh Century English Psalter in the British Museum, Arundel 60." Master's thesis, New York University, 1941.

Millier, Brett C. *Elizabeth Bishop: Life and the Memory of It*. Berkeley: University of California Press, 1993.

Mindlin, Henrique. "Alexander Calder." In *Calder in Brazil: The Tale of a Friendship,* ed. Roberta Saraiva, trans. Juliet Attwater, 54–58. São Paulo: Cosac Naify, 2006.

———. "Calder, Smith and Sculptor." In *Calder in Brazil: The Tale of a Friendship,* ed. Roberta Saraiva, trans. Juliet Attwater, 120–23. São Paulo: Cosac Naify, 2006.

Molesworth, Charles. *Marianne Moore: A Literary Life*. New York: Atheneum, 1990.

Moore, Marianne. *The Complete Prose of Marianne Moore*. Ed. Patricia C. Willis. New York: Viking Press, 1986.

———. *The Selected Letters of Marianne Moore*. Ed. Bonnie Costello and Celeste Goodridge. New York: Alfred A. Knopf, 1997.

Motherwell, Robert. "Painter's Objects." *Partisan Review* 11, no. 1 (winter 1944): 93–97.

Mullen, Richard. "Elizabeth Bishop's Surrealist Inheritance." *American Literature* 54 (March 1982): 63–80.

New, Elisa. *The Line's Eye: Poetic Experience, American Sight*. Cambridge, Mass.: Harvard University Press, 1998.

Niebuhr, Reinhold. *Beyond Tragedy: Essays on the Christian Interpretation of History*. New York: Scribner's and Sons, 1938.

Orchard, Karin. "The Eloquence of Waste: Kurt Schwitters' Work and Its Reception in America." In *Merz: In the Beginning was Merz—from Kurt Schwitters to the Present Day*, ed. Susanne Meyer-Büser and Karin Orchard. Ostfildern, Germany: Hatje Cantz, 2000.

Page, Barbara, "Elizabeth Bishop and Postmodernism." *Wallace Stevens Journal* 19, no. 2 (fall 1995): 166–79.

——. "Off-Beat Claves, Oblique Realities: The Key West Notebooks of Elizabeth Bishop." In *Elizabeth Bishop: The Geography of Gender*, ed. Marilyn May Lombardi, 196–211. Charlottesville and London: University Press of Virginia, 1993.

Panofsky, Erwin. *Studies in Iconology: Humanistic Themes in the Art of the Renaissance*. New York: Oxford University Press, 1939.

Pedrosa, Mário. "Tension and Cohesion in Calder's Work." In *Calder in Brazil: The Tale of a Friendship*, ed. Roberta Saraiva, trans. Juliet Attwater, 124–36. São Paulo: Cosac Naify, 2006.

Quinn, Alice, ed. *Edgar Allen Poe & the Juke-Box: Uncollected Poems, Drafts, and Fragments*. New York: Farrar, Straus & Giroux, 2006.

Ribeiro, Leó Gilson. "Elizabeth Bishop; The Poetess, the Cashew, and Micucu." In *Conversations with Elizabeth Bishop*, ed. George Monteiro, 14–17. Jackson: University Press of Mississippi, 1996.

Roman, Camille. *Elizabeth Bishop's World War II–Cold War View*. New York: Palgrave, 2001.

Rosenberg, Harold. "The Intrasubjectives." Exhibition Catalogue, Samuel M. Kootz Gallery, September 14–October 3, 1949.

Saraiva, Roberta. *Calder in Brazil: The Tale of a Friendship*. Trans. Juliet Attwater. São Paulo: Cosac Naify, 2006.

Schapiro, Meyer. "Fromentin as Critic." *Partisan Review* 16 (January 1949): 25–51.

——. "Matisse and Impressionism: A Review of the Retrospective Exhibition at the Museum of Modern Art, Nov. 1931." *Androcles* 1, no. 1 (February 1932): 21–36.

——. "Modern Art." In *An Introduction to Contemporary Civilization in the West: A Syllabus*, 7th ed., ed. Columbia College Associates in Economics, Government and Public Law, History and Philosophy, 270–322. New York: Columbia University Press, 1930.

Schwitters, Kurt. "Merz (1920)." In *The Dada Painters and Poets; An Anthology*, ed. Robert Motherwell, trans. Ralph Manheim, 55–65. New York: Wittenborn, Schulz, 1951.

Sheppard, Richard. *Modernism-Dada-Postmodernism*. Evanston: Northwestern University Press, 2000.

Silverman, Kaja. *The Threshold of the Visible World*. New York and London: Routledge, 1996.

Soby, James Thrall. *Paintings, Drawings, and Prints by Paul Klee from the Klee Foundation, Berne, Switzerland with additions from American Collections*. New York Museum of Modern Art, Exhibition Catalogue, 1949.

Stevens, Wallace. *Collected Poetry and Prose*. Ed. Frank Kermode and Joan Richardson. New York: Library of America, 1997.

Storace, Patricia. "Visits to St. Elizabeth's." *Parnassus: Poetry in Review* 12–13 (1985): 163–78.

Suárez-Toste, Ernesto. "'Telling It Slant': The 'Healthier' Surrealism of Elizabeth Bishop and Joseph Cornell." *Revista Canaria de Estudios Ingleses* 42 (2001): 279–88.

Summers, David. *Real Spaces: World Art History and the Rise of Western Modernism*. New York: Phaidon, 2003.

Sweeney, James Johnson. *Alexander Calder*. New York: Museum of Modern Art, 1943.

——. Alexander Calder. New York: Museum of Modern Art, 1951.

——. "Exhibitions in New York." *Parnassus* 10, no. 7 (December 1938): 10–16.

——. "New Directions in Gravure." *Bulletin of the Museum of Modern Art* 12, no. 1 (August 1944): 3–5.

Sylvester, David. "Auguries of Experience." *Tiger's Eye: On Arts and Letters* 1, no. 6 (December 1948): 48–51. Reprinted in *About Modern Art: Critical Essays, 1948–96*. London: Chatto & Windus, 1996, 35–38.

Thwaites, John A. "Paul Klee and the Object: First Part." *Parnassus* 9, no. 6 (1937): 9–11.

——. "Paul Klee and the Object: Second Part." *Parnassus* 9, no. 7 (1937): 7–9, 33–34.

Travisano, Thomas. *Elizabeth Bishop: Her Artistic Development*. Charlottesville: University Press of Virginia, 1988.

——. *Mid-Century Quartet: Bishop, Lowell, Jarrell, Berryman and the Making of a Postmodern Aesthetic*. Charlottesville and London: University of Virginia Press, 1999.

Turner, Elizabeth Hutton. "'Our Adopted Ancestor,' America's Postwar Embrace of Klee." In *Klee and America,* ed. Josef Helfenstein and Elizabeth Hutton Turner. Menil Collection. Ostfildern-Ruit, Germany: Hatje Cantz Verlag, 2006.

Umland, Anne, and Adrian Sudhalter with Scott Gerson, eds. *Dada in the Collection of the Museum of Modern Art*. New York: Museum of Modern Art, 2008.

Vitrac, Roger. "Le Regard de Paul Klee." *Cahiers d'Art* 20–21 (1945–1946): 53–54.

Williamson, Alan. "*A Cold Spring*: The Poet of Feeling." In *Elizabeth Bishop and Her Art,* ed. Lloyd Schwartz and Sybil P. Estess. Ann Arbor: University of Michigan Press, 1983, 96–108.

Zervos, Christian. "Paul Klee, 1879–1040." *Cahiers d'Art* 20–21 (1945–1946): 10–16.

Zimmerman, Lee. "The Weirdest Scale on Earth: Elizabeth Bishop and Containment." *American Imago* 61, no. 4 (winter 2004): 495–518.

INDEX

Pages numbers followed by *f* or n indicate figures or notes.

Bishop, Elizabeth (*continued*)
"The Imaginary Iceberg," 31, 143
"In the Village," 21
"In the Waiting Room,"
21, 167
"Insomnia," 137, 147, 148–52
"Invitation to Miss Marianne
Moore," 39, 131–32
"Key West," 118
"Luxembourg Gardens," 118
"Mimosas in Bloom," 75–76
"The Monument," 143
"The Moose," 85, 178, 194–97
"The Museum," 158–60, 200
North & South, 30–31
"North Haven," 178, 197–201
"O Breath," 161, 172–75
"On the *Prince of Fundy*," 71–73, 85,
185–86
"Prodigal," 137, 147, 148, 151–53
"Rain Towards Morning," 161,
166–69, 171
"The Riverman," 217n7
"Roosters," 57, 60, 62, 118, 127,
221n23
"The Sea, or, the Moderator
Modulated," 38–39
"Sestina," 102, 132
"The Shampoo," 73–75, 78, 85
"A Short, Slow Life," 208–9
"Something I've Meant to Write,"
202–4, 209–10
"Song for the Rainy Season,"
142–43, 148
"Sonnet," 202, 204–5
"Sunday, 4 A.M.," 176–77
"The Unbeliever," 149
"View of the Capital from the
Library of Congress," 132,
147–48
"While Someone Telephones," 161,
169–72
"Whitewashed," 76–78, 80, 85

see also ""Four Poems"; "Over 2000
Illustrations and a Complete
Concordance"; "Pleasure Seas"
Braque, Georges, 66, 104–5, 120
Breuning, Margaret, 217n6
Brogan, Jacqueline Vaught, 215n18
Brown, Ashley, 12, 65
Brueghal, Pieter the Younger,
176–77
Buffet-Picabia, Gabrielle, 181

Cahiers d'Art, 17–18, 63, 68, 85
Calder, Alexander, 2, 13–14, 18, 24
Bishop's combining of Schwitters'
aesthetic with, 178, 190–201
Bishop's composing motions and,
182–90
Bishop's exposure to aesthetics of,
176–79
mid-century reception of, 179–82,
186, 187, 194
Carré, Louis, 103
Claudel, Paul, 4–5, 216n5
Collage, 102–36
Miller and dissociation, 102–6
modulation, 87–136
Moore's use of aesthetics of, 8–9
Schwitters and, 26–27, 102–3,
106–21, 126–28, 131–32, 158–59,
190–91, 194–96
Composing motions, 176–201
"The Armadillo," 178, 186–87
"Arrival at Santos," 178, 184–85
Calder's aesthetic and, 176–79
Calder's and Schwitters' aesthetics
combined, 190–201
Calder's mid-century reception,
179–82
"A Cold Spring," 178,
187–94, 199
"Gypsophilia," 178, 182–84
"The Moose," 178, 194–97
"North Haven," 178, 197–201

Hayter, Stanley, 219n3
Herbert, George, 191
Hopkins, Gerard Manley, 39–40

Immersible nets, lines, fabrics,
   entanglements, 137–75
   "Argument," 155–58
   "Four Poems," 137–38, 160–75
   "Insomnia," 137, 147, 148–52
   Klee and subjectivity held in line,
      153–58
   lines incorporating objects and
      holding subjectivity, 142–48
   "Prodigal," 137, 147, 148, 151–53
   "Song for the Rainy Season,"
      142–43, 148
   surfaces, lines, membranes,
      and intimacy, 158–75
   verse as pliable net, 138–42
   verse as tilting fabric, subjectivity
      falling into extent, 148–53
   "View of the Capital from the
      Library of Congress," 147–48
Impressionism
   Bishop and, 3, 25, 43, 47, 55, 205–10
   Schapiro on, 35–36
   Seurat and, 217n6
Infiltration and suspension, 56–86,
   188–201
   Bishop's correspondence and
      discussions of Klee, 57–63, 87
   Bishop's use of Klee's aesthetic,
      25–26, 70–86, 218n5
   critical comments on Klee's use of
      eye and space, 63–70
   "Faustina, or Rock Roses," 57, 80–85
   "Gypsophilia," 78–79, 80, 85, 182–84
   "Mimosas in Bloom," 75–76
   "On the *Prince of Fundy*," 71–73, 85
   "Roosters," 57, 60, 62
   "The Shampoo," 73–75, 78, 85
   "Whitewashed" fragment, 76–78,
      80, 85

Jarrell, Randall, 1, 14, 206
"Jerboa, The" (Moore), 7
Johns, Jasper, 15

Kagan, Andrew, 143
Kahnweiler, Daniel-Henry, 87, 104–5
Kalstone, David, 21, 22
Klee, Paul, 2, 108
   Bishop's correspondence about and
      discussions of, 57–63, 87
   critical comments on use of eye and
      space, 63–70
   influence on Bishop, 10, 13–14,
      20, 24–26, 57–64, 68–86, 218n5,
      223–24n1
   lines "holding" the figure and, 143–48
   mid-century reception of, 63–70
   MoMA publication on, 17–18, 57, 63,
      64, 69, 154, 156, 218n4
   subjectivity held in line, 153–58
Klee, Paul, works
   Animals by Full Moon, 144–46, 144f
   Arab Song, 61
   Child and Aunt, 146
   "Child Consecrated to Suffering,"
      155–56
   "Demonry," 146
   "Early Sorrow," 146
   Fear, 61–63, 62f, 70, 78, 79–80, 86,
      218n3
   "Fight," 155
   Glance of a Landscape, 66f, 70, 78,
      80, 82, 84, 86
   "Insula Dulcamara," 146
   Intention, 146, 147f, 148
   Lying as Snow, 145, 146f
   The Man of Confusion, 57–60, 58f,
      62–63, 78, 86
   "The Mocker Mocked," 156
   "On Creation," 69
   A Park and the Tresspasser, 146
   "Refuge," 218n4
   Sextet of Genii, 146